BOMBING
HITLER

BOMBING HITLER

The Story of the Man Who Almost
Assassinated the Führer

HELLMUT G. HAASIS
TRANSLATED BY WILLIAM ODOM

SKYHORSE PUBLISHING

10 9 8 7 6 5 4 3 2 1

Library of Congress Cataloging-in-Publication Data

Haasis, Hellmut G., 1942-
[Hitler jag' ich in die Luft. English]
Bombing Hitler : the story of the man who almost assassinated the Fuhrer / Hellmut G. Haasis ; translated by William Odom.
    p. cm.
Translation of: Den Hitler jag' ich in die Luft.

ISBN 978-1-61608-741-8 (hardcover : alk. paper) 1. Elser, Johann Georg, 1903–1945. 2. Hitler, Adolf, 1889–1945–Assassination attempt, 1939 (November 8) 3. Anti-Nazi movement–Germany–Biography. 4. Germany–History–1933-1945. I. Title.

DD247.E6H3313 2012
943.086092–dc23
[B]

2012017676

Paperback ISBN: 978-1-63220-312-0

Cover photo © AP Images

Printed in the United States of America

This translation is dedicated to the indomitable spirit of Georg Elser.

CONTENTS

I

Hitler Speaks Under a Ticking Time Bomb

As THEY HAD done for several years, the "Old Soldiers" (*Alte Kämpfer*) gathered on November 8, 1939, in the Bürgerbräukeller beer hall in Munich, arriving around six in the evening. At least once a year, these otherwise powerless participants in the Beer Hall Putsch of 1923 could seize an opportunity to bask in glory. In earlier years, the brown shirts of the SA had dominated the hall; now it was the field gray of soldiers, about fifteen hundred of them. Since September 1, 1939, Germany had been at war. Most of those participating in the traditional celebration had been drafted into the military, but they were on leave that evening. On the podium at the front of the hall, a band was playing march music. The pub tables were filled with beer mugs. The only thing distinguishing this gathering from one of the many beer festivals held here was the presence of red Nazi flags.

For weeks, foreign printed materials—English and French leaflets—had been fluttering down over Germany, delivered by balloons or thrown from airplanes. Reading them was considered dangerous, and the Gestapo had school classes gather up the leaflets and turn them in. In October 1939, a flyer from England was distributed that stated:

> Herr Hitler rejected all offers of peace until he crushed Poland as he destroyed Czechoslovakia. It will be impossible to accept any conditions for peace which approve acts of aggression. The proposals made by the Chancellor of the German Reich in his speech are extremely unclear and indefinite.

The leaflet went on: "Experience has shown that there is no relying on the promises of the current German government." Therefore Germany would have to deliver "convincing proof of its commitment to peace" or Britain would have to fulfill its obligation—meaning war against Nazi Germany. The last line of the leaflet was, "The choice is up to Germany!"

The *Alte Kämpfer* assembled in the Bürgerbräukeller had already made their choice back in 1923: war against democracy and the rest of Europe. And Nazi society was far removed from any concerns about peace. As Propaganda Minister Joseph Goebbels noted in his diary on November 5, 1939: "Politically, all is absolutely calm. But this is probably the calm before the storm. It's even hard to find material for propaganda purposes."

In a meeting with Hitler shortly afterward, however, the mission was made clear to Goebbels: "He [Hitler] is of the opinion that England needs to receive a knockout punch. And this is true. England's power is just a lingering myth—it's no longer a reality. All the more reason it must be destroyed. Until it is, there can be no peace and quiet in the world." After Hitler had achieved his first goal of revising the Versailles Treaty of 1919, he started fantasizing about a more comprehensive objective. According to Goebbels, "Perhaps the Führer will succeed—and sooner than all of us thought—in undoing the Peace of Westphalia. Historically, that would be the crowning achievement of his life." This would mean undoing the Reformation, and repartitioning Europe under the hegemony of a far-reaching German Reich—truly delusional speculations.

On November 7, Goebbels noted the murky mood of the regime: "There are the wildest rumors going around all over the country about what will happen next." Rumors played a fundamental role in public opinion in Nazi society, which was so manipulated that nobody knew any longer what was and was not propaganda. Even Goebbels trusted less and less in the reports of the SD (*Sicherheitsdienst*—"security service," the intelligence arm of the SS).

The following day, Goebbels flew to Munich with Hitler. On board, while Hitler dictated to his secretary the speech that he would give there to his secretary, Goebbels was reading the screenplay of the anti-Semitic propaganda film *Jud Süss* (Jew Süss) by Veit Harlan.

After stopping by his Munich apartment, Hitler went to a café, then proceeded to the Bürgerbräukeller, arriving at precisely 8:00 p.m. Normally, he would have arrived at 8:30, the historically accurate time.

It was at exactly this time on November 8, 1923, that Hitler and his heavily armed rebels had stormed the meeting of the Bavarian cabinet at the Bürgerbräukeller. Like a hero in a Western, he had charged into the hall and up onto the podium with his pistol drawn, firing into the air and proclaiming the "national revolution." Every year since 1933, at exactly the same time and in the same place, in what amounted to a Party religious service, he reaffirmed this "brown revolution" with a two-hour speech. That evening, however, the Party faithful would have to make do with a speech only half as long without receiving an official clarification of the reason for the change.

Because of the impending French campaign, Hitler wanted to get back to Berlin right away; however, the weather conditions were uncertain and his personal pilot, Hans Baur, thought there would be fog. In all likelihood, Hitler would not have been able to fly out the next morning. The railway administration saw only one possibility for working Hitler's private train into the schedule—by leaving at 9:31 that same evening. Hitler would have to get to the station with his entourage on time. Forced to adapt to the schedule change, he revised his speech to take only an hour.

* * *

When Hitler arrives with his entourage, the *"Blutfahne"* (Blood Flag) is paraded in before him; this was the flag from the 1923 Putsch, supposedly spattered with the blood of those shot by police during the confrontation. This piece of cloth enjoyed cult status, and every new Party flag had to be brought into contact with this "holy banner" so that it too could acquire such sacred character.

Filing in behind Hitler are the Party dignitaries. The only high-level officials missing are Göring and Himmler; however, Goebbels, Heydrich, Hess, Ley, Rosenberg, Streicher, Frank, and Esser are present. Christian Weber, a National Socialist city councilman in Munich, who as one of those who marched in 1923 always appears with the top brass, introduces Hitler in a provincial *Lederhosen* style: halting, awkward, inarticulate, and inadvertently humorous—to be expected when combining a sense of mission and an ordinary beer festival.

"My Führer, today we have once again fallen in for roll call"—in reality they are all sitting there with their beer steins—"to the day or to the deeds of the memory of November eighth and ninth, 1923." Weber starts floundering. He has chosen to speak extemporaneously and starts rambling: "Today everything becomes unnecessary. You see, my Führer, that our hearts speak." He tries to save himself with repetition, speaking again about the "roll call," stating that Hitler has "rushed here" and thanking him "from the bottom of [his] heart." Six times, waves of *Sieg Heil* roar through the hall. They all rise to their feet, shouting *Heil* three more times. Then Weber tries to take charge, shouting *"Sieg,"* but in an instant the crowd takes over and yells *Heil* three times in a row. The attempt at coordinating the response is spoiled.

Now the speaker's platform in front of the center pillar—the load-bearing pillar for the entire hall—is free for Hitler to take over. He lowers his gaze to the text he has brought with him, which has been previously distributed to selected journalists and will be printed in its entirety in the *Völkischer Beobachter*. In reality, however, Hitler frequently does not stick to the words of the text; so the only authentic record of the speech is the recording at the German Radio Archives.

At first Hitler speaks haltingly, frequently pausing in odd places. There is a method in this: He doesn't want to stir up the crowd until later because he knows that once the applause starts there will be no holding it back. In a subdued voice, he informs his well-trained audience that now is not the time to applaud. From the start, he primarily employs devices of a simple speaking style: redundancy, repetition, and empty rhetoric.

The very first sentence comes off as overblown and pompous, and the speech continues in this vein: He, Hitler, wants to celebrate "the remembrance of a day which was of great importance for us." That would actually be sufficient, but since Hitler is so inspired by the throng, he gratuitously adds more: "Which was of importance for us, for the movement, and therefore for all the people." In this way, he can play for time and maximize the effect.

The scene at the Bürgerbräukeller is similar to a religious ceremony: The preacher, styled by Goebbels as the Messiah of the downtrodden German people, need only allude to the sacred event, and the believers will know and understand. A concrete description of how events unfolded at the Putsch of 1923 would only interfere with the hallowed mood of the moment. "It was a difficult decision that I had to make at that time"; these are the words in the written text—no mention of the fellow combatants who are sitting here in front of him and know full well that he wasn't the only one involved. While standing there at the lectern, Hitler, apparently sensing a need for scruples, adds spontaneously: "And, together with many comrades, I acted upon this decision." This could continue now, but the ritual demands deep reverence here, best achieved by repetition: "a difficult decision, but one which had to be risked."

In order to put the best face on the present, Hitler first revisits the negative past: "A dreadful catastrophe had befallen our country." The defeat of 1918, perhaps? No, it was the war that had been thrust upon us. Not a word of regret for Germany's role in the war—at most regret at not having done everything possible to build "national strength" and at having started the war too late. In order to obscure the causes of the war of 1914, Hitler engages in some reckless logic, saying that "Germany had to be dragged into war." He is aware of just how odd the phrase "had to" sounds here and therefore throws himself into it unctuously, with the full power of his voice.

From this point on, the structure of the speech becomes jumbled. Hitler suddenly lights on the enemies, apparently trying to prove their culpability for the two World Wars by labeling them "the same powers." They incited war against Germany "with the same slogans and the same lies." The defeat of 1918 was not a defeat at all, he says; it was only a clever maneuver by the adversary. Hitler doesn't even have to resort to the legend claiming that the military was "stabbed in the back" by domestic forces (*Dolchstosslegende*). "It took a great lie to rob our people of their weapons." So apparently, the armies were simply conquered by a lie, and the English and the French could never have "forced the Germans into submission on the battlefield."

Here Hitler's extreme belief in the power of will becomes evident; he even thinks he can change history by willing it to happen. The devastating consequences of yet another defeat loom—but Germany is invincible on the battlefield, and the real struggle takes place in the arena of the will. The logical consequence of such thinking is clear: In the end, he is willing to sacrifice his own country, to the point of complete annihilation.

Freely associating, Hitler again jumps track, right in the middle of a paragraph. What is the source, he asks, of his "great self-confidence"? Now Hitler gives his undivided attention to his veterans, to the soldiers seated before him; he fires them up, yet simultaneously he is driving them to their death. He himself found his self-confidence he says, "on the field of battle." Death becomes a great companion. No enemy has been superior to German soldiers. And why? Again, because of will: "Neither the French nor the English had more courage; neither summoned up more deadly force than the German soldier!"

Hitler then loses the thread, so takes to repeating himself. But the audience is working up a head of steam, which it is accustomed to letting off by clapping. When Hitler first says that today Churchill is facing "a different government" than in 1914, he cannot prevent the applause.

The ice is broken. From this point on, the speech is interrupted by salvos of laughter and storms of applause—sixty-three times during the final fifty minutes, an average of once every forty-five seconds. Hitler gathers momentum—it does him good to be applauded by the Party faithful. His tone becomes lighter, he starts using irony, even sarcasm; he demonstrates his acting skills. At some points he turns the Bürgerbräukeller into a cabaret—a Bavarian one, to be sure. Of Germany's enemies, only England is mentioned. Hitler doesn't seem to realize that he's the one who picked this fight called a World War. England is subjected to ridicule—the audience is delighted. Amusement and beery spirits usher in the war.

Again and again Hitler returns to the First World War, and then to the humiliating Treaty of Versailles. When moving on to the claim that England's greatness is due to its colonies, he becomes dramatic, speaking faster and shouting. The audience catches on: The applause is more frequent—four times in one minute. Hitler pins his many broken promises on England—England can't be trusted, he says.

Hitler jumps around, relying on whim. He returns to Germany's catastrophe—at first he meant by this the outbreak of war, now he means the postwar period. He interprets the defeat only in terms of national expansion. He laments Germany's loss of its colonies, of trade, of its naval fleet, of its territories—in the process making the maudlin declaration: "We were thrust into deepest misery." This provides an ideal opportunity to bring up the Party: "And out of this misery arose the National Socialist movement." In fact, it was not until 1929 during the Great Depression that many citizens, insecure and concerned, grasped at his party like a straw, out of opposition to the left—a detail that Hitler obscures by casting his "movement" as a chronicle of redemption.

The increasing volume of Hitler's voice indicates that a raw nerve in his power complex has been exposed. He roars when the subject turns to renunciation of force, calling it "renunciation of life." He can only imagine life as constant struggle, as an uninterrupted series of acts of violence. For this reason he wants to assure that "the life" of the German people "will prevail."

At this point Hitler's ideas about expansion—*"Lebensraum"*—start coming through. Any limit to this expansion is not discernible—infinite territory on all sides. A nation is exploding, right in the middle of Europe.

Closing scene of Hitler's address at the Bürgerbräukeller on November 8, 1939. The swastika flag behind Hitler obscures the pillar with the bomb.

Around the middle of this memorable speech, Hitler's megalomania manifests itself. Germany is strong, Hitler shouts—the actual standard of living is of no interest to him—Germany is the greatest military power. During these passages one wave of shouting and applause after another washes through the hall. The crowd goes wild, stirred up not only by the speaker but by its own enthusiasm. The *Alte Kämpfer* want to go to war. The people are united as never before, says the supreme commander.

Hitler takes yet another shot at England, claiming that the English hate Germany because of its progressive social policies. When he then states that the English hate "the Germany that has eliminated class differences," it is not quite clear what the brown-shirted veterans will find to applaud about. But the content no longer matters here, just tough words spoken in a shrill voice by the agitator in chief. In the course of one segment he hammers home the word "hate," repeating it eighteen times as he recounts everything that the English supposedly hate about Germany. In a calmer setting, the tone of voice alone would be enough to establish who exactly is consumed by hate. He resorts to even the most banal sort of prejudice, claiming that the English don't wash their children and let them become lice infested.

The crowd has now become so completely agitated and ready for war that Hitler can start wrapping things up. Even with all the rhetorical chaos, there is an inner logic to the speech: The objective is to get people fired up for war. When Hitler shouts into the hall that in this new world war "England will definitely not be the victor," the roar from the audience is louder than at any point so far—the first vocal climax. Then follows another show of strength, at the same volume, when Hitler stumbles off into a collective death wish: "No matter how long the war lasts, Germany will never, never capitulate—not now, and not three years from now." With the repetition of "never," Hitler starts to rant; his voice rises rapidly, then falters and is lost in the sudden roar of the throng. Total war is being foreshadowed here, a war until the *Götterdämmerung*. Berliners were not the first, in 1943, to shout to Goebbels that they wanted total war; in 1939 the people of Munich—those in the Bürgerbräukeller—demonstrated just how ready they were. There is one more bloodcurdling roar as

Hitler makes a prophecy: "Here [in this war] only one can win—and we are the one!"

The soldiers are ready for self-sacrifice, and Hitler digs deep into his bag of mystical ideology: "Whatever may be demanded of us individually in this period of sacrifice, we know that this shall pass ... it is of no import. The crucial aim is and will remain victory!"

The church service is drawing to a close. Hitler expresses his gratitude to "Providence," which he cloaks in a swastika. From the history of the Party he concludes that "What has happened was the will of Providence!" He expresses his gratitude to the fallen soldiers (everyone in the audience stands up; the sound of chairs scraping goes on and on). Their sacrifices helped make it possible to overwhelm Poland in thirty days. The mystique of death once more reduces Hitler's language to a muddle: "What we National Socialists have taken with us as realization and as pledge from the bloodbath of November 9 into the history of our movement, that is, that what the first sixteen died for is worth, if necessary, sending many others to die for—this realization shall not forsake us, not now nor in the future." One must read this sentence several times before the fog clears a bit.

Hitler ends his speech at 9:07 p.m. In order to reach his private train on time he must hurry to the main station with his entourage. Besotted with thoughts of victory, Goebbels writes in his diary: "Mad enthusiasm rocks the hall. This speech will become a sensation all over the world."

But someone else, the Swabian woodworker Georg Elser, was to steal the show from Hitler. While the supreme commander of the German *Wehrmacht* was roaring praise to the next World War, the two clock mechanisms in Elser's bomb were ticking. By this time the assassin had intended to be across the border in safety.

II

The Assassin Is Foiled
at the Border

Gᴇᴏʀɢ Eʟsᴇʀ ᴄᴏᴜʟᴅ in fact have sneaked across the border on November 6, 1939, three days before Hitler's speech, but after three months of nerve-wracking, exhausting labor in the Munich Bürgerbräukeller, he had lost his sense of urgency. Leaving his homeland was harder than anticipated. After a long period of loneliness in Munich, he longed to see family and friends again. He had originally planned to take a quick trip to Königsbronn to say good-bye to his father, who was in poor health, as well as to the Schmauder family in Schnaitheim, with whom he had lived when he began working on his explosive device. He would pay dearly for this sentimentality.

On November 6, he visited the family of his sister, Maria Hirth, who lived at Lerchenstrasse 52 in Stuttgart. He told them only that he had to go "over the fence" (i.e., the border), but did not reveal the true reason, even after they asked. He felt no need to unburden himself, being at peace with himself and his self-assigned task. While his sister assumed that he intended to desert, Elser acted as if he simply wanted to take a trip and look for work in Switzerland. This was believable, since the time he had spent at Lake Constance had imbued him with enthusiasm for Switzerland. When asked about his reasons for leaving, he said only, "I must. It can't be changed." Given his well-known stubbornness, there was no point in quizzing him any further.

On the evening of the 6th, Elser went to bed early. Feeling completely drained, he slept until quite late the next morning. The work was done, all the tension had left him, he had no further goals—the final one, the border, seemed a simple matter to him. He had entrusted the most important task, yet to be completed, to an ignition system which was secured against failure.

The two clocks were ticking.

From the outset, he had intended to recheck the explosive device before fleeing to Switzerland. He had a reputation among his superiors for going back to customers after a job had been completed to make sure that everything was in working order. Later they would joke about his "check-o-mania." As a tinkerer with a tendency to perfectionism, Elser did not want to risk undermining a year's effort because of carelessness or error. As a clock expert, he knew that a pendulum clock could stop if there were even a slight inclination in the floor. Under difficult circumstances and using primitive means, he had leveled the base of the bomb chamber in the pitch-black hall, using only a flashlight covered with a dark handkerchief. He had mixed the plaster using his own urine and was not able to use a level for the finishing work.

On November 7, he took the 4:00 p.m. express train from Stuttgart to Munich, in order to arrive late. He would no longer have time for his customary supper in the Bürgerbräustübl next to the large hall, the Bürgerbräukeller. And perhaps on his last evening he didn't want to be seen by the waitresses again, who had come to know him all too well. At the end of his three-month stint working as an "inventor" (which he claimed to be throughout his stay in Munich), he arrived in Stuttgart with only ten marks in his pocket. His sister gave him thirty marks as thanks for the tools, clocks, and clothes that he had left with her. These few possessions would prove to be a fatal gift.

* * *

At the Swiss border, Georg Elser had exactly five marks left.

In order to avoid being seen, Elser entered the Bürgerbräukeller in Munich through the main entrance on Rosenheimer Strasse, around 10:00 p.m., shortly before closing time. It was to his advantage that, in spite of its cult status as a Nazi hangout, the locals liked to use the gigantic hall as a shortcut between Rosenheimer Strasse and Kellerstrasse. It was an altogether unusual location, ideal for a silent assassin in the midst of a state presumed to maintain total surveillance of its citizens.

Elser strolled through the hall to the end of the gallery, and then turned to see if anyone else was in the room. Once the coast was clear, he disappeared into a storage space behind a screen, as he had done so often during the previous months. After the doors to the hall were locked, he waited to see whether anyone else was around. He then moved toward his pillar in the middle of the hall above the podium where Hitler would speak the next evening, and opened his "secret door" in the pillar. Both clocks were correct to the minute. Whatever he could accomplish as a craftsman and inventor had been finished. For the rest of the night he dozed as usual in the chair in his hiding place.

At 6:30 a.m., he stepped unobserved out onto Kellerstrasse through the emergency exit next to the kitchen, and had breakfast at a kiosk near the Isartor. Elser had a reason to celebrate, and the thrifty Swabian treated himself to two cups of coffee rather than his usual single cup.

Georg Elser loved regularity. In pubs, for example, he always liked to sit at the same table. But with no real reason for doing so, that morning he decided to stop by Türkenstrasse 59 to see master joiner Brög, with whom he had gotten along so well. Elser had been allowed to use Brög's bench and even to spend the night at his home on occasion. Elser wanted to say good-bye to him one last time, but since Brög was not in his workshop, Elser went to see his landlady, Rosa Lehmann, who lived close by at Türkenstrasse 94. He had moved out the week before, explaining that he was going back home. Now he was standing outside her window wearing a black hat and looking somewhat threatening, as Rosa Lehmann would later recount after the war. But by then, she was caught up in the assassination drama, and her recollection may have been influenced by gossip or fear of harassment by the police, journalists, and her own neighbors. Elser called up to her to ask whether he had gotten any mail—a nonsensical question, since he hadn't written anyone in a long time.

No, she said, there was no mail for him. So at 10:00 a.m. he boarded a local train at the main station, traveling third class to Ulm, where he transferred to an express train headed for Lake Constance, arriving around 6:00 p.m. at the harbor train station in Friedrichshafen. He still had a half hour and went looking for a barber. He wanted to be clean shaven in order to make a good impression as a political refugee at the border crossing. The ship to Konstanz departed at 6:30 p.m. According to the schedule, it should have arrived at 8:05 p.m.; however, it might have been a few minutes late because of the fog.

Once Elser was on shore at Konstanz, he started making mistakes—or so we might think today. In actuality, the errors had been made a long time ago. They lay in his false perception of the border situation, in his stubborn rejection of all assistance, and in his profound state of exhaustion. His mood might have been compared to the feelings once expressed by the French prisoner Rovan, who, upon his release from Dachau, proclaimed: "Now that there was no longer a reason to be afraid I felt a great emptiness within me, an abyss of exhaustion, which, so it seemed to me, I would never be able to climb out of." Elser had been seized by the "melancholy of fulfillment," in the words of the philosopher Ernst Bloch. And he knew Switzerland only superficially from the six-month summer idyll he had spent in the village of Bottighofen near Kreuzlingen.

In a similar vein, the playwright Rolf Hochhuth, attempting to put himself in Elser's place, once remarked: "He had now used up all his energy; from this point on, he made only careless or foolish moves . . . positively dazed from emotional exhaustion, he simply stumbled into the clutches of the customs officials." But the errors had already been made, largely as a result of his isolation. In the fall of 1938, Elser had indeed made a short trip to Konstanz in order to determine whether the border crossing he intended to use was still unmanned, as he had recalled it being in 1930. And it is possible that he in fact found this stretch of border unguarded; for in 1938, war had not yet broken out—the situation had even eased somewhat since Czechoslovakia had been abandoned by England. Now, however, Germany was in the third month of war, and war might break out any day on the Western Front. Elser did not consider soliciting Communists with experience to help with the escape—he wanted absolutely no one else to be involved in the assassination. Besides, he didn't belong to the Party nor was he some official in danger who needed to be taken along secret routes by couriers across the green border.

From the harbor in Konstanz, Elser now took the most direct path to the border, almost like a sleepwalker: Konzil, straight ahead across the Marktstätte, left onto Rosgartenstrasse, past the Dreifaltigkeits-kirche, across Bodanplatz to Hüetlinstrasse, and across Kreuzlinger Strasse to the small border street, Schwedenschanze. His destina-tion was the big park at the Wessenbergheim. There the border was marked by a fence approximately two meters high and topped by two rows of barbed wire. It didn't occur to Elser to first determine the location of the border patrol and the route taken during patrols. To the left of the spot where the Elser memorial plaque stands today, he passed through an unlocked gate, walked down the left side of the house, and quickly approached the border fence.

What happened next is not in doubt, as many have maintained. Most reliable are the reports of the border patrol officers who stopped Elser twenty-five meters from the border fence. Xaver Rieger and Waldemar Zipperer began their patrol at 8:00 p.m., walking from the Kreuzlinger customs office to the Wessenberggarten along the Schwedenschanze. Five weeks later, when it was clear what a catch they had made, Rieger wrote:

> We entered the property at 8:05 p.m. Our position was chosen so that we could keep the entire stretch of border in our section under surveillance. . . . Between 8:40 and 8:45, a figure stepped out from behind the building and, after quickly surveying the area, made for the border, moving stealthily, yet very rapidly. The distance between me and the figure was about fifteen to twenty meters. When I saw the figure, I immediately ran quickly and cautiously toward the man, while simultaneously readying my carbine. When I was confident that I would be heard, I shouted at him "Hello, where are you going?" . . . In accordance with the guidelines regarding such a scenario, I considered it best not to make the man suspicious by telling him that he was under arrest. Since in response to my shout the man claimed to be looking for an acquaintance by the name of Feuchtelhuber, with the Konstanz Tra-ditional Dress Club, of which he had been a member some years ago, I let him think that I wanted to be of assistance to him. . . . I therefore told him

that I wanted to take him to a man who was more familiar with Konstanz
and would surely know the acquaintance in question. Should, however, this
man not know the acquaintance, then he would have to work it out on his
own. . . . I hereby managed to gain his trust, and he came along willingly.
I instructed adjutant border guard Zipperer to remain at his post and to maintain a sharp lookout, since I suspected that there were other individuals behind
Elser who would also attempt to cross the border illegally. I had this suspicion
because earlier we had observed a man in a light-colored coat on the Swiss
side of the border doing something at the fence and walking back and forth in
a conspicuous manner. As I was escorting Elser, I watched carefully to be sure
that he did not discard any objects. Before being taken into the border patrol
office, Elser stopped again at the door and took another look in the direction of
Switzerland. It gave one the impression that at the last minute he might flee to
Switzerland. However, when Elser saw my carbine at the ready and I said to
him firmly "Here's the door," he followed willingly into the inspection room.
The thorough physical inspection undertaken here, with Elser stripped down
to his shirt, yielded the following results: In his pockets Elser carried wire cutters and a sealed envelope, which contained numerous notes with sketches per-
taining to the production of grenades and fuses, heat and hardness coefficients,
and the labeling of ammunition crates, as well as their color, contents, and
destination. In addition, Elser had parts of an ignition device with him (firing
pins, spring, etc.) and a postcard with an interior view of the Bürgerbräukeller in color. The card bore the official seal of the Nazi Party and contained no
writing. At the conclusion, Customs Secretary Traber, who participated in the
inspection, found concealed under Elser's coat lapel the former insignia of
the Red Front. In answer to questions as to why he had the insignia and the
postcard with him, he said, "Out of sympathy." During the entire search and
interrogation Elser appeared very cooperative and extremely calm. Elser was
then turned over to the border police.

    This report serves as the basic text for Elser's failed border cross-
ing. Later on, the event was taken over by legends as wild and tangled
as the rose bushes around Sleeping Beauty's castle. The exact location and activity of the patrol remain unclear. The guards positioned
themselves behind the house on the south side, in such a way that they
were able to see over the border fence. From the living room on the
ground floor they heard through an open window the radio broadcast

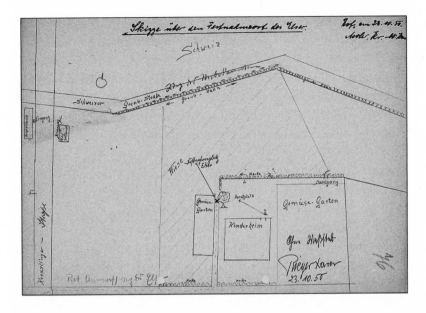

of Hitler's speech from the Bürgerbräukeller. They were not able to see into the neighbors' backyards on the left side—and here might have lain Elser's chance. If he had arrived in Konstanz earlier and had observed the changing of the guard—for the previous watch in the Wessenberggarten had been relieved just a bit earlier—he might have actually made it. At 8:25, Elser could not have known of this trap behind the house. Unconcerned, he walked past the house without looking to the right. The border guards were standing in the shadow of an old pear tree off the right corner of the house—while twenty-five meters beyond the fence the Swiss border street was brightly lit.

Elser was no fool. When the customs officers stopped him, he knew to quickly assume his trusting and harmless manner. He mentioned the name of the former chairman of the Traditional Dress Club and said he was looking for him. Regarding the man in the light-colored coat on the Swiss side of the border, the clairvoyant Gestapo later claimed it was a British Secret Service man, Otto Strasser, or another contact. After that, the Gestapo interrogations focused for weeks solely on the question of whether this man had been wearing a hat or a cap. Rieger spoke of a hat, while others, including, interestingly, some who had not been there, said under intense pressure from the Gestapo, that it was a cap. The Gestapo was in a state of permanent paranoia. From this point on, anyone who had seen or might have seen anything suspicious was under the Gestapo's constant watch and subject to interrogation, using methods garnered from the GPU (the Soviet secret police) and administered by the admitted GPU disciple Heinrich Müller, known as Gestapo Müller. The paranoia was so widespread that long after the interrogations of Elser, even Xaver Rieger was kept under surveillance by a Gestapo informant to see whether he might meet with the British Secret Service or Otto Strasser.

At the Kreuzlingen customs office, Elser looked toward Switzerland, perhaps with longing, perhaps with regret. In any case, he lacked the energy to run the last eight meters from the customs building to the border. There was at that time no barrier across the border, only a chain. Would the border patrol have fired? Most certainly—the Nazis had no qualms when it came to dealing with violations of the border with Switzerland. But Elser was drained. He had never been an athlete and didn't have an athletic build. His strength lay in the years spent in his shop doing delicate work, hiding behind a calm and natural exterior. And with these skills, he had come far.

What finally led to his downfall was the bodily search. The contents of his pockets suggested that Elser must be a spy, a saboteur, and a Communist. Later on, the Berlin Gestapo would include in its interrogation record Elser's excuse that he had simply forgotten about these things. However, *Reichskriminaldirektor* Arthur Nebe came to the correct conclusion: that Elser had wanted to use the contents of his pockets to secure asylum in Switzerland. Elser had taken the materials and information relating to munitions from the Waldenmaier Company in Heidenheim where he had worked. He wanted to prove to the Swiss that war matériel was being produced in Germany. This was of course old news since the war had already begun and would have been of little interest to Switzerland since it was engaging in arms trading with Germany. But Elser still clung to the notion of an old Swiss Confederation that no longer existed. The insignia of the Communist *Rotfrontkämpferbund* (Red Front) would likely have hastened his deportation, since the Swiss treatment of their own Communists was not exactly in accord with their constitution.

There was only one item in his pockets that belonged to Elser: the wire cutters. With these, he would have gotten through the border fence in only a few minutes. Perhaps once there he would have been considered a refugee. Perhaps in the cantons of Baselstadt or Schaffhausen, which were governed by the Social Democrats, but certainly not in Thurgau. Here the sentiment was inclined toward Hitler—with a good dose of anti-Semitism and enmity toward the left. In the best-case scenario, Elser might have been shunted off to France, as was Otto Strasser the next day. Through physical evidence of his work, Elser wanted to lay creative claim to the explosion in the Bürgerbräukeller. But the Gestapo would have immediately demanded of the Swiss that he be extradited as a felon, and the police in Bern would have complied with the demand. Elser's itinerary would have remained the same: Berlin, Sachsenhausen, Dachau.

Viewing the border episode this way places it in a new light. If Elser had succeeded in fleeing to Switzerland, his fate would not likely have been any different than it was following his capture in Konstanz. The case of Maurice Bavaud demonstrates that the Swiss at that time had no sympathy for a Hitler assassin. The Swiss ambassador in Berlin, Hans Frölicher, could have arranged to exchange Bavaud, who had planned to kill Hitler with a pistol in 1938, for several Gestapo spies imprisoned in Switzerland. But he didn't want to. So Bavaud was executed by guillotine in Berlin-Plötzensee in 1941.

While Elser was being searched, he was threatened with beatings because he tried to pass off the detonator parts as clock parts. The threats were left out of the interrogation record, as they were considered standard tools of the trade. From this point on, until he was delivered to Sachsenhausen—more than a year later—Elser received frequent beatings; most were severe and sometimes life threatening.

When they were done, the customs officials called Gestapo headquarters, located at Mainaustrasse 29 in the former Villa Rokka, and Gestapo officer Otto Grethe was sent to pick up Elser and bring him there for further questioning. Grethe's impression of Elser was that he was "an unremarkable man, at most 1.6 m. (5' 2") tall—wavy hair, haggard, sullen expression." From this point forward, Elser was addressed by his first name and *du*, the familiar form for "you." (This would later be interpreted by some of Elser's prison inmates to mean that he was somehow entangled with the SS.)

Grethe interrogated Elser on the second floor at Gestapo headquarters. He believed none of Elser's excuses and noticed right away that he was "very unapproachable" and would admit nothing. Elser resisted the pressure, divulging nothing and giving out meaningless information as a defense. He even became "hostile," claiming he had been arrested without cause and banging his fist on the table.

Around 11:00 p.m., after an hour of interrogation, which had produced nothing of substance for the Gestapo, news of the assassination attempt in the Bürgerbräukeller came in over the teletype, with instructions to close the borders and maintain strict surveillance.

Georg Elser appeared uninterested as one teletype after another containing the words "bomb attack" arrived at the Gestapo headquarters. There was no indication at this point whether or not Hitler was dead.

The Gestapo continued their interrogation of Elser until 4:00 a.m., when they finally locked him into a holding cell on the ground floor. Because he had detonator parts in his wallet, Elser would be interrogated by the next level of command. A message from the Gestapo central office in Karlsruhe was forwarded to Gestapo headquarters in Berlin and to the Special Commission in Munich. The same day, Elser was transferred in a Gestapo car to Munich.

Later, in Berlin, the Gestapo asked Elser what he felt when challenged by the patrol at the border. His dry answer: "Annoyance at myself and my thoughtlessness." He regretted not having first looked around more carefully—a mistake he had not previously allowed himself. For the deed itself had been superbly prepared—his explosive device had functioned with great precision.

III

The Explosion

EVEN BEFORE HITLER arrived at the main train station in Munich, the Bürgerbräukeller lay in ruins. Hitler knew nothing more than that. The explosion that occurred at 9:20 p.m. was experienced by the eyewitnesses in very different ways, depending on their position in the hall and what they were doing at the time.

It was waitress Maria Strobl's job to wait on Hitler's table, but not on Hitler himself. In 1959 she told a journalist about that night. During Hitler's speech, she and some of her coworkers—there were thirty on duty—were standing near the restrooms smoking. At the end, when "Deutschland über alles" started up, they went to the entrance of the hall. The sound of chairs being pushed back was their cue to clear away the beer mugs and collect payment from the customers. The hall was emptying out quickly—Hitler was of course already gone, and there were only about 120 people left, including many musicians and technical support staff.

I wanted to clear the table, so I picked up ten large mugs. It was right by the column where Hitler was—I was waiting on those tables. I picked up the ten mugs and all of a sudden there was a blast that knocked me through the door into the entranceway. Rocks and all kinds of junk were falling on my head. Then I went out to the doctor's room. We thought a bomb had fallen somewhere. We didn't know anything. Then I got a cop to take me home.

The wreckage of the Bürgerbräukeller after the debris had been cleared.

When she got home, Maria Strobl realized that she had forgotten her purse and papers at the restaurant, so she had to go back. In the meantime, the SS had arrived. "It wasn't until then that I saw how the hall looked—everything had collapsed; the SS guys were making a fuss because somebody was smoking—nobody was supposed to smoke because they didn't know what was going on, right?" At first it was thought to be a poison gas bomb.

For a long time afterward, Maria Strobl could not hear and she suffered a serious nervous breakdown. She ended up experiencing permanent damage due to the blast. Night and day she could hear a rushing sound in her ears, and later on she became deaf in her left ear. And because of the abrupt end of the event, the men had not paid their tabs. Maria had to go to Party headquarters (known as the "Brown House") nine times before someone finally agreed to cover the tabs run up by those who had skipped out on them that evening.

Four of the waitresses had to go to the hospital. Part-time waitress Maria Henle was killed immediately. A coworker who was clearing tables with her on the gallery said the whole gallery was rocking so hard during the explosion that she had the feeling she was on a swing.

In the days that followed, political elements began to creep into the recollections of the eyewitnesses, elements that had previously hardly been present at all. For example, on November 11, after returning from Munich, a recipient of the Nazi *Blutorden* (Blood Order) from Hamburg reported to the *Hamburger Tagblatt* that at the Bürgerbräukeller that evening, just as he was going through a door into the Bürgerbräustübl to get a snack, he was hurled to the floor by the blast. "At first, I didn't know what had happened," he said. And then the *ex post facto* ideology sets in; everyone's first suspicion—that it was a bomb dropped from a plane—has now been pushed aside:

Our very first thought was: Thank God nothing happened to the Führer! From the scene of the tragedy we could hear the cries of pain from our injured Party comrades, men and women. Their cries for help sounded like a heartrending outcry against the bloody assassins who had carried out this attempt on the life of the Führer and thereby on Germany itself. . . . After they had been told repeatedly that nothing had happened to the Führer, their eyes filled with tears of deep gratitude to Providence and then they appeared to forget all their pain.

The first report from the hospital mixed medical information with eyewitness accounts. The injured were covered with thick dust; the faces of many were bloody; most had injuries to the upper body—bruises, abrasions, skull fractures—caused as the ceiling and walls collapsed and the chandelier fell. The blast alone had had devastating consequences. "Several *Alte Kampfer* were hurled from the gallery twenty feet down into the hall. Others were thrown under the tables with enormous force, and yet more were struck by falling beams." As many recalled, "[. . .] a gigantic flame seemed to shoot up over the column where the Führer had been standing just a short while before. Then a mighty cloud of dust shrouded the hall in an impenetrable darkness. For several seconds longer, one could hear the masonry crumbling and the columns bursting. And throughout, loud cries for help reverberated through the hall."

A prescient eyewitness, who had already been quoted in the *Münchner Neueste Nachrichten* on November 9, expressed a suspicion not commonly heard at first: "There was a time bomb in the hall!" and, in true Hitler fashion, he drew the conclusion "The Führer was to be murdered—my God, what bestial mind could conceive and execute such horrors?"

In the *Berliner Lokalanzeiger* of November 11, other eyewitness reports appeared. An engineer named Jakob Royer, also a recipient of the *Blutorden,* was lucky. At the moment of the explosion, he was "about twenty feet away from the pillar and was flung unconscious under a table by the blast, thus being protected from the falling debris." When he regained consciousness, he thought a bomb had been dropped, but he realized his error when he saw flames leaping head-high in the back of the hall.

Another witness, Emil Wipfel, was an engineer employed by the *Reichsautozug Deutschland,* a technical division of the SA which was responsible for providing power and water at mass assemblies of the Party. During the explosion, this group was in the process of disassembling the PA system and was therefore in the vicinity of the speaker's platform.

Suddenly, there was a brief, bright fiery glow around us. At the same moment, we heard a horrific bang. I was knocked back about six feet and landed on some debris; then everything started cracking and crashing down on me. When things quieted down, I was lying on my belly with my arm around the foot of my comrade Schachta. At that moment I was not yet aware that he was already dead. I couldn't move my left arm, and my feet were completely pinned down. It's astounding how cool one can remain in such a dire situation. At first, I had only one thought: that I had to remain still in order to prevent any further shifting of the beams or other debris lying on top of me. As I later learned, a part of the ceiling that had collapsed on the spot where the Führer's podium had been was lying on top of me. I suspect that it was supported just enough by a smashed table that was next to me—and maybe also by the body of my dead comrade—that I was not crushed. I could hardly breathe. Very close to me I soon heard the cries of trapped comrades and then started to call attention to myself. Over and over we shouted that no one should walk on the debris on top of us. However, it took a considerable time until the police could get us out because the debris was especially deep at precisely the location where we were trapped by it.

The most extensive eyewitness report was written by Dr. Wilhelm Kaffl, editor-in-chief of the National Socialist weekly, *Die Post*, and a staunch supporter of Hitler:

For a fraction of a second, it's eerily quiet and dark. But a few light bulbs have remained intact—I see the first people pushing through the exit—dark figures, totally covered in dust! Mechanically, I reach for my coat, which the deathly pale attendant has just tossed to me. Screaming loudly, a young girl, who is probably coming from the nearby kitchen, rushes past me. I'm still standing there shouting, asking what's happening. Understandably, I receive no answer. A couple of people close to me run to the entrance to the hall—as do I! But we can't swim against the stream now flooding out of the hall. But even worse: A yellowish-gray opaque wall—probably made up of dust and residue from the explosion—moves toward us. The indescribable stench of the fog causes someone next to me to shout: "Air attack—poison gas—everybody out!" I already have my hand over my nose and mouth and am digging for a handkerchief. I give up trying to get into the hall. From somewhere there came a shout: "Lock everything—nobody leaves the premises!" I try to make myself useful and join with others to form a barrier. In the meantime, it has become clear that there had been no air attack and that no gas bombs had been dropped—rather, that something far more horrible must have happened: *a crime, an assassination attempt, a murderous attack on the Führer!* We were seized by a nameless rage. Where are *the murderers*, who are they? We have no time to think. Covered in blood, some of the wounded have dragged themselves out of the hall. That was shortly before 9:30, and the explosion had happened perhaps five minutes before. Did I say wounded? Correct! God knows what else might have happened there in the hall. We have to help! We quickly break away from our human chain. The way into the hall, which is almost dark, is open. Our eyes take a moment to adjust. *Then we see what happened here.* Our first concern: *wounded comrades.* We find them: in a corner, on a broken chair, lying in broken glass and debris. And we get waitresses out as well. In the meantime it has cleared up somewhat—or perhaps it just seems that way to us. Suddenly there are medics among us with stretchers and bandages. Several women in nurse uniforms are setting about their work quickly yet calmly. From the courtyard we hear the bell of the fire department and the sirens of the bomb attack squad. At last! Those few minutes of waiting after the alarm seemed like hours to us. Now at last we find time to look around us in the hall: a picture of gruesome destruction. A good part of the suspended ceiling has crashed down into the hall. A mountain of debris—boards, iron girders, broken chairs and tables—is piled high as a man from the main entrance to the middle of the hall. *Yes, to the middle of the hall*—right to the spot where, twenty minutes before, the Führer was standing and speaking, where Rudolf Hess, Dr. Goebbels, Alfred Rosenberg, and many more of our leaders were sitting—all the way to this point the wreckage was piled, standing in indictment of one of the most vile and brutal crimes in the history of the world. *The Führer lives!* Three words—we spoke them as the most fervent prayer ever to issue from our hearts and mouths. The hatred, the malevolence of this criminal rabble—were shattered by him. *He lives*—and we shall stamp out this pestilence which threatens to take over this world, sending out its putrid breath against justice, honor, and manliness, and stopping at nothing, however base or low.

At the site of the speaker's platform, the debris was about ten feet high. The ceiling had fallen in on itself and an exterior wall about fifty feet long had collapsed inward. Hitler would not have survived the blast. The Nuremberg *Gauleiter* (District Leader) Julius Streicher quickly went back into the hall and took a look at the spot where he had been sitting a short while before. "Tables and chairs have been reduced to thousands and thousands of splinters, and right where my chair was there is now an iron beam weighing hundreds of pounds."

After the initial confusion, police and Gestapo sealed off the entire area with the help of the SS and SA, many of whom were wearing steel helmets. Inside the collapsed hall, the National Labor Service went about the business of rescue and recovery. For the time being, they could not consider shoring up the remaining part of the hanging ceiling—they did not have the necessary boards. Ambulances, police cars, and fire trucks were constantly arriving with sirens wailing. Wild rumors were flying around the neighborhood, where people had clearly heard the detonation. Outgoing telephone connections in the city were blocked for a long time. At one in the morning the Gestapo ordered a shutdown that affected even central facilities such as Army Intelligence in Berlin.

A very objective radio report was recorded and broadcast by National Radio in Munich on the morning of November 9. This source lies unpublished in the Radio Archive in Frankfurt and is given here in some detail. The reporter does not embellish his report with outrage at the assassination attempt or grief for the victims. Instead, his intent is for listeners to gain an authentic impression of the gruesome scene. While he talks calmly, in the background we can hear shovels scraping up the debris:

Upon entering the courtyard in the rear, one finds an enormous pile of beams—a gigantic tangle of beams; a mountain of bricks; broken tables and chairs strewn all around; smashed beer glasses, stained grayish black with plaster and filth. And now we are here inside the former hall: above us a gigantic hole, the sky clearly visible through it. The work of debris removal is in progress. The ceiling came down—it fell in, partially collapsed. Pieces of plaster are still hanging on it, some of it crumbling away. The chandeliers are hanging at a sharp angle, dented and missing bulbs . . . a jumble of bricks . . . splintered wood. The blast obviously smashed all the window panes—pushed them outward. It is a scene of terrible destruction . . . here large piles of debris. We are now standing about ten feet from the spot where yesterday the Führer's platform stood. Reed matting is hanging down . . . parts of the wall are still standing. An I-beam has tilted into the room at an angle . . . above us, as we said, there's open sky. Snarls of wire, girders, paneling, support columns . . . lying everywhere. The floor above has fallen down, and up there beams are jutting from every direction into the room like skewers. As we have said, it is a terrible scene, and one must struggle to find the words to describe something like this.

The reporter then interviews Party member Frank, a Swabian technician or architect who was there during the explosion. This man clearly delights in precision and objective coolness. His technical curiosity informs his report, and he even lets two distinct compliments to the assassin slip out—not at all in keeping with the ranting of the press about instigators behind the scenes. This is the classic technical clinician speaking, unperturbed by the politically tinged surroundings:

I was just about to leave the hall and was perhaps three feet from the exit, when suddenly there was a flash up above in the room. In the same instant [I felt] a hard push from behind . . . not actually a blow—it felt like I was being shoved forward, and in the next instant I found myself five or six feet closer to the exit. At the same moment there was a thunderous noise, a [he imitates the sound]; and then it was all over, actually. Before you could figure out what was going on, you were standing there in a cloud of dust so thick that first, you couldn't see anything at all, and second, you couldn't breathe. At first, we couldn't think about what had happened—we just put our handkerchiefs over our mouths and made sure we got to the exit. Out in the cloakroom it became possible to breathe a little; then, as quickly as possible, we turned around and headed back into the hall. On the ground floor, where the windows were still intact, we broke out the glass in order to get some fresh air in there. And then, after a minute or maybe a minute and a half, the dust began to settle; that's when we discovered that the ceiling had caved in. And then immediately the first of the injured started coming out, those who had been able to free themselves from under tables or chairs. They were somewhat better off since they were able to get to safety. But the more seriously injured ones we had to gradually dig out.

The reporter then asked him how this all happened, and Frank replied:

After the flash, we could see that it came from above. That means the blast definitely didn't come from below, from the floor; the explosive charge must have been placed at the gallery level, in the first pillar on the side where the Führer's podium was located—at the gallery level. That is the pillar where we are standing now, which was about ten feet to the right of the Führer's podium; that's where the explosive charge [must have been placed]. You see the girders up there are bent and cracked—up here we see the effects of the explosion. So the charge must have been situated on the gallery either under the plank flooring or under the wood paneling on the wall. First, this support beam came down. . . . And since the support beam was gone, the longitudinal beams, which provided support between the gallery and the hall itself, came loose and sagged down. There were two of these: This one here, with stone still attached to it, was at the level of the gallery floor, and the large iron T-girder we see there . . . it tipped downward because the upper part of this vertical beam here also gave way after it had been cracked by the explosion.

Infected now by curiosity, the reporter asked innocently, "So that was the spot from which someone was able to bring down the entire hall?"

Frank had no reservations about expressing praise for the assassin:

Yes, this was technically the most effective spot . . . besides the two longitudinal beams a large transverse beam dislodged—it came loose too and fell down. And lying on top of this transverse beam there was also a steel girder that spanned the middle of the hall and wasn't supported by the next beam, but was attached to the next beam only by rivets and side plates and supported from above by the roof structure. And because of this structure, which gave way, the girder tilted down; the spot here where it was riveted gave way—the rivets were ripped out—the girder came down, the next one dropped; in addition, the whole roof structure was brought down because that was what the girder was attached to. And therefore an extraordinarily comprehensive collapse could be achieved.

There were no arrests made on the evening of November 8, as there was still a great deal of uncertainty: Who could it have been? Three people died immediately, four of the injured died soon thereafter in the hospital where an additional sixty-three injured people were being treated. On November 13 an eighth died of his injuries.

For a long time afterward, postwar Germany refused to admit that the attempt on Hitler's life was justified and dwelled instead on the eight "innocent victims" killed in the collapse of the Bürgerbräukeller, rather than on the millions murdered by Hitler in the camps, or the "euthanasia" victims, or the fifty million victims of World War II.

A glance at the *Völkischer Beobachter* might have dampened this sympathy. Except for the part-time waitress Maria Henle, the dead were all members of the Nazi Party or the SA. In the obituaries, the Party and the families indicated their pride in these recipients of the *Blutorden.* Many had belonged to the *Freikorps* Epp and to the *Stoss-trupp* Adolf Hitler, which in 1923 had set out to destroy the Republic and establish a dictatorship. The obituaries of Michael Wilhelm Weber can serve to illustrate this. As his widow wrote, he had died "for his beloved Führer, for his free Germany." Weber was the owner of the large perfume concern Bavaria, a Party member, recipient of the *Blutorden*, recipient of the *EKII* (Iron Cross 2nd Class) and the Bavarian Military Service Cross, a *Freikorps* veteran, a Hitler supporter since 1920, a *Hauptsturmführer* in the *NSKK* (National Socialist Motor Corps), and deputy Führer of the *NSKK-Motorstandarte* 86.

Three of the victims who died in the vicinity of Hitler's podium were members of the *Reichsautozug* (the organization responsible for motorcade logistics) and were *SA Hauptsturmführer* or *Truppführer*. They were on duty. According to Nazi values, one did not need to mourn those who died in the service of the Party; they were accepted into the ranks of Party heroes. Their deaths were considered a noble contribution to the victory of the "Movement." As Hitler's followers were told at the official state ceremony of November 11, the tragedy of the individual meant nothing, as long as the Führer was alive.

IV

Searching the Rubble

Hitler had arrived with his entourage at the main station in Munich five minutes before the train was to depart. The "simple corporal," as he liked to think of himself, had as usual exactly a dozen suitcases. At 9:31 p.m. the private train left for Berlin. The mood in the parlor car was cheerful, even boisterous. The topic, as always after such events, was the glorious past of the Party before 1933—the "*Kampfzeit*" (Time of Struggle). And now there was the *Blitzkrieg* against Poland, the second country in the East to be conquered in just a few weeks. Hitler had always been right; now he was assured of the absolute support of his people. So what if there was some reluctance in the military? The General Staff officers had always had reservations—they never wanted to take any risks, but he had always gotten his way. And now they were to move against England. First, however, they needed to invade France and occupy Paris in another *Blitzkrieg*.

In the car they were intoxicated with victory. Hitler, as always, drank mineral water, but several in the entourage were deeply into the alcohol. The train would not arrive at the Anhalter Station in Berlin until 10:20 a.m., so there would be plenty of time to sleep it off. Along the route, two stationmasters, one of them in Augsburg, tried in vain to stop the train to tell Hitler about the attack—the engineer kept going in order to maintain the tight schedule.

There was no stop planned until Nürnberg, where Goebbels got off to have some teletypes dispatched and returned as white as a sheet. But Hitler thought the news about the Bürgerbräukeller was a macabre joke—Goebbels after all had a bit of a mischievous bent. Before the bombing, Hitler's officers had discussed the risk of an attack many times. Hitler was prone to wade into a crowd to bask in the adulation of his followers. His security forces broke out in a cold sweat every time he ignored safety measures in order to have contact with his admirers, accept flowers, or let people get close to his car— any one of them might someday toss a grenade.

However, at this moment the pallor on Goebbels's face and his seriousness spoke against the possibility of a joke. Hitler wondered if it was simply a false report. But the propaganda minister had already excluded this possibility by contacting Berlin. So indeed, at the very site of the self-glorification of the Party, someone had been out to get Hitler. But the mood on the train was so cheerful, with victory so close, that Hitler reacted in a way that yields deep insight into his mentality. His spontaneous comment was, "A man has to be lucky"— the attitude of a gambler. Until then he had always gotten by with that. Now he wanted to verify the news for himself and got off the train to phone the men directing the operation at the Bürgerbräukeller: Gauleiter Adolf Wagner and Munich chief of police Friedrich Karl Freiherr von Eberstein.

When Hitler returned he looked transformed, according to his secretary. His face, she reported, took on "a determined and hardened appearance. . . . In his eyes there glowed the mystical fire that I had so often seen in him at times of great decisions." In a flash Hitler determined that any attempt on his life proved to be an even greater victory for him, and he shouted into the parlor car: "Now I am completely at peace! My leaving the Bürgerbräu earlier than usual is proof to me that Providence wants me to reach my goal."

Thoughts turned next to the instigators. Hitler was still so filled with hatred toward England from his speech that his suspicion immediately fell on the British Secret Service. At the following train stations, where new reports from Munich awaited them, the first orders were given out. All night long, it was so hectic aboard the train that Goebbels only managed to get one hour of sleep before they arrived in Berlin. During the night Himmler had launched inquiries. Hitler demanded the best experts for the criminal investigation and charged Arthur Nebe, *Reichskriminaldirektor* (Commissioner of the Criminal Police, or Kripo) and chief of Office V of the *Reichssicherheitshauptamt* (Central Office of Reich Security) in Berlin, with undertaking the investigation.

Hitler's idea of holding the British Secret Service responsible was transmitted to Berlin by Goebbels that night. By the next day, November 9, the press releases of the National Socialist news agency DNB (*Deutsches Nachrichten Büro*) had established the Party line. It wasn't until November 21 that Hitler gave the press another angle: that the mastermind of the Munich attempt was Otto Strasser, a left-leaning National Socialist, who at the time was living as an emigrant in Switzerland. Strasser had been an opponent of Hitler since 1930, and his brother Gregor had been murdered in connection with the bloody assault against the SA in 1934. Otto Strasser had already been held responsible for other assassination attempts in Germany, and Hitler had sent several murderers out after him in Czechoslovakia.

By midnight of November 9, two explosives experts had begun their investigation at the scene of the crime, supervised by Dr. Albrecht Böhme, chief of the central Kripo office (*Kripo leit stelle*) in Munich. The Munich Gestapo chief actually responsible for investigating incidents of assassination and sabotage was away at the time and was later booted out of his position. Böhme had the Kripo people undertake other investigative duties such as securing evidence, especially fragments of any kind, and using spotlights to take photographs, which would of course have to be taken again the next day in daylight. While working on recovering the dead from under the debris, the fire department had already discovered suspicious brass parts. This convinced Böhme to carefully sift the entire mountain of debris the next morning.

The first suspicion about the origin of the attack came from the *Alte Kämpfer*, who had to defend themselves against the accusation that they had failed to protect the hall and the people in it. They claimed that the explosion lay outside their purview—after all, it had occurred only after they had lifted the security around the hall. When the experts found pieces of the timed detonator, this claim completely fell apart. For a few days, they shored up their public image with the speculation that the explosion had taken place in an empty space above the gallery or in the roof beams. This notion flitted through the domestic and foreign press as news.

In contrast, by 4:00 a.m. on November 9, the explosives experts felt confident of their findings and in their report reached a conclusion, which largely conformed with the observations that eyewitness Frank had made on the radio: "Based on these initial findings, it was assumed that the point of the explosion must have been located here at this column, up on the gallery level." If the explosive charge had been out in the open, then some fifty kilos would have been required. It would surely have been impossible for the assassin to smuggle so much explosive into the hall and store it unnoticed. This thought steered the experts onto the right path: "It is therefore likely that the quantity of explosive packed into the column would have totaled, in accordance with the standard formula, 8–10 kg." The modifications necessary for the installation led to the conclusion that "the attack had been prepared far in advance." The assassin had enhanced the effect enormously by not placing the explosive in the open but instead building it into a pillar—in technical terms, "confining" it—and on top of that, putting it into a load-bearing pillar that supported the ceiling of the hall and the roof.

The experts surmised that:

Since the gallery was covered with wood paneling, both on the side facing the hall and the side toward the exterior wall, it would have been possible for the perpetrator to work without attracting attention by repeatedly removing the paneling and then replacing it while constructing the bomb chamber. He must, in any case, have been familiar with the conditions at the location as well as the routine procedures of the business. As soon as the bomb chamber had been completed, all that remained to do was install the timing device and then set it.

Thus the experts assumed that this was a timed detonation, calling it a "*Höllenmaschine*" (Hell's machine)—a time bomb. Fitting in with their conclusion were the "spiral springs, cogs, and other metal parts" that had been "found on the gallery floor, which was still intact. . . . Given the location where these items were found, it could be concluded that the site of the explosion was also at the level of the gallery floor." According to the report, the charge was located behind the paneling, "approximately in the center of the pillar." The experts were seriously mistaken about only one issue, however: They claimed that "an extraordinarily powerful explosive was used, which was far superior to the customary commercial explosives."

Munich police chief von Eberstein, in his first report of November 9, declared enthusiastically "that this was definitely not a primitive apparatus; it was clearly the product of superior workmanship." He then dutifully dampened his somewhat grotesque enthusiasm by expressing the suspicion that the perpetrators were "an as-yet-unknown terrorist group." The police chief expected further revelations from interrogations of Bürgerbräu staff, sanitation department employees temporarily housed in the hall, and all companies that might have had anything to do with construction work, renovation, or interior decoration of the Bürgerbräukeller and might therefore have come into possession of the building plans.

When Dr. Böhme ordered the piles of debris searched for fragments of the explosive device that morning, the Munich watchmakers guild offered him their assistance and sent forty apprentices from the watch-making school. The men from the fire department and the Reich Labor Service carefully shoveled through the debris and secured the area against collapse. In the middle of a dust cloud, which obstructed vision and breathing, the students searched the debris with their trained eyes and skilled fingers. Police commissars plotted the locations where metal parts and other parts were found onto a plan of the hall so that it soon became clear where the explosion came from and with what force. In all, the apprentices found 300 parts made of brass and other metals. In addition, pieces of insulation were found that contained a company stamp and could thus provide an important clue as to the seller of the material and, through him, to the purchaser—the assassin.

From the very beginning, various agencies squabbled over the investigation. This was typical of the governing style of the National Socialists. By having various offices compete against each other, Hitler felt he could ensure his absolute authority. Thus at 2:30 a.m., without being called, the prosecutor general and the senior public prosecutor appeared at the scene in order to initiate the judicial inquiry. The Gestapo allowed them to proceed, until on November 15, probably after an audience Himmler had with Hitler, there came a categorical declaration, which intelligence officer Groscurth noted in his journal: "Heydrich informed Senior Reich Prosecutor Lautz that it was out of the question for Justice to participate in the investigation of the assassination attempt. Likewise, on orders from above, *Reichskriminaldirektor* Nebe has rejected the involvement of the prosecutor general in Munich." A high-level SS officer justified the exclusion of Justice from the investigation of the assassination attempt: "It's wartime now; all crimes and other such matters should be referred directly to the Gestapo."

There were further clashes over securing the evidence. When Police Chief Eberstein read the first report by Böhme that morning, he contemptuously tapped his forehead with his finger and lashed out at the Kripo chief: "You think you're going to find a political crime in this debris?!" He would have much preferred to have everything at the scene cleared away immediately. Böhme made clear that that would be "an inexcusable dereliction of duty." When Böhme asked what should be done instead, his boss had no answer. The sifting continued. In the morning some *Alte Kämpfer* came by, wanting to get involved in the investigation, but they were turned away with the warning that there was "danger of collapse" of the building.

On November 9 at 11:00 a.m., Arthur Nebe arrived from Berlin by plane at Munich-Riem, with his entourage of six Kripo officers. Himmler, head of the SS and the police, had during the night ordered the establishment of a "Bürgerbräukeller Special Commission," with a "crime scene commission" under Section Chief Hans Lobbes from the Reich Criminal Police, and a "suspect commission," for which, after a day and a half of fruitless interrogations, a former expert for the Munich Political Police was called in from Vienna—Franz-Josef

Huber, chief of Gestapo Headquarters in Vienna. Huber was a good friend of the much-feared Heinrich Müller, who had been head of the Gestapo in Berlin since 1937. The office of the Special Commission was at the Munich Gestapo headquarters in Wittelsbacher Palace at the corner of Briennerstrasse and Türkenstrasse, an area which today includes the chic and affluent district of Schwabing.

A wave of arrests, which had already started that night, went on for weeks. The total number of people detained cannot be determined, but it must have been at least a thousand. That first night alone there were 120 arrests just at the border crossings. All Communists who weren't already behind bars were apprehended. Anyone hanging around the scene out of curiosity was dragged to Wittelsbacher Palace for interrogation. During the next few weeks, anyone in Germany who said anything about the attempt that didn't conform to the Party line fell into the hands of the Gestapo. There was such a bumper crop of denunciations that even the Gestapo was overwhelmed—people trying to settle old scores were reporting their enemies. At first, all names were checked at the Reich security office in Berlin, where a central catalog of suspects was established. In addition, Himmler ordered the employees of the Bürgerbräu—approximately fifty—to be arrested and interrogated. The waitress Maria Strobl was able to avoid arrest only because of her injuries. Instead, Gestapo people, armed with a typewriter, sought her out at home and for days asked her the same questions over and over again, then despite her objections dragged her to Wittelsbacher Palace five or six times for interrogations. Many of those involved, most notably the innkeeper of the Bürgerbräukeller, remained in custody for three months.

Kripo director Nebe, who for years had maintained loose contacts with the military opposition, initially feared that rebellious firebrands from the General Staff might have acted on their own. The timing of the attempt would appear to indicate this, because in the event of war with France, assassination plans had already been worked out by an opposition group within the General Staff. But General Staff Chief of the Army Franz Halder thought and thought, hemmed and hawed and delayed, then pushed the job off on Chief of Intelligence (*Abwehr*) Canaris, but he, in turn, was too patriotic and scrupulous. Intelligence officer Groscurth wrote in his personal diary: "These indecisive leaders make you sick." On November 1, Major General Hans Oster, the head of Army Intelligence and one of the most active of the military resistance fighters, declared to the diplomat Erich Kordt: "We don't have anybody we can get to throw the bomb and liberate our generals from their scruples."

Nebe became even more concerned when he heard on the radio that morning that British explosives had been used in the attempt. This version also made its way into the *Wochenschau*, the weekly newsreel from UFA. And indeed the German military opposition favored using British Explosive material because it was more volatile and more easily workable—the subject never got beyond the discussion stage in these circles.

When Nebe read the explosives report around noon, he took a deep breath. Now it seemed impossible that the rival Gestapo could, through manipulation, pin the attempt on Intelligence. From this point on, Nebe had not the slightest interest in going easy on the assassin. Duty was duty. According to testimony by Gisevius, it took him until 1944 to recognize that only the Bürgerbräu assassin had the right stuff to get rid of Hitler.

V

Reaction to the Attack

Hitler's Propaganda Minister Joseph Goebbels appeared to be unfazed by the attack. He dryly wrote in his diary, "If the rally had gone off according to plan, as it always had before, then none of us would be alive." Then he took on the voice of a preacher: "He [Hitler] is, after all, under the protection of the Almighty. He will not die until his mission is accomplished." On November 10 Goebbels noted with satisfaction: "The mood in the country is excellent." At the time he was editing the script for the film *Jud Süss* by Veit Harlan.

General Rommel, who was one of Hitler's greatest admirers, wrote on November 15: "The Führer is very determined. The Munich attack has strengthened his resolve." And in the next line he reveals that he shares Hitler's delight in war: "It is a pleasure to participate in this experience."

This pleasure, however, was not shared by Party philosopher Alfred Rosenberg, who had been seated close to the Führer and the ticking bomb. He wrote in his diary on November 11: "We are all still feeling the effects of the assassination attempt in Munich." If Hitler had not ended his speech sooner than usual, Rosenberg surmised, "we would have all been buried under the rubble." During the bombing he recalled the failed Putsch of 1923: "[…]Sixteen years ago I went with Adolf Hitler, pistol in hand, to this same podium where death now awaited us. . . . For fourteen years we had risked our necks—now the same enemies, apparently foreigners, are at work trying to get rid of us for good." It was clear that the assassination attempt had made him uneasy, and his thoughts turned to his own fate: "If I look at my house, I see that it would be a simple matter in that remote area to toss a bomb into my bedroom window at night."

Goebbels, on the other hand, was a professional optimist, and he used his influence to shape public opinion through newspapers, radio, and the film industry. The top headline in the *Berliner Lokalanzeiger* of November 10 read: "All Germany Reeling from this Dastardly Crime." The next headline announced: "Civilized World Outraged." The third article about the bombing—"Wave of Fanatical Outrage Sweeps Reich"—heightened the drama even more. ("Fanatical" was a favorite word of Hitler's and hence of Nazi journalists.)

With its network of volunteer members, the *Sicherheitsdienst*— the intelligence arm of the SS and the Party—was able to gauge the real mood of the people. The SD was often better informed and more realistic in its assessments than the somewhat removed Party leadership. Describing the mood in the days leading up to the Munich attack, the SD reported on October 23, 1939: "Throughout the Reich, it can be confirmed that trust in official reports in press, film, and radio continues at a gratifyingly high level and that the people support and embrace the current manner of conducting propaganda, especially with regard to foreign countries." And two days later: "The German people are convinced that the battle against England must be continued." According to their reports, almost no opposition to the war could be found anywhere in the country. This was hardly surprising: Anyone speaking out for peace risked being sent to a concentration camp. Since 1934, any dissenting views fell under the *Heimtückegesetz* (sedition law); after the start of the war, listening to enemy broadcasts became a punishable offense.

In its report issued two days after the attack, the SD registered, with some satisfaction, a wave of outrage among German citizens. At first there was mistrust toward the press, then the rumor mill went into gear, reporting that Hitler had been badly injured and that "leading men of the Party and the government" had been killed. When it turned out that there was nothing to these reports, the bitterness shifted to "the English and the Jews"—they must surely be behind it. In the report, it was stated that "in some areas there were demonstrations against Jews" and that workers were exhorting Göring to send the Luftwaffe to "reduce London to rubble." Hitler considered his speech at the Bürgerbräukeller so essential to his mission that he had it issued as a lavishly illustrated brochure, with three million copies distributed throughout Germany.

Just how deeply the hearts of the Germans were affected by the attack can be gauged from private documents, which mainly conveyed the Party line. A professor wrote Hitler's chief adjutant Brückner: "All of our people are deeply filled with gratitude to Providence. An individual cannot express it to the Führer; but to you, the guardian of the vestibule to the heart of the Führer, who conduct so many streams from the people to him, I may say it . . . it was for me the happiest moment of my long life when I knew the Führer was safe . . ." And the wife of Austrian Fascist Othmar Spann-Rheinisch wrote:

Once again God's angels have protected the Chosen One of the German soul. Thanks be to God and to you, o my Führer! What happens to people is in accord with what they are. What happens to you is in accord with your being, with your destiny: Your being is one with the German spirit, which has brought you forth from the obscurity of your forebears and made you into our heart and our head! May friend and foe alike see that you are invincible, like the German spirit, as invulnerable as Siegfried!

Similar sentiments were on display in businesses throughout Germany. On December 13 the SD announced, "Since the outbreak of war and especially since the Munich attack, business owners in many locations have placed pictures of the Führer in their shop windows." A liquor store in Kiel inserted a photo of Hitler among a large number of liquor bottles, with a sign that said "We'll never capitulate!"

Many German women, however, were not as confident—the same SD report noted that miscarriages and abortions were on the increase. Many women who had recently become pregnant seemed to be worried about the future—what if their children's providers did not return from the war? And so they took matters into their own hands.

Concerning the bombing itself, Himmler issued orders in the newspapers that any suspicious remark should be reported to the police. This was unlikely to elicit any concrete results from the rumor mill that was constantly churning among the people. Given the wave of denunciations and the increasing number of detainees, the Gestapo was already overburdened.

Many rumors and misstatements resulted in a large number of arrests. On the night of the attack, the police put up numerous road blocks in and around Munich in an effort to catch the assassins. The rural police in Unterhaching stopped a taxi at 5:00 a.m. on November 9. While they were checking papers, the passenger, completely drunk, mumbled, "I didn't mean to shoot the Führer." Only because he was able to identify himself, and because he had a doctorate and was a reserve officer, was he allowed to go home.

A woman from Ottobrunn remembered a local mechanic telling her in 1936 that "if right now somebody would get out there and mingle with the crowd, he could easily get off a shot at him [Hitler]." This same man, who lived on the road that Hitler had traveled to get to the Obersalzberg, told another witness that "somebody could easily lie in the woods and open fire from there when he [Hitler] passed by." Someone else had observed this man carrying "a military weapon that could easily be disassembled." The head administrator for the district forwarded the charges to the senior public prosecutor.

In Moorenweis, a village near Fürstenfeldbruck, a postal worker, who was also a Party member, was overheard saying something in local dialect that the police interpreted as "it would have been no loss if Hitler had been dead." When he was sent to the Gestapo in Munich over the issue, he claimed to have heard the remark from two farm women. When these two women were questioned, it turned out they had heard something quite different. And on it went. Finally the local police officer threw in the towel, realizing that he had been led on a wild goose chase.

In Berlin, the SD district office itself confirmed how little of the propaganda regarding the positive mood in Berlin was accurate. They collected such statements as "during the period around November 9, great radical changes could be expected." In Wilmersdorf, there was a rumor that on November 9 Hermann Göring would be named Führer.

A sales clerk in a radio shop in Weissensee snitched on a man who made the threatening remark: "Just you wait till the eighth or ninth of November!" The date of the traditional gathering in Munich seemed to have already acquired an almost mythical quality.

After the assassination attempt, a master painter in Berlin expressed regret: "Too bad it failed!" A metal worker doubted that the English Secret Service had carried out the attack, underscoring his political intuition with the remark: "The people were responsible for the attempt—don't believe that the people are 100 percent behind Hitler!"

Hitler supporters in Berlin felt some measure of *Schadenfreude* directed at them because of the attack. Any number of people assumed that Hitler and others would soon be shot to death. A shop owner, who according to the sign in his window served Jews only between 12:00 and 1:00 p.m., received a threatening postcard on November 11 that read, "You son of a bitch, how is it that you refuse to allow Jewish people to shop until after twelve? Have you completely forgotten that 100 percent of your business used to come from Jewish customers? Get rid of this sign fast, or the glass will fly just like it did yesterday in Munich, where the lousy Nazis got bombed."

Starting in November, subversive anti-Nazi literature increased dramatically. A sticker found on a front door in Berlin contained the following message: "Christians, remember the Sermon on the Mount! Declare war on war!" This was very much in line with the motivation of the assassin.

Deutschland-Berichte (Reports from Germany), a publication of the Social Democratic Party in exile, also painted a picture of the chaotic thinking prevalent among Germans after the attempt, a picture that included civil unrest, wild rumors, mistrust toward the Nazi press, adoption of English phrases, and, above all, reports of people keeping their heads down in fear. From the German underground the Party leadership received five reports, which revealed no uniform assessment of the mood. According to the first report, the popular imagination had taken the English line and creatively modified it: The "Göring clique" had instigated the attempt, and the military had carried it out. Finally, however, people returned to the Gestapo myth of an English conspiracy: What forces are behind this attack and what forces could have succeeded in deceiving Himmler's Gestapo or in concealing from it that this was about to happen? Somehow, Hitler had to be behind it, they reasoned.

Another report contained speculation as to why, after the initial spate of conflicting opinions, Nazi propaganda was able to prevail so quickly. It came to the following conclusion: "The notion that all are in the same boat is too widespread and the belief in the promises made previously by the antiwar faction too shaken for the proverbial 'little man' to wish that the bomb had achieved the desired result. Besides, people reason, such an attack can never get all the 'Führers' at the same time and is therefore pointless. In the best-case scenario, it would result only in internal confusion; and the beneficiary would be the enemy, the war would be lost, and the misery would be even greater than after Versailles—all the efforts since 1933 would have been in vain." The point was devastating: "So it is with complete amazement that one must conclude that, whoever threw the bomb, the Nazis were the beneficiaries." The English claim that the attack was "a second Reichstag fire," i.e., carried out by the Nazis, was given no credence in the report.

However, this line of reasoning continued to flourish underground. Once the assassin had acquired a name, a biography, and a profession, this was the very angle used by those carrying out the assault on his integrity. He would come to be regarded as the stooge of the Nazis.

The SD report closed by asking what, if anything, could change the political situation. Answer: only "the decisive military defeat of the Reich." This view was also shared by some elements of the military resistance.

The bloodbath of the years to come might have been averted if the assassination attempt at the Bürgerbräukeller had been successful.

For many of the resistance fighters and members of the opposition, the assassination attempt served as a clarion call. The SD report of November 10 announced that in Berlin "at the shop of the Photo-Hoffmann company at Kochstrasse 10, a shop window had been shattered by a stone. The only items on display in the window were pictures of the Führer." The Czechs, too, could not conceal their satisfaction. "Among the Czech minority in the Sudetenland the *Schadenfreude* at the Munich attack was universally apparent."

The SD reports did not have much to say about statements by those who supported the attack—this was the purview of the Gestapo. There may have been several hundred Gestapo investigations of people who made remarks about the Munich attack that were suspicious or even supportive. But Gestapo records of reactions to the attacks have been preserved only in Düsseldorf (with seventy files), Würzburg (sixteen files), and Speyer (fifty-eight files).

One of the few cases to become famous was that of Wilhelm Jung, an innkeeper in Neunkirchen and a former member of the SD. When he read the newspaper report about the attempt while sitting in his pub on November 9, he said to a neighbor: "If the Führer and his closest associates had died in the attack, things would already be looking a lot different in Germany." He went on to say that the assassin, even if he were sitting there in the bar, would not be turned in by anybody. Jung was a little too sure of himself. His views circulated, he was taken into custody, and the witness stuck to her "patriotic" statement in spite of pleas from Mrs. Jung. Jung, a war invalid, was sentenced by a special court to two years in prison, after which he was transferred, at the age of sixty years and in poor health, to the concentration camp at Sachsenhausen and later to Auschwitz, where he died in 1942.

The effects of the bomb attack even spread as far as the concentration camps. On the one hand, political prisoners gained hope that someone might one day succeed in eliminating Hitler; on the other hand, the SS guards were in such a rage that they took it out on the prisoners. Immediately after the guards in Buchenwald heard about the attack, they took several Jews out to a quarry and shot them.

A former political prisoner named Rudolf Wunderlich provided further evidence that the SS guards at the concentration camp in Sachsenhausen were quite agitated about the attack. Around November 14, according to his testimony, Dr. Tuppy, a former prosecutor in Vienna, was taken there as a prisoner. The Nazis still had a score to settle with Tuppy. In accordance with prevailing law, he had at one time brought charges against the National Socialist murderers of the Austrian chancellor, Engelbert Dollfuss. Now, upon entering the "Political Department," (Gestapo headquarters inside the camp), he was almost bludgeoned to death. Later that evening he died in the infirmary.

The news of the Bürgerbräu attack left everyone in a confused state. The Nazis exerted relentless pressure to conform—anyone whose statements attracted attention was turned over to the Gestapo, yet anyone who was reticent could be considered suspicious. Those who had always been vulnerable, such as the Jews, were better off withdrawing completely, avoiding dangerous people or keeping quiet. The only organizations that had not yet been brought into line and could still take a stand—even if it was only to remain silent—were the churches. In the SD Report of November 15, the SS was already taking note that the Protestant Church and the Catholic Church were reacting differently to the attack. The Catholic clergy were content to avoid taking a position, while many Protestants sharply condemned it. In the Protestant churches there were "services thanking God for saving the Führer" and proclamations from the pulpit praising Hitler. As an example, the report described a church service in Stuttgart. The pastor went far beyond thanking God; he emphasized Hitler's service in the First World War, the "brave act of November 9, 1923," and the "struggle for political power." And he asked God to "grant our people *Lebensraum*." The old God of the Christians had been given an armband with a swastika—he had been placed into the ranks of the *Alte Kämpfer.*

On November 22, the SD followed up with another notice, stating that the Catholic Church had consented to adopt a position condemning the attack. The notice went on to report that the newsletters for the bishoprics of Passau and Freiburg had published statements on November 19 expressing thanks that the Führer's life had been spared. In Freiburg they repeated the Nazi gospel that "foreign powers" were at work, citing Himmler as a source.

Internally, the SS did not suppress the fact that there were doubts among the Catholic clergy about the Party line on the attack. An informant reported from an assembly of priests in Fulda that they believed the claim made by the radio station in Strasbourg that the attack could be traced to Party circles. A few wise members of the clergy expressed the opinion "that it was premature for the death of the Führer since he would have become a martyr of the people."

Among the Protestants, the bishop of the state of Württemberg, Theophil Wurm, really went overboard. Like the majority of his pastors, he was staunchly nationalistic and anti-Semitic as well. He declared: "Together with all the German people we are deeply shaken by the criminal attempt on the life of the Führer in Munich. The clergy will take the opportunity in services this coming Sunday to give thanks to God for His merciful protection and renew our fervent prayer that God may continue to keep watch over the Führer and our people." Wurm was apparently in a state of shock over the attack. In his eyes, Hitler had been protected by God despite whatever unjust or criminal acts he may have committed.

The reactions of the other pastors in Württemberg fell into a gray zone. At many church services there were informants for the Gestapo—those there on an official basis as well as many volunteers. The bishop had left it up to the pastors how they were to proceed. It would have been possible to address the assassination attempt in the prayer of intercession at the end of the service—a text that is not customarily preserved in the record. But no proclamations about the attack were recorded, even though, starting on November 12, hordes of Gestapo officials descended on the community, interrogating and arresting dozens of residents.

In the Catholic Church, the reaction was delayed. The newsletter of the bishopric of Freiburg ran a remarkably extensive text, which gave the impression that the delay should be offset with more commitment. The twenty-four lines comprising the first section might well have appeared in the *Völkischer Beobachter*, judging by the content and the choice of words. The second section expressed thanks to "God's Providence," but it was not until the third section that the text declared that Pope Pius XII, through the Apostolic Nuncio in Berlin, had expressed to Hitler his "best wishes."

The newsletter of the bishopric of Limburg claimed that the attack had been planned by a "diabolically murderous mind," but that "Divine Providence" had thwarted the plan and "God's hand guides history."

And then Rudolf Hess delivered his lengthy speech at the official state ceremony commemorating the dead. God was "with the righteous cause," he said, and would therefore "let the Germany of Adolf Hitler prevail."

It should be taken into consideration that this position was to be heard in the Catholic Church only at the higher levels, and not in all dioceses. Nothing of a similar nature was reported from the bishoprics of Rottenburg and Trier. In contrast to the Protestant clergy, there were, even at that time, numerous German priests in concentration camps. By the end of the war there were almost five hundred in Dachau alone. Many of them provided assistance to other prisoners while there and even assumed the duties of the prisoners. They did not, however, allow the SS to use them in their persecution of the Communists.

VI

The Evidence Mounts

WHILE STILL ON his private train the night of the attack, Hitler ordered Himmler to put the police crime division in charge of the investigation. He did not trust the SS or the Gestapo with the work of gathering detailed information. At first, Reich director of criminal investigation Nebe suspected a "Party maneuver"; but once Hitler demanded a serious investigation, this option was eliminated.

Alongside the rather politically motivated search for evidence there was a less conspicuous line of investigation being conducted that addressed the question: How was such an attack even possible, given that the Gestapo was responsible for organizing security everywhere, especially security for Hitler? There soon emerged a body of evidence that was quickly buried, causing repercussions that persist today. There was no long-term security service for the Bürgerbräukeller. Throughout the year, there was no one to conduct security inspections of the hall, which was used not only for Party functions, but for dances as well. Even the night before the memorial celebration, no guard had gone through the hall. The *Alte Kämpfer* Josef Gerum, an official in the central office of the Gestapo in Munich who was in charge of security matters, appeared just an hour before people were admitted in order to inspect the entire building from roof to cellar. He looked for any explosives that might be lying around, but never thought of looking at the pillars in the hall.

Until then, a comprehensive security service for Hitler had been considered unnecessary—and every year it had been demonstrated anew that this view was correct. The dictatorship relied on two myths that had sufficed for protection. One myth presented the Führer as sent by God to fulfill his historic mission as the Savior of Germany. So far, each encounter with danger had proved that the Führer stood under the protection of "Providence"—however one might want to interpret this term. Wherever Holiness was present, such mundane matters as security had no place—Providence would take care of things. The second myth was the Gestapo myth: the belief in a perfect police state. Not only the Germans, who were directly affected, but foreign observers as well assumed that the Gestapo (*Geheime Staatspolizei* or "Secret State Police") had created a seamless police state that was infallible, invincible, and omniscient. Even the *St. Galler Tagblatt*, a Swiss newspaper otherwise cautious in its use of Nazi sources, seemed to be taken in by the story that the assassin had gotten through "three armed Gestapo lines of defense." At first, the thought of a time bomb occurred to no one.

Security at the hall on the day of Hitler's appearance was—as it had always been—the prerogative of the *Alte Kämpfer*. This led to rivalries with the police, but Hitler had already decided years before that at the Bürgerbräukeller the responsibility of the police ended at the hall entrance—inside he would be protected by his old comrades.

The generally positive attitude toward the regime led the security apparatus to believe that such an assassination attempt would be unlikely. Hitler was not in any particular need of protection; he could remain relatively confident of the people's support—at least as long as he did not lead them into a devastating defeat. Hitler himself, who fostered the legend that he could sense any danger of assassination, actually felt more threatened in the Bürgerbräukeller by the mineral water he consumed there among all the beer drinkers. The waitress who was assigned to his table was instructed to serve his companions their beer, while he had his own water, which was brought along especially for this purpose. In the hall, the best personal protection was provided by the cheering crowd itself, *Blutorden* recipients one and all. Even high-level officials of the Party, the government, or the

Wehrmacht were admitted only if they had taken part in the Putsch of 1923 and had subsequently received the *Blutorden* from Hitler for their participation. Anyone not wearing the medal was brusquely denied admission at the door. After the war began, exceptions had to be made, and local dignitaries were admitted, in part so that the hall could be filled. Hitler declined to impose sanctions for the failure of his security forces that evening.

During the night of the attack, Himmler offered a reward of 500,000 marks "for the capture of the perpetrators"; another 100,000 marks was added to this, ostensibly from private sources. For informants abroad, 100,000 marks in foreign currency was supposedly made available at the German embassies. The money remained unclaimed. Two customs officers in Konstanz had performed their duties correctly.

Although Arthur Nebe was responsible for the Bürgerbräukeller Special Commission, he reported directly to Himmler, and Himmler assigned control of the investigation to the Gestapo's Heinrich Müller. Thus from the very beginning, the dominance of the Kripo ordered by Hitler was undermined by the Gestapo. Before Nebe arrived at the Munich airport at 11:00 a.m. on November 9, Müller had called from Berlin at 10:00 a.m. and issued orders that he should be kept informed of developments by telephone. Müller was in fact in charge of the case; Nebe oversaw only the detailed work of the technical investigation assigned to him. So Müller, in the name of Himmler, immediately ordered the arrest of all employees of the Bürgerbräukeller.

At first Hitler steered the investigation toward evidence that supposedly pointed to England, but Nebe knew from the first day that the conventional explosive did not fit in with this theory. Himmler and Heydrich, who was head of SS security services and Nebe's immediate superior, at first pursued a suspicion that had been discussed that night on Hitler's private train: a group of Bavarian monarchists (also known as legitimists) was responsible. Heydrich, who was also considering the possibility of embittered *Alte Kämpfer,* is said to have initially ordered monarchists to be shot, apparently after the example of the Röhm bloodbath of 1934, but Hitler was not so inclined. He wanted exact information.

The Bavarian minister of the interior was allowed to pursue the monarchist angle. He berated the Gestapo command post for not including Catholic clergy on their list of monarchists. To appease him, they were added immediately, as was the former mayor of Nürnberg. On another occasion the minister also wished to see on the list "personal acquaintances of the former crown prince."

The SS constantly got in the way of the investigation. On the afternoon of November 9, their secret service group led by the head of SD interior defense, Walter Schellenberg, met with Sigismund Payne Best and R. H. Stevens of the British Intelligence Service just across the German-Dutch border in Venlo. The SD people identified themselves as representatives of a resistance group of German generals and tried to coax the names of resistance generals out of the Englishmen.

At a time when British secret agents could have known about the Bürgerbräu attack from newspapers and radio, Best and Stevens were lured into a café thirty yards from the German border. Without any cover from their own people or Dutch security forces, they quickly fell prey to an armed SD riot squad. They were at first kept in custody in the prison at Moabit, then at the headquarters for Reich security, and afterward in the concentration camp Sachsenhausen, in the same cell block that later housed Georg Elser. After a lengthy and terrifying term of imprisonment, they got out alive. The memoirs Best wrote while imprisoned were later used against Elser.

The SS and Hitler seized upon the opportunity to cast the two Englishmen as Elser's backers, even though Hitler surely understood the crassness of this lie. Swiss newspapers recognized this as rank nonsense—if the two agents had actually had anything to do with the attempt, would they have gone to the German border on the day after "their" attack? After years of manipulation by the Nazi propaganda machine, readers of German newspapers were no longer capable of recognizing the lies surrounding the Venlo story.

The truth regarding the attack soon became apparent. In the piles of debris, brass plates from the two clocks were found, still bearing parts of their patent numbers. The mystery of the clocks in the explosive device was quickly resolved. According to the opinion issued by the patent office, one of the clocks was manufactured between 1925 and 1929 by the firm Haller Benzing AG in Schwenningen. With this evidence, searching for clues abroad seemed pointless. Nonetheless, Himmler released a statement to the Saturday papers that "the composition of individual metal parts" pointed to "foreign origins." Elser had either received the clocks in Meersburg as compensation for back pay or had ordered them and had them sent to him in Königsbronn. In any event, he used clockworks from the Black Forest.

Things were in a state of turmoil at the Munich Gestapo headquarters located at Brienner Strasse 50; the mass arrests were creating a hectic situation. The Catholic priest Rupert Mayer, who was imprisoned in the cellar (and later on, while imprisoned in Sachsenhausen, proved a brave witness of his faith) noted on the evening of November 9 "an unidentifiable agitation and unrest" that continued the whole night. The next morning there was "enormous unrest in the courtyard of the Gestapo prison"; all cars were quickly readied and soon left with Gestapo officials in them. Most returned that evening.

* * *

Georg Elser, fetched up to Munich from Konstanz, did not attract attention for quite a while. He was considered a deserter and spy—a small fish. He was also helped by his appearance of harmlessness. After November 12, however, the situation became more threatening for him as a series of face-to-face meetings with Bürgerbräu personnel took place. At first, the waitress Maria Strobl couldn't remember Elser. Only after she talked to the other women under arrest did she recall who Elser was: He was usually poorly dressed, ate the regular worker's meal for sixty pfennigs, and—this was suspicious—he never ordered anything to drink. Elser himself, however, claimed that he had always had a beer with his meal. But in a Munich beer hall, what does one beer amount to? He could not conceal that he was opposed to alcohol. These meetings continued without any changes in the participants' responses. Since they were repeated ad nauseum, sooner or later the desired result had to be achieved. Elser's clever approach of gaining access to the building as a harmless regular customer was now entrapping him. A plan that originally offered him protection and a chance to get away if he should ever be caught on the gallery now worked against him. The endless interrogations revealed more evidence: Elser had identified himself as a craftsman who was either taking a course or working on an invention. And he couldn't hide his Swabian dialect—he spoke the broad Swabian of the Ostalb. On the basis of this dialect he was ultimately recognized by a shopkeeper who had sold him a "sound-damping insulation plate," with which Elser made the ticking of his clocks less audible.

On the evening of November 10, Nebe called Franz-Josef Huber in Vienna, who had once been with the Munich police and was now head of the Vienna Gestapo. Huber was an old friend of Gestapo Müller's from the Munich days and a good friend of Nebe's as well. With a couple of top officers and his secretary, who would take down testimony at the interrogations, Huber got on the night train to Munich and was picked up the next morning by Heydrich and Müller at the main station.

When he arrived on the scene, Huber wondered how the assassin must have worked on the bomb chamber—surely on his knees, given its location right above the gallery floor. So when he interrogated Elser, he ordered him to drop his trousers, and noticed traces of old bruises on one of his knees. Elser had in fact suffered from the bruises on his knees for quite a while.

Immediately afterward, Elser asked what one got for doing such a thing—he meant the assassination attempt. Huber answered noncommittally that it depended on the circumstances. Then he said that Elser was ready to make a confession, which he then did, "voluntarily."

In fact, even before Huber's appearance, the Commission had been closing in on Elser, largely through the testimony of the Bürgerbräu personnel. Based on this, Himmler had an arrest warrant issued, which stated that the preparations for the attack had begun as early as August. "Under strong suspicion in this matter is an individual who frequently appeared at the Bürgerbräukeller, supposedly as a craftsman, and busied himself there on the gallery in the hall." Description: "5' 5"–5' 7" tall, thirty to thirty-five years old, normal build, dark hair, not parted. Clothing: dirty yellowish gray-brown work smock, reportedly knee breeches and sport socks." When Maria

Schmauder heard this description on the radio news in Schnaitheim at 7:00 a.m. on Sunday, November 12, she was startled and told her mother that Elser was definitely the assassin at the Bürgerbräukeller.

On the evening of November 11 or early in the morning of November 12, the attention of the Special Commission lit upon a clue—the Swabian dialect. Finally they looked around in their own cellar and discovered the prisoner from Konstanz who had been forgotten until now. Bringing the innkeeper of the Bürgerbräu and the night watchman to Elser provided a further connection: It turned out they had once stopped Elser on the gallery, but he had had the presence of mind to talk his way out of it.

On Monday, November 13, the Gestapo announced: "The evidence is steadily mounting." The previous day the Stuttgart Gestapo had found important clues of Elser's preparations in Heidenheim-Schnaitheim at the Schmauders' residence. Bits of information like this were driving Elser more and more into a corner. In the end this was why he made a "voluntary" confession. But to describe the confession as "voluntary" is a painful lie.

Germany would not have been a Gestapo state if the investigation had relied solely on circumstantial evidence. It was after all Himmler who was heading up the proceedings. On his own initiative and without the consent of Kripo boss Nebe, he ordered up a full-fledged Gestapo interrogation and involved himself in it right away. What Elser was subjected to next is to this day still cloaked in the euphemistic language of suppression known as "intensified interrogations." These consisted of bouts of questioning accompanied by the most brutal abuse, including torture sessions in which he was beaten to a bloody pulp. Even so, to this day no police officer associated with the Elser case has ever been brought before a court and sentenced.

Only one person lifted the veil of silence—the head of the Munich Kripo, Dr. Albrecht Böhme, who was a jurist, not a police officer. He was responsible for securing the evidence and did not feel himself bound by the code of the Gestapo. During the course of events, he wound up joining the resistance struggle in Bavaria. Dr. Böhme attested to the atmosphere prevailing during Elser's torment:

I saw him [Elser] only once; I never spoke with him. When I saw the prisoner, I by coincidence became witness to a brutal scene that was playing out—in the presence of Nebe and me—between SS Reichsführer and Chief of the German Police Heinrich Himmler and the prisoner Georg Elser. Elser was bound up, and Himmler was kicking him hard with his boots and cursing wildly. Then he had a Gestapo man unknown to me drag him into the washroom of the Munich Gestapo chief and beat him there with a whip or (I couldn't see it) some similar instrument, so that he cried out in pain. Then he was hustled, quick time, before Himmler, who kicked him again and cursed at him. Then he was dragged back to the washroom, where he was beaten again horribly, then brought back to Himmler and kicked again. But Elser, who was groaning and bleeding profusely from his mouth and nose, made no confession; he would probably not have been physically able to, even if he had wanted to.

The next day, police president von Eberstein informed Dr. Böhme that the Gestapo had "yet again demonstrated their clumsiness by apparently beating Elser horribly," so now Elser would probably not confess anything. Dr. Böhme remarked that Himmler himself had been present at the beating. For Eberstein, this rash criticism might have been very dangerous. According to Böhme, "Von Eberstein grew pale and said in a fearful tone to me: 'Oh, Herr Böhme, please completely disregard my remark about the beating.' I was then treated with courtesy—with unaccustomed courtesy—as I was shown out."

On the night of November 13, Elser was so battered that he saw no further point in continuing his denial. Only out of ignorance could one make the claim, as Rothfels, Hassel, and others have done, that Elser unnecessarily made a complete confession. Even hardened resistance fighters such as Communists or military opposition leaders had a rule of thumb: Nobody could withstand the savage torture of the Gestapo for more than twenty-four hours—and live.

In the meantime, the Gestapo had made progress along another path. On the morning of November 12, an order arrived via teletype at the office of the Stuttgart Gestapo to proceed immediately to Königsbronn and inquire into Elser's personal and political background. His family members were to be taken into custody as a precaution. If former Gestapo man Wilhelm Rauschenberger recalled

Georg Elser during the Berlin interrogation, November 19–23, 1939. The man interrogating him is probably Arthur Nebe.

correctly in 1950, the teletype mentioned only that when Elser was detained at the border crossing he had in his possession grenade detonator parts, which he had taken from the Waldenmaier company.

The counterespionage arm of the Gestapo, in the person of Otto Rappold, took charge of the matter. He and Rauschenberger went immediately by car to Königsbronn, where at the town hall they acquired personal information on the family members, with the intention to start making arrests on November 13. Rauschenberger struck pay dirt right away at the Schmauder residence in Schnaitheim at Benzstrasse 18, where Elser had spent the final months before his departure for Munich. The daughter, Maria, only sixteen, turned out to be very chatty. Elser had certainly not told her anything about his assassination plans, but he had teased her a bit with all his secret doings. Once, when she discovered him opening the secret compartment of his wooden suitcase with the false bottom where he kept his sketches, he became a funny, mischievous storyteller. The sketches, he had told her, were for his invention, "a new kind of device for display windows, which had to be able to automatically lift a weight of about 1 1/2 pounds." He said he had been working on the invention for months and wanted to apply for a patent on it in Munich. She said he had told her that "if this thing works and it gets patented in Munich, he would become a rich man with 2 1/2 million marks. He said he would go straight from Munich to Switzerland, and then he would bring her to Switzerland and marry her." In actuality the two were still quite formal with each other, using the German *Sie*; Elser was still attached to Elsa Härlen, whose photograph remained on his table in his cell block at the concentration camp Sachsenhausen.

Things got worse when Maria started talking about Elser working at the quarry and having something to do with gunpowder. She said that he had been in the Munich Bürgerbräukeller in 1938 and that he "had finished drinking a glass of water that Hitler had not finished," that he knew the hall well and had shown her photographs of the Bürgerbräukeller taken November 8 and 9, 1938. So when she heard the radio report that morning, she became suspicious.

The Stuttgart Gestapo officials changed their schedule and spent the rest of that Sunday interrogating Maria Schmauder at the Kripo office in Heidenheim. The suspicion of Elser's guilt continued to grow; the news went immediately to Stuttgart and from there to Munich, so that by the evening of November 12 Elser's probable involvement was known in Munich. By this time at the latest, Elser was repeatedly being tortured.

Georg Elser's fingerprints, taken November 15, 1939, in Munich and containing Elser's signature.

For her willingness to cooperate, Maria Schmauder received special treatment: On the orders of Gestapo Müller, she was taken into "informal custody." In Stuttgart, unlike the Elsers, she did not have to go to the Gestapo prison on Büchsenstrasse, but was sent instead to the family of a prison warden as a maid—nonetheless under house arrest. The Schmauders were otherwise treated more gently, even though Elser had worked out the construction of his bomb right in their house and had conducted explosives tests from there. The Elsers, on the other hand, who had nothing to do with the attack, were imprisoned, threatened at times with death, and tyrannized for months, with lingering effects that continued well into the postwar period.

Town hall in Königsbronn, where the Stuttgart Gestapo began its investigation on November 13.

The next morning, Monday, November 13, the Gestapo stormed into Königsbronn. Five or six Gestapo people moved into the König Karl in Heidenheim, and two to four of them were housed at the Hirsch in Oberkochen. Above and beyond family members, everyone was questioned who had known Elser: people involved with the zither club, the glee club, or the dancing lessons; workers from the quarry; all relatives. There might have been well over a hundred individuals—almost every family was affected. Under the watchful eyes of the Gestapo, the town felt compelled to collectively renounce this dangerous man.

After the Gestapo had shown themselves to be negligent in guarding the Bürgerbräukeller, they now wanted to cast the unassuming Georg Elser in the fiendish image of a born assassin. The Gestapo wanted to leave no instant of Elser's life uninvestigated. Incapable of establishing priorities, they went after every minuscule detail. Thus one of the Gestapo people had as his duty to trace Elser's childhood and youth, from childhood diseases to toys. Georg Holl, who did social work with the parish, was perhaps one of the few who, after the war, was able to view this pressure on the residents of Königsbronn with some humor: "A wonder that they didn't interrogate the midwife who was there at his birth!" The Gestapo fell victim to its guilty conscience, its "biologistic" view of life, and its global conspiracy theory. It was impossible for the people of Königsbronn to comprehend this world of madness. Anywhere—even on the playground or in the laundry room—an agent for the English might have been hiding, or perhaps a tendency toward criminal behavior or some perverse interest had become apparent. The story of the Elsers became the subject of "research into criminal biology" (criminal tendencies were considered hereditary). And in fact everyone in Königsbronn appeared as a borderline accomplice in the crime—this kind of thing was catching.

After months of investigation, Stuttgart Gestapo official Rappold arrived at a view that reflected the efforts of the threatened community around Elser to distance itself: "Georg Elser was a very talented craftsman, but in his private life he was an eccentric." The birth of the legend of Elser the eccentric, which still lives on, can be traced to the sense of helplessness felt by those being interrogated as they sat in the presence of the omniscient and unscrupulous Gestapo and saw themselves being treated as accomplices.

VII

From Königsbronn to Berlin

O<small>N THE MORNING</small> of November 13, 1939, the Gestapo invaded Königsbronn, making arrests: Georg Elser's parents, his siblings, his relatives, and their spouses were all brought in. Everything had to be done in a great rush—simply in order to increase the atmosphere of intimidation. So Georg's brother, who worked at the Königsbronn ironworks, was not allowed to remove his work apron or change clothes; he was taken as he was to Stuttgart. It was not until November 28 that those arrested were to return to Königsbronn from Berlin.

A reason for the arrests was never given. Although they remained top secret, word about them got around. On the first day, people in Königsbronn were rounded up and placed in custody in Heidenheim; in the evening they were transported in cars by the Gestapo to Stuttgart, where they were imprisoned at Gestapo headquarters on Büchsenstrasse. While Georg's mother, Maria Elser, was placed in a common cell with five other women, most of the others were placed in single cells. All were kept isolated from each other. Maria was interrogated once or twice daily, always by a different person. She didn't believe that her Georg was the assassin. (And as late as 1950 she still had doubts—perhaps he had just been used by someone else.

She would later report that her husband, who died in 1942, had been assaulted during the interrogations, and that he had talked "a little too much, which he shouldn't have done.")

Maria Elser was sent alone on the night train to Berlin before the others, where she was taken to the prison at Moabit, brought face to face with Georg, and then, like the other family members who followed, locked up in the Hotel Kaiserhof—in a kind of "informal custody."

Georg's sister Maria Hirth was subjected to the worst treatment. The reason for this was the baggage that Georg had left with her as well as his last visit to her on November 6. Maria Hirth was considered a co-conspirator because the large suitcase with the false bottom contained sketches, clock parts, detonators, and the like, and in the tool chest there was almost everything that the assassin had used. Thus Georg's sister fell victim to an old saying about the people of Württemberg: They can't throw anything away, especially not when someone has given his all to acquire it and use it regularly. If Elser had taken the tools, sketches, and bomb-making materials and thrown them into the deepest part of the Isar River in Munich, he would have spared his sister much terror and trauma. Georg was a superb craftsman and well experienced at keeping quiet, but he had no concept of the internal workings of the terror apparatus—he lacked the political experience.

In her witness testimony after the war, Maria Hirth said only that she had been "treated very severely" during the interrogations in Stuttgart—a gross understatement by a woman who had clearly been intimidated. Only her sister Anna Lober dared to tell the truth: "During the interrogations, my sister Maria Hirth, who lives in Stuttgart, was the only one they threatened to kill if she didn't tell the truth." Her tormentor was the notorious Gestapo official Paul Bässler, who subsequently was kept longer than anyone else in Allied internment camps because of his mistreatment of people in the cellars of the Stuttgart Gestapo. Maria Hirth, the one most seriously affected, was, like all the others from Königsbronn, taken at first to the detention prison in Moabit, then a few days later to the Kaiserhof.

Her sister Anna Lober and her husband were arrested in Stuttgart-Zuffenhausen on November 13, taken to Gestapo headquarters on Büchsenstrasse, and booked in like all the others, with fingerprints and photographs. The Elsers, one and all, were considered to be criminals. Despite her inquiries, Anna Lober was given no reason for the arrest, "which really made me angry," as she stated to the Kripo for the record after the war in a remark truly worthy of her dead brother. But she too did not originally want to believe that Georg Elser had blown up the Bürgerbräukeller; she too was interrogated "in a very harsh manner." After the war, now without the Gestapo on her back, she managed to reach a conclusion: "It is believable that my brother came up with the idea of executing this attack; he was unquestionably in a position to undertake the technical preparations for the attack on his own." She nevertheless still had some suspicions that others might have been involved in the instigation and financing of the attack. None of the siblings could see inside Georg—there was a wall of silence between them. It was a family that, according to Georg Elser's statements, was apolitical. From an early age, he had preferred not to speak of politics at home, where there was always strife anyway because of his father's drinking and violent tendencies.

Like his siblings, Leonhard Elser, the youngest, was arrested on November 13, and his wife a few days later. When the Gestapo tried to take her out of the laundry in her work clothes, she insisted adamantly that she had to change, and went up into her apartment. The two secret service men, not wanting to let her out of their sight, tried to follow her into her bedroom. She explained that she wanted to be alone, and quickly shut the door and locked it—a gesture that, with a bit of courage, was possible even in a Gestapo state.

On November 15, Elser's girlfriend Elsa Härlen was also arrested, at her mother's place in Göppingen-Jebenhausen. On the same day, the quarry owner Georg Vollmer was picked up in Königsbronn along with his son Ernst, as well as the explosives expert Kolb and the bookkeeper.

Around November 23, the Gestapo moved all of the relatives being held in the Stuttgart police jail along with Elsa Härlen to

Hotel Kaiserhof in Berlin around 1930, where Elser's relatives were kept under arrest for a week in November 1939.

Berlin, transporting them on the night train in a special car. Each person was in a separate compartment—only the married couples stayed together. Guards were stationed left and right; not a word could be spoken; even a trip to the toilet could not be made unaccompanied. It gradually became clear to the Elsers that they were on a family trip—to Berlin, for interrogations. In the morning they were first taken from the Anhalter train station to the Moabit prison, then a few days later to the Hotel Kaiserhof, the finest hotel in the government district, located at Ziethenplatz 4 between Wilhelmstrasse and Mauerstrasse. Before the First World War, the massive complex had been the preferred hotel for diplomats and the aristocracy. Before 1933, Hitler had his headquarters at the hotel, and he still liked to stay there—he was fond of the Hungarian orchestra that often performed there.

So the Elsers were in first-class accommodations but under house arrest, with a Gestapo guard outside every door. Anyone who wanted to go to the toilet had to knock and wait to be accompanied; meals were taken in a room together, but no speaking was permitted.

Only Elsa Härlen, the outsider in the group, got her meals brought to her room. In the finest hotel, in the center of the capital, directly across from Hitler's Reich Chancellery, the Gestapo had transformed an entire floor into a temporary luxury prison. The inmates were taken by police van to the interrogation sessions, which were conducted, generally at night, in the nearby Reich Security Headquarters at Prinz-Albrecht-Strasse 8. Everyone noticed that the tone here was markedly more polite than it had been in Stuttgart.

Gestapo headquarters could assume different guises; this time, orders had come from above to put on a friendly face with the prisoners. At the same time, however, down in the cellar a hellish atmosphere prevailed. The cells were filled to overflowing: The prisoners were crawling over each other in a dreadful stench; they weren't able to wash and were covered with bugs and filth. The preferential treatment of the Elser family reflects the direct involvement of Hitler, for whom this assassin constituted a psychological enigma. Hitler wanted to keep the whole family in custody, but he wanted to do it with style. It is possible that the transfer to the luxury hotel was connected with the conclusion of Elser's interrogation on November 23.

Most important were the face-to-face meetings with Georg Elser, to which only Elser's mother, his sister Maria Hirth, her husband Karl, and his girlfriend Elsa Härlen were subjected. In the account of the assassination attempt, these encounters have been left out. Elser's mother was the first to be brought in, on either November 20 or 21. Elser was supposed to be gripped by emotion. However, since the dispute over his claims regarding the new house, he had wanted to see neither his mother nor most of the rest of the family except for his father and Maria. In 1950 Maria recalled the situation:

> Here in Berlin I was taken into a large room once, where my son Georg was sitting at a long table. I was seated across from him and asked whether this was my son Georg and whether I believed that he had carried out the attack. Here, too, I expressed my conviction that I didn't believe Georg had done such a thing. I didn't speak with Georg himself because I didn't know whether I was allowed to speak with him or not; that's why I didn't dare

say anything to him. During this meeting in Berlin, Georg looked good; I didn't notice that he showed any signs of physical mistreatment. Georg cried when I was brought in, but he didn't speak to me.

Vienna Gestapo chief Huber was present at the meeting, which took place in the conference room at Reich Security Headquarters. For propaganda purposes, Huber was supposed to interrogate Elser once more, in the presence of his mother. A film camera for the weekly news had been set up out of sight. Elser's confession was to be shown at movie theaters. But the assassin was "in an obstinate period," as Huber expressed it, and would not answer at all or only reluctantly. Elser saw through the ruse and didn't want to be turned into a monkey in some Gestapo zoo.

Maria Hirth, who was at first interrogated by Gestapo Müller, learned from her brother the true story of the attempt; unfortunately, her voice was soon lost in a sea of rumors. She later reported:

In Berlin I was also interrogated in the presence of my brother. My brother also had to describe the attack in my presence; he said that he had done the attack alone. I can't remember the details anymore, but I am completely convinced that he executed it alone. At this hearing, my brother still looked good. When I was later taken to see him two or three times, his head had been shaved and his face was completely swollen. Whether his face was swollen because of beatings, I can't say. During the hearing my brother told how he had worked at night in the Bürgerbräukeller and had taken out the debris in a carpet. And in fact, this carpet was among the things that he had sent us from Munich. And so then he said he built a clock into the hole that he had hollowed out. After the meeting with my brother I had a nervous breakdown, and I still have problems because of it.

At the meeting with his brother-in-law Karl Hirth, Elser told the same story. In the words of Hirth: "His face was swollen and one eye had a bruise under it. I assume that this disfiguring was caused by beatings." According to Hirth, Elser said he had carried out the attempt alone and had told no one about it. Another confrontation in the presence of Himmler produced nothing new. Afterward, Karl Hirth was of the opinion that Georg Elser was solely responsible for the attack.

Finally Elser's girlfriend Elsa Härlen, who had been so harshly interrogated that she collapsed, sat before the wreck of a man created by Gestapo terror. This was the worst of the meetings; there is hardly a more chilling description to come out of Gestapo headquarters in Berlin. If Elsa Härlen remembered correctly in 1950, the version she got to hear was the version that suited the Nazis the best and one given by Elser only for a brief period and only after extreme violence had been used.

He was sitting on a chair in the middle of the room, and I would definitely not have recognized him as my fo[rmer] fiancé in the condition he was in. His face was swollen and beaten black and blue. His eyes were bulging out of their sockets, and I was horrified by his appearance. And his feet were swollen, and I believe the only reason he was sitting on the chair was that he was no longer able to stand. In each corner of the room there was a Kripo officer standing with his pistol drawn. An officer said to Elser: "Here is your fo[rmer] fiancée. She is still convinced that you did not commit this attack. Now tell her yourself that you committed it." An officer placed himself behind Elser and, to make him talk, he kept striking him on the back or on the back of his head. I am convinced that he talked only because he had been physically broken and feared the beatings. Even then he spoke only in fragments and they forced him to keep talking by continually hitting him. What he said was approximately this: He had taken black powder from the Vollmer Co[mpany], and with this he had built a time bomb. He had been induced to do this by foreign agents and had acted on their orders. He had established contact with the agents while working at the Waldenmaier Company, where, as an employee in the shipping department, he had come into contact with people from abroad. I was not able to learn more details—he couldn't talk because they kept hitting him; on the other hand, they kept hitting him in order to make him talk. . . . Before the meeting was ended, a Kripo officer told me that I could now ask Elser something. But the only thing I could ask was: "Georg, did *you* do this?" At first Elser didn't answer but just stared at me with an expression that I will never forget. Then slowly, he opened his mouth and said: Elsa . . . at that moment he was struck on the back of the head by the officer standing behind him and was not allowed to continue speaking. I was convinced at that time, and I am still convinced today, that Elser wanted to say he was innocent. As his former fiancée, I was able to read that much from his expression and his gestures.

Several days earlier, on November 23, during his last interrogation, Elser had said he firmly believed that, in accordance with his religious beliefs, he had committed no sin with his assassination attempt against Hitler. This was likely what Elsa Härlen had read in his gestures.

Heinrich Himmler frequently injected himself into the interrogations of the Königsbronn group. On one occasion, he had them all brought face to face with Georg at the same time, but with no results. One night Elsa Härlen was awakened at 1:30 a.m. and taken to Himmler's office. He was strikingly pleasant to her and had her tell him the smallest details: the troubles with her ex-husband, who drank, and how friendly Elser was by contrast. Himmler rarely interrupted her and did not appear mistrustful or haughty. She did not perceive the situation as an interrogation. After two or three hours, Himmler stood up, patted her on the shoulder, and said approvingly: "Hats off to you, Frau Härlen; you are truly a fine Swabian woman!"

Two days later at noontime she was taken by car to the Reich Chancellery to see Hitler. After leading her down endless corridors and past many rooms, two SS men flung open a door and Elsa Härlen was suddenly standing in a large office. At a desk sat Hitler in a field-gray uniform. Not looking up, he continued reading. An SS man announced Frau Härlen; Hitler glanced up but said nothing. She wanted to raise her arm in salute, but she couldn't. She got a poke in the ribs from the SS man, but all she could manage to do was stammer, "My Führer!" Her arm wouldn't react—it was as if it had become lame. One thought raced through her mind, a mixture of comedy and horror. Seeing Hitler there before her, the only thing she could think of was: "Der Schnurrbart-August!" ("Mustache August"[1]). Charlie Chaplin would surely have been pleased with her.

Now Hitler began to interrogate Elsa Härlen, but, unlike Himmler, he wanted to twist her every remark, make her feel guilty. He insinuated that she had maintained contact with Elser when he was in Munich.

---

[1] The reference in this mocking remark by Härlen is not clear, possibly a popular clown figure or cartoon character.

She determinedly stuck to the truth: "No, my Führer, that's not how it was." Hitler expressed interest in Elser's character and habits; he wanted to know everything about him. The interrogation with Hitler lasted until around 8:00 p.m., without a meal break. At the end Hitler started playing tough, threatening her, saying that he wanted to talk to her again, that she was still hiding something from him. She made reference to the friendlier tone used by Himmler, saying also that he had believed her.

A few days later, Elsa Härlen was interrogated by Martin Bormann, again in the Reich Chancellery. Bormann too was pleasant, she stated. Hitler and Himmler had anticipated that the hot-and-cold treatment of terror and luxurious comfort, punishing interrogations and friendly attention by top-level Nazi officials, would so confuse the little people from the Ostalb that they would say whatever was required of them. But the elaborate undertaking in Berlin was a failure—not a single detail was revealed that was not already known. Above all, Elser could not in any consistent way be forced to dream up foreign agents of some kind nor to implicate others whom he had intentionally excluded from his plans.

On November 28, all those from Königsbronn except for Maria and Karl Hirth were released, but first they had to execute the customary agreement to maintain absolute silence. As they were returning home unaccompanied, the Elsers did not speak a word to Elsa Härlen. She had never been considered one of them. As a divorced woman, she had always been rejected, thereby once again making Georg Elser's isolation within the family clear. Once they were back at home, the interrogations started again in earnest and went on for six months—over and over the same humiliating trip to the Gestapo, over and over the same mindless questions that had already been answered dozens of times. The Elsers, with their country ways and lack of education, looked far brighter than the vaunted Gestapo. At least at the Stuttgart Gestapo, the conclusion was finally reached that Georg Elser had acted alone.

Maria Hirth and her husband were not released from Gestapo custody in Berlin and allowed to return home until February 20, 1940. For a long time afterward, both remained out of work—no one wanted to employ family members of the assassin. Then after her nervous breakdown, Maria was not able to work at all for some time.

VIII

Confession and Interrogation

In the Gestapo cellar during the night of November 13 or early morning of November 14, 1939, Elser concluded that there was no way to escape the interrogations, which were becoming increasingly coercive and brutal. The mistreatment had taken a heavy toll on a body severely weakened by months of working at night. Even the Kripo was not able to protect Elser from the torture ordered by Himmler, despite the fact that Kripo chief Nebe had reportedly ordered that the violence be stopped. Nebe's word carried weight only in the absence of Himmler and Gestapo Müller.

Elser's explanations for his three-month stay in Munich and the attempted border crossing were gradually falling apart. In Munich, he claimed, he had intended to take a course and then go work abroad as a skilled craftsman; but he couldn't give a description of the course. He also indicated that he wanted to go abroad in order to "get out of paying support for a child born out of wedlock." But the contents of his pockets pointed to work in espionage and explosives. In addition, Elser was recognized by more and more employees of the Bürgerbräukeller, including the former errand boy, whose job he tried to get in exchange for a payment of some fifty marks—easily more than a week's salary for a skilled worker. And then he was recognized by the man who sold him the insulation plate that had been found in the pile of debris. There were simply no loopholes left.

One thing was accomplished by the friendly approach of the Kripo officers under Nebe. They had experience in dealing with an untalkative type who had been driven into a corner; they knew how to soften him up by taking the right tone—by being soothing and encouraging, by making promises.

Huber was a master at this. With his knowledge of the area—he was from Munich—he had frequently taken Elser on imagined walks around the city, including the Bürgerbräukeller. He became suspicious when Elser, with his peasant shrewdness, "misheard" it as "Löwenbräukeller." This had to be a weak spot.

On November 14, Elser was brought face-to-face with Maria Schmauder from Schnaitheim. When he saw her, although it was only briefly and in passing, Nebe, Müller, and other Gestapo men noticed that he winced and turned pale—a fairly flimsy "clue." At other times, an informant was placed in the cell with Elser in order to prevent any attempt at escape or suicide. Elser had no interest in either—it was the informant who brought up the subject.

Finally, Elser declared to a commissar that he wanted to make a confession. The interrogation was interrupted immediately. Present at the ensuing night interrogation were Nebe, Huber, Lobbes, and Huber's secretary. It lasted from 12:30 a.m. until 4:00 a.m. on November 15. Huber later said that Elser had simply been allowed to talk without being interrogated. This was not really believable since Elser was anything but talkative. But Elser possibly had more of an opportunity to present his own view here than he had later on at the five-day interrogation in Berlin. He may also have believed that here he was talking to save his neck, that he might still get off—the understandable hope of a man destined to die.

In Huber's version given in 1966, the confession occurred in an almost relaxed atmosphere:

We were all sitting around a table. Frau Kranz was handling the transcription splendidly—she even captured the Swabian dialect as in a photograph [!]. I knew Swabian dialect as well, and that may have been one reason why I was able to establish a good relationship with Elser from the start. . . . At the beginning Elser said something like: 'Well, it was me!' Then he began to talk; he was awkward and confused at first, but after a while he spoke easily. He related the details of the precision work that he had performed. He said nothing at all about his reasons or any possible instigators. We also asked no questions; we just occasionally said, "Aha," or asked, "And how did it go from there?" Elser was obviously under great strain. During this time, he drank two entire bottles of seltzer. He also told us about having a small hiding place on the gallery. There was all kinds of junk lying around there; the work apron he left there along with a chisel and a drill attracted no attention. When using his tools, by the way, he always wrapped them in cloth in order to avoid creating unnecessary noise. He also told us about befriending Ajaxel, the innkeeper's dog.

The transcript of Elser's confession was clearly not satisfactory, and it must have been filled with Swabian expressions which would never do in Berlin. So on November 15, a proper written confession was created. After listening to the prisoner, a commissar reformulated the sentences himself and dictated them directly to a typist.

What Elser said during these two days in Munich must have gone into the final two-volume report of the Special Commission, which appeared in a limited edition bound in red, for internal use only. All Gestapo stations received a copy for training purposes. Unfortunately, not a single copy has survived. At the end of the war, these volumes vanished either in the bombardments or in the mountains of files that the Gestapo burned in order to destroy the records of their crimes.

Hitler, who even today still has the reputation of having good intuition when it came to assassination attempts, declared to Goebbels on November 14, "Probably the perpetrators . . . are probably long since out of the country."

On November 15, Goebbels noted: "Himmler has now found the first of the Munich assassins—a technician from Württemberg. But we're still missing the instigators. For this reason, we will not yet publish anything." The Gestapo worked on proving that Elser was a stooge of the British Intelligence Service and of Otto Strasser, a member of the Nazi opposition.

Since November 9, the matter of the Venlo abduction of the two British Secret Service men had continued to simmer. Heydrich, the man in charge, kept his plans secret for days, even from Kripo boss Nebe. Even Army Intelligence did not learn about it until November 15. The Gestapo interpretation made its way into Goebbel's diary on November 16: "[. . .] the actual assassin is a minion of Otto Strasser, who was in Switzerland during the crucial period. After the attempt he made tracks for England, apparently to report to those issuing the orders and the payoffs—the work of the Secret Service. We're still keeping everything secret in order not to tip off the instigators."

All the connections were wildly invented. Strasser had already been expelled by the Swiss political police on November 9, before the Nazis had even brought him into the picture. The expulsion had already been decided upon sometime before this date. Later on, it was postulated that Elser had gone to Zurich for several days to see Strasser—another theory the Gestapo dreamed up. Nebe's criminal division did not buy this foolishness.

After Elser's written confession was made, the Kripo wanted to visit the scene of the crime with the perpetrator. Elser considered this superfluous; he said he knew the premises well enough and still had the measurements in his head, including those for his explosive device. Later, on November 16 and 17, under the close watch of the Kripo, he filled several large pages with sketches. Unfortunately, these components of the confession were destroyed as well. During the Berlin interrogations of November 19 through 23, he made five new sketches, on a life-size scale, but these too were lost during the war or in the postwar period.

Why did Elser go so far in cooperating with the Kripo? It had nothing to do with some self-important desire to tell all or a sudden eagerness to confess. Elser had been declared guilty, so he saw no reason to withhold technical details. Of course, his artisan's pride had probably been stirred. The Nazis simply didn't consider this man, the little cabinetmaker from the Ostalb, capable of such a sensational deed. By producing precise sketches out of his head he demonstrated two things: the high level of his technical skills and—more important to him—his sole responsibility for the attack. The more extensively he described his activities, the more indisputable it became that he had been the only one involved. This made it possible for him to keep others out of the proceedings who might have had some peripheral connection to the preparations. He wanted to assume full responsibility and not drag anyone else into his misfortune.

This was a basic tenet of the best resistance fighters, from the military opposition to the Communists: If one of them had to go to the gallows, then he went alone and took no one else with him. Elser developed this tenet out of his own fundamental sense of ethics—he almost certainly never had any contact with resistance movements. His greatest success during the entire ordeal was probably that he was able to convince the Kripo and even the Gestapo of his sole involvement in the commission of the act. Under this regime, which saw in every individual only a puppet manipulated by outside forces, this was an extraordinary accomplishment.

Elser was probably transferred by the Gestapo to Reich Security Headquarters in Berlin on November 18. Over the next five days—November 19 to 23—he was subjected to a comprehensive interrogation. The record of these sessions needs to be viewed from a particular perspective here, as it shows evidence of Elser's tenacity in his discussions with the Gestapo commissars, resulting in some successes for him with regard to wording and permitting inferences as to the conditions under which Elser was being interrogated. What Elser actually admitted to will be dealt with at a later point.

* * *

The center of Nazi terror at Prinz-Albrecht-Strasse 8 lay in ruins after the war and by 1956 had so completely disappeared from the public consciousness that it was simply demolished. The need to forget, forgive, and let the grass grow over things was great. In the days of the SS and the Gestapo, the cellar of the building was supposed to hold only fifty detainees; in reality, the cells were unbearably crowded. Torture and cries of pain at any time of day or night were routine there. The light was kept on in the cells all

night. Prisoners slept only for brief stretches because they were
constantly awakened and asked their names and the charges against
them. Summer and winter, the heating system was turned on full
blast—the heat was insufferable. The prisoners were deprived of
water to slake their thirst, and hunger tore at their guts. Every day
prisoners were screamed at, threatened with death, and told of the
suffering of others. They wore tight shackles which chafed and
caused serious wounds. In a change of routine, they were sometimes promised a reduction of their sentence if they admitted to
one thing or another, then all of a sudden the beatings resumed.
They were beaten around the face until their teeth were broken out,
or struck on the back with sticks or whips. And then there was the
formal four-step torture, which was described by resistance fighter
Fabian von Schlabrendorff.

A record of which tools in this satanic arsenal Elser was forced to
suffer under has not been preserved. But he was here because of his
attempt on the life of the "dear Führer." Himmler, head of the SS and
the Gestapo and a consummate sadist, wanted to squeeze out of Elser
everything regarding his cooperation with the British Secret Service
and Otto Strasser. In his case, any and all means were justified.

It was in this environment that Elser was interrogated between
November 19 and November 23, for a total of forty-five hours—nine
hours a day, after deducting time for any breaks. The interrogations
took place during the day, starting at 8:30 a.m. and ending at 7:00 or
8:00 p.m. On one particularly intensive day with visits from high-
level Nazis, the questioning even went on until 11:30 p.m. What happened to Elser at night is not recorded.

In the printed version of the Stuttgart edition, the record takes
up a total of 130 pages. The daily records vary in length, depending on how much resistance was offered by Elser or what kinds of
things were going on. On the third day, November 21, many high-
level Nazi functionaries were present in order to observe Elser being
interrogated. It is also possible that he was brought face-to-face with
his mother on this date. The prisoner seemed to be primed for pres-
entation, to the public or even on the weekly news. The next day,
the newspapers ran the sensational announcement that the assassin

had been captured—hardly a sensation, since he had already been in custody for two weeks.

Every day the Gestapo people wrung out of Elser between twenty and thirty-one recorded pages. For one page they needed an average of twenty-one minutes; a normal speaker takes three minutes to read a page aloud. From these statistics alone one can glean how steadfast and effective Elser was in his resistance. He could not be rattled; he retracted wording or took back a statement he had just made. The Gestapo didn't have it easy with him. Elser was anything but chatty; he doggedly stuck to his interrogation strategy. And when there was no other way, he had the ability to simply remain silent. Huber called this "a period of obstinacy."

Elser sat across from three Kripo commissars, one of whom was Herbert Kappler, who would later become the notorious police chief of Rome convicted by an Italian court of shooting hostages and imprisoned as a war criminal in the military prison at Gaeta. Even though Elser was completely inexperienced in the police environment, he became intuitively attuned to a rule of thumb Nebe constantly pounded into his friends in the resistance:

. . . as soon as possible, whether by making a partial confession or declaring remorse, take control of the questioning—so you clumsily admit something that is clearly known or indisputable, dictate the record yourself, make mistakes and then correct yourself, distort the circumstances. But above all, create distractions—one distraction after another until, through their impatience or their curiosity, they perhaps permit some insight into what they wanted to hear or what their interests are, or might be, or were at some point.

Hitler, who read the records of the interrogations, could sense in them the small victories achieved by Elser. In his headquarters at the Wolf's Lair, on March 26, 1942, he admitted in a belated compliment that Elser was "very crafty. He says only what has already been learned from other sources."

The record of the Berlin interrogations was not taken down first in shorthand, like Elser's first informal conversation in Munich. There are no notes; here the Gestapo commissar dictated—usually exactly what he wanted to hear. It is not a word-for-word record, with questions and answers; instead, it is a kind of record of results. A stenographer typed what was dictated straight into a typewriter—nothing was corrected. Today one can still sense the pace of the interrogation from the many breaks in the halting style of the text.

It is not until the third day in the record—sometime after he had described his trip to Munich on November 8, 1938—that he remembers going to Oktoberfest once in 1919. This is nothing but a distraction, which just piques the curiosity of the commissars. A bit later, in a supplemental entry, they focus on an outburst by Elser that surely did not take place. The subject is Elser's free time in Munich and his tours of the city, "always on foot." He made no acquaintances, he says, except for the errand boy and an unknown official who "accompanied him once." He prefers not to mention his interest in young women. Now he is asked about the waitresses, who have already mentioned his name. The Gestapo official depicts Elser making an effort at remembering, "Wait, now I remember, I was talking to three serving girls in the Bürgerbräukeller," then going on to say that he had taken a group photograph of them.

Immediately there are questions about his camera and who he got it from, even though the Gestapo already knew it was Maria Schmauder. The actual interrogation is riddled with countless supplemental questions, which can be recognized in the text as such only when one looks behind the formulation of the sentences. The record reflects a constant struggle between the prisoner, who is trying to stall for time, and the commissars, who keep pressuring him. An analysis of the text formation would reveal hundreds of these supplemental questions. One sentence is usually the result of cobbling together three, four, or five bits of questioning; thus, what we have here is an artificial record produced by the Gestapo, in which we can nonetheless, with effort and interpretation, hear Elser's voice.

The commissars are not able to adapt everything to their language style. We occasionally encounter a Swabian turn of phrase. In reference to his termination of employment at the Wachter woodworking shop in Bernried near Lake Constance, where the master was reluctant to let him go, Elser says in his simple and direct way: "But quarrel we had none on account of that." Asked why he had given up zither lessons in Konstanz, he responds like the proverbial frugal Swabian: "[...]it was the money." At two marks, he found the lesson too expensive; his own hourly wage was barely half that. On the crucial third day of the interrogation, when the room was filled at times with voyeurs who wanted to glimpse a real firebrand of an *Untermensch*, he is asked about his motives for the assassination attempt. He tells them about the dissatisfaction of workers with the regime—a sensitive subject. The Gestapo becomes uncertain when Elser lashes out in Swabian that working people had "'a real rage' against the government." Being made uneasy by the statement and not able to translate it into their jargon, the Gestapo finally resorts to quotation marks.

Less Gestapo influence is exhibited when Elser is asked about things that fall more within his range of interests—his speech becomes more fluid, almost breezy. Gone are the space-fillers he used when he got stuck, phrases like "if you're asking," or "if I recall correctly." We learn about his interests and his interrogation strategy. He prefers to talk about ordinary things, and is definitely not cut out for political discussions. He speaks most easily when talking about his profession, any technical matters, music, work activities, his "tinkering," the Waldenmaier Company, acquiring explosives at the Vollmer Quarry in Königsbronn, and the move to Schnaitheim. When expressing political views, he speaks fluidly and extensively only about workers' economic criticism of the regime—the Gestapo doesn't have to drag this out of him.

The interrogations reach their most important point on the third day, November 21, when the topic turns to the preparations for the attack. The Gestapo commissars have clearly gotten used to the assassin—they pay careful attention as his life story unfolds, and little by little their detachment diminishes. Frequently the technical aspects take precedence, as they did during the eyewitness accounts given in the wreckage of the hall or the reports of explosives experts. The ideology, the negative portrayal of the assassin and his actions start to diminish, and Elser himself can be distinctly heard.

At first, they put words in his mouth, e.g., "national revolution" for Hitler's assumption of power—Elser would never have uttered such words. But as soon as the subject turns to the explosive device and its ignition mechanism, more objectivity becomes possible. The Gestapo renders "ignition mechanism" with an awkward Teutonic construction, adding afterward the word *Höllenmaschine* (Hell's machine), a term that Elser avoided using.

But the Gestapo's language increasingly conforms to that of Elser—an indicator of the effect Elser's behavior is having on his adversaries. Now we read that Elser "got hold of" powder "for the planned attack"; the forced negative tone is gone. Regarding breaking into Vollmer's explosives shed, Elser shows his foxiness. Downplaying becomes his motto—he calls each of the burglaries a "visit." Five times in a row he makes "visits" to the explosives stockpile.

The influence of both Elser's cautious manner of speaking and the intense nature of the subject matter continue into the fourth day. What Elser was doing at night in the Bürgerbräukeller was simply "working." The reprehensible nature of the purpose has disappeared from the language. Hollowing out the pillar is part of the "preparatory work." Even on the final day of the interrogation, the commissars respectfully use the word "work" in their regular dictation.

Only later, when the Gestapo commissars consider it necessary to address the technical issues in a "notation," do they regain their ideological footing: Elser's "apparatus" is then a *Höllenmaschine*. But when the interrogation reaches the decisive phase of the preparations and setting the two clocks, the commissars are once again caught up in Elser's language: He let "matters take their course." This creates the impression of a just cause, certainly Elser's view of the matter.

An opportunity arises for the Gestapo to regain some of their lost detachment when they confront Elser with the eight victims of his attack. In order best to capture the essence of Elser, they change the form of the interrogation from the piecemeal results-oriented style of establishing the record to a question-and-answer type of procedure. They want to soften him up with crocodile tears, but he is unimpressed and maintains the poise he has now cultivated for so long. After five days of interrogation, after extensive beatings, after many a night spent in fear, his demeanor stands out as evidence of his self-confidence and his moral certitude.

What were his thoughts when he finally closed the door in the pillar? He dodges the question—he can no longer recall. "At the time, what did you think the results of the attack would be?" His answer is noncommittal: "I had already thought that through several times." They are unable to extract more out of him. "Did you consider that a number of people could be killed?" Elser responds with a provocatively simple "Yes."

The Gestapo interrogators seem flustered and have to repeat a question that has already been answered: "Is that what you wanted?" Then the Gestapo makes a mistake that offers Elser the opportunity to state his goal bluntly. "And who were you trying to hit?" Elser: "Well, I wanted to get the leadership." The policemen, who themselves work under the most dreadful terror apparatus, would like to hear that Elser occasionally had doubts about his actions. Regarding his scruples, they note down that the prisoner thought for a long time. Finally Elser says: "I no longer recall whether or not at some time I had doubts." Continuing this thought, he states: "But I don't think I ever had any."

The attempt to maneuver Elser into making some statement of regret does not work. The commissar can no longer conceal his annoyance and asks again how Elser feels about his actions in light of his failure and the eight people killed. Elser responds: "I would never do that again"—hardly a grand gesture, considering that he was now in the hands of the police. Now angry, the commissar lashes out pedantically: "That is not an answer to my question." Elser does not yield—he remains the rational craftsman: "The objective was not achieved." The Gestapo resorts more and more to moralizing, asking whether the deaths of eight people were of no consequence to him. These men of the Gestapo were the right ones to be asking; however, they still didn't go as far as the newspapers and use the term "murder." But then they turn to trickery, asking: "What would you do if, for some reason, you were to be released?"—knowing full well, of course, that such a thing would never happen. Retaining his composure, Elser responds: "I would try to make up for the things I did wrong." He pauses again, then the commissar probes further: "How? By doing what?"

It is not until this point that Elser tries to reflect the prevailing ideology—he has simply had enough: "By making the effort to be part of the *Volksgemeinschaft* ("people's community," in Nazi ideology) and to work within it." Inevitably he is asked whether he could do this. Elser's response: "I've changed my views." What changed them, they want to know—his arrest? The Gestapo commissars realize how absurd it seems to argue with one who has been defeated. Now Elser works himself up to the final sentence of the entire written record, a self-criticism based on the course of history, a secularized determinism. The Nazis had prated about "Providence"; now Elser states: "No, I definitely believe that my plan would have succeeded if I had had the correct views. After it failed, I became convinced that it was not meant to succeed and that my views were wrong." Only his *views* were wrong—perhaps about setting the two clocks? The act itself stands oddly apart—the hatred of Hitler has in no way been recanted. Anyone reading the transcript will find no indication of changed views. Elser seeks to appease with empty words; there is no trace of repentance and contrition.

For the Gestapo the interrogation was a grim disappointment because Elser refused to invent any instigators. When Himmler read the final report and saw that his expectations had not been fulfilled, he flew into a rage and scrawled in the green ink reserved for him on the red cover of the printed report: "What idiot created this report?" The "idiots" were *Reichskriminaldirektor* Nebe and the leaders of the two subgroups of the Bürgerbräu Special Commission.

The voyeurism of the Nazi brass on day three of the interrogation led to an unexpected result. A journalist from the DNB agency, from which the press took its reports in lockstep, was so impressed with Elser's integrity that he erected a written monument to the assassin. In his report on Elser's guilt, the journalist allowed his impressions to take precedence over his political convictions:

We have seen this man. He is the murderer; the dead are the victims of his dreadful plan. This is the man whose intended target was the Führer and with him the leadership of the Reich. All of these things we must always bear in mind, for this man does not have the obvious physiognomy of a criminal; rather, he has intelligent eyes and expresses himself in a way that reveals cautious reflection. The hearings go on interminably. He weighs each word carefully and at length before he gives his answer; and when one observes him doing so, one forgets for a moment what a satanic monster this is and what a ghastly burden this conscience is apparently capable of bearing with ease.

IX

Cult of Death: The Official Ceremony of November 11

IN ORDER TO understand the assassination attempt not just as an isolated event but in the larger context of the effect it had, one must not ignore the extent to which the regime made the victims into instruments of propaganda.

Since its new beginning following Hitler's release from prison in Landsberg at the end of 1924, the Nazi Party had developed a cult in which defeat and death could be transformed into victories. If the original intention was to counteract the low morale following the failed Putsch of 1923, the Putsch was recast after the Nazi assumption of power as a preliminary step on the way to victory: the bloody end on the street in a hail of bullets fired by the Bavarian state police became glorified as the beginning of a triumphal march to power. Hitler's escape and disappearance were converted by the Nazi lie into heroism. The memorial ceremonies for the Putsch were blended into the ceremonies commemorating the fallen of the World War. Thus the failure of the march on the Feldherrnhalle gained national significance; the Putsch appeared as a first attempt to erase the defeat in the World War and expunge the "shame of Versailles." Mourning became militarized with the presence of high-ranking officers and military formations—all in all it was an occasion for standing at attention and marching around to the sound of lively music.

As might be expected, the main celebration always took place in Munich. The nighttime general assembly before the Feldherrnhalle began after Hitler's speech in the Bürgerbräukeller; the rousing words were accompanied by lighting effects. Sheathed in red and brown, there were funerary columns in the ancient Egyptian style, each topped with a large shallow vessel containing a burning flame. Attached to the columns were plaques, each containing the words "Last Roll Call" and the name of one of the sixteen killed in the Putsch. Thus the religious ur-experience of the numinous became a public staged event, a theatrical production for the masses, with a political purpose.

Grief was transformed into glorification of the victims; reflecting on the historic defeat became a celebration of Nazi triumph. This moral and political exploitation culminated in the call to emulate those who had died. During this period, the dead were in general considered to be the greatest—there was, apparently, nothing finer than to die for the "movement." Anyone at all who lost his life had sacrificed himself for Hitler so that Hitler could live on and be Germany's salvation. There were no tears of widows or children here. Everything was manly, bursting with the will to prevail. The faces were stony; all were silent. Except for Hitler, the high priest of the Party, no one was called upon to speak. There they were, the rank and file in huge formations as if cast in bronze—thousands of boots, their stamping like the gigantic drumbeats of a death march.

The Party insinuated itself into the spiritual history of salvation. The Christian religion served as a model; Christian liturgy was constantly plundered in the design of theatrical events. It was only a short symbolic step from the sacrifices of the *Alte Kämpfer* and those fallen to the sacrificial death of Jesus: the historic defeat became the Good Friday of the Party, and the victory its Resurrection, a national Easter. In this scenario the notion of "victory" could be expanded:

first the acquisition of power, soon a victory over England, and at the end victory over all the evil forces in the world until Germany finally achieved salvation. This inversion of defeat and death into victory and new life draws upon Pauline theology—it is on the cross, in death, that the victory of faith has its foundations.

On November 9 around noontime, columns of men clad in brown and in black moved in—the Hitler Youth, accompanied by the somber thump of the Landsknecht drums. The only evidence of the cult remaining at the Feldherrnhalle was a memorial, which was guarded year round by two SS sentries. A sixteen-gun salute was fired in honor of the sixteen who died in the Putsch. For the first time, the procession from the Bürgerbräukeller to the Feldherrnhalle did not take place—too many *Alte Kämpfer* were at the front. Moreover, the wreckage that was once the hall was now in the hands of the Special Commission; with the extensive damage, it had lost its sacred character. The leaders, under the command of Rudolf Hess, subsequently proceeded to Königsplatz for the laying of the wreath. Three years before, the sixteen sarcophagi had been brought here and placed in the two pantheons located on the narrow side of the newly remodeled square. At Königsplatz, Hess welcomed individually the family members of those killed in 1923.

Two days later, on November 11, it is necessary to hold another ceremony in the same style. On the evening of the previous day at 9:45 p.m., a procession begins that takes the seven coffins with the victims of the assassination attempt to lie in state. By 9:00 p.m., three hundred Hitler Youth are waiting in the courtyard of the Residenz with torches, ready to accompany the coffins, which are to be placed at the Hofgartentor by 9:40. The coffins are followed by fourteen *Alte Kämpfer* carrying seven wreaths from Hitler.

At 10:00 p.m., accompanied by the roll of drums, the Combat Support Force appears, surrounding the square and thus making it into a "holy space." The procession of torchbearers and *Alte Kämpfer* bearing wreaths moves to the square before the Feldherrnhalle. The SS presents arms and a marching band plays the *Präsentiermarsch*. The wreath bearers place their wreaths at the coffins, and then step

Official ceremony for the victims of the assassination attempt in the Bürgerbräukeller—
November 11, 1939, at the Feldherrnhalle.

behind the coffins. Now the SA guard takes up its position and remains there the entire night.

The coffins are placed in front of the hall; from a vessel within the hall, a commemorative flame casts an eerie light. "Germany is cloaked in darkness," proclaimed a grandiloquent article in the *Völkischer Beobachter*, "since this brazen declaration of war. In the smoldering flame from this single vessel, our pain—the collective pain of all Germans—appears to burn unabated." A swastika-emblazoned flag drapes each coffin. "Motionless, SA men stand silent watch." Then for hours on end the people of Munich file past the coffins. As they pass, in their thoughts they "hold discourse with the dead, and a manly answer to the eternal question 'Why?' may be found in these solemn moments." The dark night and the single flame are the stuff of mass religious spectacle—the square is "a vast nighttime cathedral."

In the darkness, a mystical bond is established: "The never-ending queue of mourners continues quietly past. From the darkness of the city it emerges, moving into the mournful light of the flame, then disappearing again into the darkness. And so it is: A great people pays its last respects to the mortal remains of the victims and lays down its thoughts, its pain, and its sadness there with the dead. We, all of us, were in this procession." This marks the end of the lying in state on November 10.

For the official ceremony on the following day, November 11, orders have been issued to fly all flags at half staff on public buildings throughout the Reich. At private residences flags are hoisted to half staff as well. At the Feldherrnhalle, the "altar of the movement," it is reported that ten thousand people have gathered—for a city the size of Munich, this is a relatively small number. Starting at ten o'clock that morning, honor guards of the Party, including the Reich Labor Service with spades on their shoulders, march from the north across Ludwigstrasse onto Theatinerstrasse. From the south come units from the SS, the Wehrmacht and the Luftwaffe. The SA guard standing night watch over the coffins is relieved. Approaching from Residenzstrasse are the hearses, each escorted by a dozen *Alte Kämpfer*; accompanying the hearse of the waitress killed in the attack are members of the Nazi Women's League.

The organization of the assembly in the "holy space" originates at the Feldherrnhalle. Located directly in front of the hall is the podium for the main speaker, Hess. Arranged in a row before the podium are the seven coffins—the eighth victim has not yet died—and beside each coffin an *Alter Kämpfer*, or a woman from the Nazi Women's League. Seated on chairs before the coffins are the family members of the victims and, in two groups, guests of honor of the government, the Party, and the military.

Shortly before 11:00 a.m. the Grossdeutsche Rundfunk (Greater German Radio) begins its broadcast. Millions are listening. At first it is difficult to make out anything but a few commands being barked out, such as "Formations, attention!" or "Present arms!" and the sound of boots slapping the pavement. The *Alte Kämpfer* march in from the Hofgartentor in the rear, and then the family members of those killed take their seats on the chairs in front of the coffins.

Next the holiest of objects is carried in: the *Blutfahne* (Blood Flag), the flag from the 1923 Putsch, spattered with the blood of those shot during the confrontation. It is carried here by Grimminger, a participant in the 1923 Putsch and a Nazi Party city council member. As the *Blutfahne* enters the Feldherrnhalle and is planted in front of a large pylon in the "altar room" behind the central arch, the *Präsentiermarsch* is played. Then there is silence, in anticipation of the arrival of Hess and Brückner, Hitler's adjutants. An announcer fills the time by giving the names of the deceased and highlights of their political biographies. They were all, according to the announcer, "fervent defenders of the ideas of the Führer."

The bells on the nearby Theatinerkirche strike eleven; the congregation is assembled and the Party church service can begin. The second announcer proclaims: "Flanked by the deputy Führer and Gauleiter Wagner, Adolf Hitler himself now returns to his fallen comrades. The Führer is here." There is some movement in the crowd, evidence of joyous feelings as Hitler appears, wearing a field-gray overcoat and a black band of mourning on his left arm.

There follows a lengthy pause. Silently, Hitler assumes the position of the high priest—only he may enter the space between the family members and the coffins. The announcer: "Adolf Hitler stands before the victims torn from our midst by a cowardly act of murder." During the entire speech by Hess—over half an hour—Hitler stands motionless. Then softly, the orchestra starts to play a melody beloved by the German culture of mourning of that time, "Aase's Death" by Edvard Grieg.

Rudolf Hess speaks with greater dignity than Hitler did in the Bürgerbräukeller—more slowly and evenly, in the manner of an experienced priest, with many repetitions for rhetorical emphasis. The

Völkische Beobachter published an edited transcript of the speech, from which the repetitions are deleted.

"At this time," Hess intones, "the German people take their sad leave of the victims of a gruesome crime, a crime almost unparalleled in history." On the one hand, the attack was a "ruthless act of murder"; on the other hand, the dead were victims of a preordained fate—they were "destined to die" at the Bürgerbräukeller. It was the loyalty of these seven, he proclaims, that made it possible for Hitler to "steer the movement through all storms." Germany owes a debt of gratitude to the *Alte Kämpfer,* who have "made it possible to withstand this attack by foreign enemies." It is only because of the *Alte Kämpfer,* says Hess, that Hitler was able to build the great Wehrmacht and liberate Germany.

Hess addresses the dead directly with the bold assertion that "all of Germany" is in mourning, and with the stock promise never to forget. "Eternal is the river of blood that flows for Germany, eternal the commitment of German men to their people; thus, Germany, too, will be eternal—this Germany for which you gave your lives."

But Hess also manages to extract from these deaths some folk wisdom and political benefit—the attack has its good side. The deaths of these seven victims have served to "fully arouse the bitterness and the passion of the German people," he says, adding: "The perpetrators of this crime have succeeded in teaching the German people to hate. They have heightened immeasurably the commitment of the German people to this battle that has been forced upon them, as well as its willingness to give its all to the cause." The spirit prevailing among the German people, he goes on, is best expressed in the words of the wives of two of the victims. Hess does not shrink from exploiting the widows in their grief—it is after all the duty of the individual to subordinate himself to the overall political purpose. He declares that two of them had said: "What the death of our husbands means to us can be felt only by those who have lost their closest loved ones. But more important than the lives of our husbands is knowing that the Führer is alive."

No feelings are expressed for the bereaved—these are all reserved for Hitler's deliverance. Hess then makes allusions to Hitler as Germany's messiah: "With the miracle of his salvation, our faith has become unshakable: Providence has protected our Führer; and Providence will continue to protect our Führer, for it is Providence that sent him to us." Next, as in Christian liturgy, comes a statement of faith, paralleling that of the Apostles' Creed:

In recent days, Providence has protected our Hitler from harm, as it protected him during his service in the World War—in the drumfire of the World War; as it protected him on the march to the Feldherrnhalle; as it protected him while he repeatedly risked his life in battle, and now in the Polish campaign. Providence was always at the side of the Führer; and whatever his enemies plotted against him, Providence ultimately turned all to his advantage and thereby to the advantage of the German people.

As the faithful disciple of his lord, Hess is "of the rock-solid conviction that . . . this enormous crime, this war which was forced upon us, will turn out in favor of the Führer, in favor of Germany—in favor of Germany and of the entire world." Hitler will bring about utopia for mankind and establish eternal peace—but apparently only for the Germans. "But to our enemies, the perpetrators of this crime, we call out: You attempted to take our Führer from us, but you brought him closer to us than ever. You wanted to make us weaker, but have only made us stronger than ever. You hoped you could rob us of our belief in the future, but have only strengthened our belief in a Providence which is on the side of Germany. You hoped you could take away our confidence in victory . . ." Never, Hess claims, have the German people been "more certain of victory" than on this day. At the end, Hess even challenges the netherworld: "And if you put the forces of Hell itself into motion, victory will still be ours. For victory will be our thanks to the dead."

Next the offerings to the victims are presented: the wreathbearers take position in front of the coffins and we hear the sounds of "Der gute Kamerad," long the favorite song of the German military crowd. As soon as Hitler steps in front of one of the coffins, an honor guard standing in the Hofgarten fires off a salute, which echoes off the walls of the surrounding buildings. Hitler places a wreath of chrysanthemums at each coffin, then steps back and lifts his arm in salute.

Then, very slowly, "Deutschland über alles" is played, followed by the Party anthem the "Horst Wessel Lied" at a much brisker tempo, intended after all the standing to put people in a marching mood. Hitler shakes hands with each of the family members. "Silently, he looks into the eyes of each one," according to the *Völkischer Beobachter*. Then he expresses his sympathy to them. It ends as it began—military units swarm across the square: "Formations, halt!"; "Present arms!"; "Shoulder arms!"; "Funeral procession, march!"; "By the right flank, march!". The sound of boots, the *Präsentier- marsch*, the church clock striking eleven-thirty. Leading off the departing procession is the *Blutfahne*, followed by funeral cars carrying participants in the 1923 march, and finally by formations from the Wehrmacht and the Party.

The funeral procession wends its way along the hour-long route across the Odeonsplatz and Ludwigstrasse, out through the Siegestor, and across Leopoldstrasse and Ungererstrasse to the Nordfriedhof (North Cemetery)—to the alternating accompaniment of drum rolls and funeral marches. Curious onlookers line the streets—according to the official reports, "all of Munich." However, as the SD of the SS admitted: "The participation by the citizens of Munich in the state funeral for the victims of the attack was relatively weak; only at Odeonsplatz were larger crowds observed, and they did not appear to be particularly moved by the occasion."

Goebbels' propaganda machine managed to extract from the irra- tionality of the death cult one bit of rationality: A film of the ceremo- nies was made, which was shown to Elser shortly before the end of his interrogation in Berlin in an effort to shock him into revealing the names of the instigators behind the attack.

At the Nordfriedhof the entire ceremony is repeated, but in a shorter version. Up until the end everything remains firmly in the hands of the Party—the *Blutfahne* is at the gravesite as well. The "program" approaches its conclusion: "The coffins are set down. The family members and the bereaved assume their positions. When they are in place, Party member Wenzel gives the sign to lower the coffins. As the coffins are being lowered, the Trapp Chamber Orchestra very solemnly plays the song 'Hakenkreuz am Stahlhelm' ('Swastika on the Steel Helmet')."

X

The Search for the Instigators

O N THE NIGHT of the attack, while on their private train, Hitler and his followers had already speculated about possible instigators behind the attack. Hitler's "chain of agitators," as he had called them in his Bürgerbräu speech, led him immediately to suspect England. Later on he thought of Otto Strasser as well, with whom a feud had been raging for a long time. From a freedom radio station in Czechoslovakia, Strasser had broadcast attacks on the regime, and from time to time he had succeeded in planting explosives in Germany.

In Hitler's view, an effective attack like the one in the Bürgerbräukeller was unimaginable without instigators behind the scenes. The assumption that there were powerful people involved seemed particularly likely to him, since without such power he would have remained a nobody. After all, Hitler had been able to rise so rapidly only because of benefactors and patrons in the justice system, in the government, in the police, and most of all in influential and wealthy circles. Left on his own, he probably couldn't have even earned a living for himself.

In the search for the identity of the assassin, the Nazi leadership fell victim to its own strategy: They had so barricaded themselves against the outside world that wherever they looked they saw only enemies. Deciding on one or the other became an arbitrary choice.

In spite of all the propaganda generated over many years, Hitler suddenly lost sight of his chief enemy: Why shouldn't Jews be behind the attack? Herschel Grynszpan's assassination of German diplomat Ernst vom Rath in Paris the year before—one of the few successful attempts—had proved that a Jew was capable of such an act. And why shouldn't bolshevists have plotted the assassination? The GPU had people at its disposal who had the necessary training. In fact, as a routine part of its investigation, the Gestapo in Munich went after Communists, thereby proving its total ignorance of the Communist resistance strategy, which did not include bomb attacks. In any event, the Communists were paralyzed because of the German-Soviet Pact.

If a future wartime enemy like England was supposed to be the mastermind behind the attack, why wasn't France also considered? In the Alsatian city of Strasbourg, there was a well-organized radio station that broadcast to foreign audiences and was influential in the south of Germany. It never occurred to anyone in Hitler's coterie that the attack might have been planned in France. Hitler kept his gaze fixed on England like a snake charmer staring at his cobra.

All the serious evidence that the Special Commission gradually assembled pointed internally to the area within the Reich, thus contradicting Hitler's anti-English conspiracy theory. As interesting as the details were regarding the nature of the explosive device, the construction of the device, or the Munich craftsmen who unknowingly rendered assistance, none of this had anything to do with the political big picture as Hitler needed to see it. The Gestapo, on the other hand, mistakenly focused on two avenues of suspicion leading abroad, thereby demonstrating whose intellectual offspring they were, even in matters of criminology. The false trail leading to Switzerland has to this day been ignored, and it adds an odd aspect to the entire account of the assassination attempt.

On November 22, 1939, all German newspapers ran the same article, in which Himmler portrayed Elser as the assassin. But without a shred of evidence in support, he simultaneously put out a lie: "The principals and financiers of this operation were from the British Intelligence Service; the crime was organized by Otto Strasser." Edited to match this article was the report on the Venlo abduction, which appeared at the same time. The British Secret Service agents Best and Stevens, who were taken at gunpoint on Dutch soil and transported to Germany, were touted as "instigators." The SS gloated "how England's Secret Service was outwitted." According to them, the pair had crossed the border into Germany in order to make contact with the German opposition. The assault and abduction were kept quiet.

At the same time, DNB, the Nazi press agency—which otherwise showed little sign of activity abroad—issued an announcement intended for Switzerland that was not allowed to appear in Germany. It stated that on November 5, Elser had crossed the border and traveled to Zurich in order to meet with his employer, Otto Strasser.

The following day, the Nazi press reported that the Gestapo had tricked the English Secret Service into carrying on radio contact for twenty-one days via a secret transmitter that, interestingly, had been delivered by the English themselves to the supposed German resistance group, which then ambushed the two feckless spies at Venlo. Bold headlines smugly heralded the success: "Radio Contact Maintained Between Gestapo and British Secret Service until Yesterday: How the London Masterminds Behind the Attack Were Exposed." Himmler could not resist expressing his *Schadenfreude* in print, reporting the final radio communication as follows: "After a while it becomes boring to converse with such arrogant and foolish people. You will understand why we are signing off. Best wishes from your friendly 'German Opposition.' The German Gestapo."

At Prinz-Albrecht-Strasse 8—Gestapo headquarters in Berlin— the jokesters were probably splitting their sides laughing. Everything else in the press was usually fabricated by the Gestapo. More interesting was what the papers had to say about Otto Strasser; Germans got to hear for the first time about his resistance activities. The press let down its guard enough to admit that in 1935 two German SS men had illegally entered Czechoslovakia and destroyed Strasser's radio transmitter.

Upon seeing the allegation that Strasser had organized the attack from a location in Switzerland, the newspapers in Switzerland took on the issue. Even the mere suspicion could become dangerous; their German neighbor was well known to be violent—and feared. Starting in 1933, individuals had frequently been abducted in Switzerland and taken to Germany; not only German emigrants—Swiss citizens considered "inconvenient" were also taken.

On November 23, the *Appenzeller Zeitung* in Herisau ran an article on Strasser that mentioned his last published work, in which he made the plea for a new Europe, "a Europe of freedom, justice, and peace." According to the article, Strasser had in the meantime moved on to Paris, where he had given an interview stating, "I don't know Elser, and it is certain that he is not one of my people. I knew neither Best nor Stevens." He considered it "an honor" that the Gestapo accused Strasser's organization *Schwarze Front* (Black Front) of being involved. He stated further that the Gestapo had attempted several times to murder him, and that the last time he had been warned by a Gestapo official.

The *Appenzeller Zeitung* reported on investigations by the Swiss Federal Prosecutor's Office in Bern and by the Political Police. In Bern the concern primarily seemed to be for precautionary obedience to its violent neighbor. Immediately after the attack, the Federal Prosecutor's Office independently initiated an inquiry into any possible Swiss connections, focusing not only on Strasser, "but also on other elements unfavorably disposed toward the present-day German government." The results were negative.

Immediately after the Munich attack, however, the Federal Prosecutor's Office ordered Strasser to leave Switzerland within four hours—since the Nazi raid in Czechoslovakia, he had been living without authorization as a refugee in the canton of Zurich.

Strasser moved on to Paris on November 13. Once there, he seized the opportunity to pin the blame for the Munich attack on the Nazis. His evidence was shaky—a few weeks before the attack, the owners of the Bürgerbräu had taken out insurance in Switzerland on the building. Then, impressed by Elser's attack, Strasser got carried away, predicting that the Reich was "ready for a revolution against Hitler." However, this could only happen under certain conditions: "First, Germany must experience the horrors of war; the Third Reich must suffer its first military defeat; and the effects of the blockade must be palpable." As a time frame for his predictions he projected early 1940.

Articles like this, and the Swiss German-language press in general, infuriated Berlin. On November 10, 1939, the Ministry of Propaganda weighed the possibility of banning altogether the importation of Swiss newspapers to Germany. It didn't even matter that few newspapers made critical comments about the Nazis—most simply knuckled under, adapted to the circumstances, or avoided the subject.

The Gestapo waited until the end of January 1940 before it demanded massive investigations in Bern. Information on these machinations was yielded by a file on Elser only recently discovered among the Strasser records in the Federal Archives in Bern. This file is a genuine treasure trove; here we learn of matters regarding which records in Berlin were lost and which clearly demonstrate the unscrupulous tactics of the Gestapo. The file also contains Elser's fingerprints, taken on November 15, 1939, and a large number of significant photographs from police records that exist nowhere else.

Reich Security Headquarters in Berlin demanded answers from the Swiss police to an eighteen-page catalog of questions entitled *Requisitorial*. Most of the questions revolved around the Munich attack; a few concerned the fire aboard the steamer *Deutschland*. The head of the Swiss police, Dr. Heinrich Rothmund, known for his close cooperation with the Nazis, especially on refugee matters, wrote on February 1, 1940, in a cover letter to the Federal Prosecutor's Office that the "Munich explosive attack" was not "a purely political crime," but that in Germany everything was nevertheless also being investigated from the political perspective: "We therefore strongly urge restraint and caution in dealing with the *Requisitorial*, as well as consultation with us and the Foreign Department before answering any questions."

The *Requisitorial* assailed the Swiss police with 163 questions. In the first part regarding Elser's relationship to Strasser and in the final part covering Elser's arrest at the border, items were mentioned that appeared in no other interrogation and that were never corroborated by others. Only in the middle section did the Gestapo ask relatively objective questions about details of Elser's life at Lake Constance.

At first it is difficult to decide whether Elser made up the astounding statements while being brutally tortured, simply in order to gain relief, or whether the Gestapo, after receiving the file from the Special Commission on November 20, invented them. The tone of the passages suggests that the Gestapo acted as if the officers of the Swiss police were already under its command, and that its intent was to discover holes in the latter's findings. Basically, the *Requisitorial* was not an official request—rather, it was a blunt interrogation that was being conducted against a sovereign state.

In order to prepare this offensive on Bern, the Gestapo had presumably instructed its foreign service to gather general information, allegations, and accusations from the Zurich area with regard to Strasser—or simply to round up rumors. The foreign arm of the Gestapo in Switzerland was run from Stuttgart and maintained a sizable network of spies in the Swiss Confederation, German as well as Swiss. On Swiss territory, the German embassy in Bern was in charge of these informers. This arrangement enabled the Gestapo to appear to already know the important information and thus need only official confirmation of it.

According to the Gestapo, Georg Elser stated "among other things, that he had been visited by an associate of Strasser's in May, September, and October—or perhaps November, 1939." In the Gestapo version, this man told him that if the Munich attack did not succeed, another could be arranged. Elser had met this person, according to the report, in 1938 in Konstanz.

Even this opening section appears remarkably senseless. In 1938 Elser had already been living in Königsbronn for a long time and was employed there by Waldenmaier. If he went to Konstanz, it was only for brief visits, in order to check out the border situation. It would not have been possible for him to find the time for protracted visits with the purpose of planning an attack.

Then the Gestapo began to besiege the Swiss police with questions, wanting to know everything about Strasser's travels: where he went, with whom, when, by what route, why. They also asked about his activities and connections. They even asked about his neighbors, his visitors, his financial expenditures, his landlady, any vehicle he might have, his contacts while traveling, and any visitors from Germany. They make the bold claim that Strasser had frequently been visited by Germans. Then, the Gestapo demanded the names of all Germans who were in Zurich at the time and the records of where they stayed.

The next group of questions focused on hearsay. According to one story, two people were driving to Vaduz on November 8, when their conversation was overheard. One allegedly said to the other, "I hope it works out this evening. Too bad we can't be there," and the other allegedly replied, "In any case, we'll hear about it on the radio—it will probably be on all the stations." The Gestapo speculated about the involvement these two may have had.

The Gestapo also had information on another conversation about the Bürgerbräukeller that occurred ten days before the attack at a Viennese café in Bern, in which one person said to another, "It must succeed." (A staff member mentioned that one of them had a "Jewish appearance.") Based on this alone, the Gestapo wanted to know what kind of people frequented the café and what circles they moved in. What kinds of observations were made by the staff?

A Gestapo informant reported from Switzerland that a woman from the area of Lake Geneva had supposedly said, "Hitler will be murdered soon." At that time in Europe, many people hoped and said such things—even the Gestapo had to know that. Now, however, the Gestapo wanted to find out everything they could about this woman.

When the subject turned to Elser's time spent at Lake Constance, the questions took on a less paranoid tone. On the subject of Elser's employment at Schönholzer, a small cabinetmaking shop in Bottighofen in the vicinity of Kreuzlingen, the Gestapo asked two dozen detailed questions. Not a single moment, not a single contact was left unexamined.

Following this were questions about a bar in Kreuzlingen for non-drinkers that Elser frequented, a festival for traditional dress that he attended, the smuggling of everyday items, two abortion attempts by his girlfriend Mathilde Niedermann, and purchases Elser made in a grocery store in Kreuzlingen. More questions dealt with the trumped-up claim that the Zurich music-store operator Karl Kuch was involved in the attack. (In the local lore of the Ostalb region, Kuch is to this day occasionally identified as the leader of a group of Communists planning a bomb attack.)

The Swiss Federal Prosecutor's Office answered in a submissive tone (they had pulled Strasser in even before the intervention of the Gestapo): "After the Swiss authorities confirmed around the end of October 1939 that Dr. Strasser had made disparaging remarks about the Chancellor of the German Reich in a foreign newspaper and had furthermore railed against the relationship between Germany and Switzerland, his immediate expulsion was ordered, and said order was made known to him at the beginning of November 1939." On November 13, Strasser was taken by car to the French border, which he then had to cross alone. It was no longer possible, according to the report, to determine whether Strasser had received mail from Germany at certain points; a search of his house turned up no evidence.

The owner of Strasser's apartment in Wetzwil-Herrliberg was a woman named Johanna Lehmann (perhaps a relative of Elser's landlady, Rosa Lehmann, the Gestapo might have wondered). At the end of this investigation, all that the Gestapo really learned was a lot of trivial information. For example, that the "dangerous woman" at Lake Geneva had died. That Elser got the job in Bottighofen through the employment office in Kreuzlingen. That Elser's old boss was also dead. That Schönholzer's son had described Elser as "hardworking, quiet, and respectable." It struck the Schönholzers as a little strange that Elser frequently left his workbench in the afternoon to go swimming. "But he always more than made up for this time off by working in the evening." It was a revealing testimony to Elser's independent spirit.

XI

Assassinville

O<small>NCE IT WAS</small> clear to the Gestapo that Königsbronn was the place where somebody had hatched a plan to get rid of Hitler, they descended on the village in droves. Officers came from Stuttgart, from Munich, and from State Security Headquarters in Berlin. In Königsbronn, the pressure mounted to a nightmarish level that crippled the quiet little town. In the months following the attack, many were repeatedly picked up for questioning. Over and over they were pummeled with the same questions; and with each interrogation they became increasingly aware that all the previous answers which had been truthfully provided and duly recorded had been a waste of time. The upper echelons of the Gestapo were united in the view that the entire village was a nest of criminals, that nobody was telling the truth, and that only relentless and repeated questioning until subjects collapsed could advance their purpose.

From this point on, the village was stigmatized. Any spot of ground where Elser had set foot or any house that he had entered was feared to be contaminated. In the south, in the wake of the Gestapo, areas of "scorched earth" developed, large and small, in Konstanz, Meersburg, Munich, and Stuttgart. By shining a light on even the most ordinary aspects of life and uncovering any contact, however coincidental, the Gestapo assumed they could track down the ring of agents in league with Elser.

The Gestapo did not need to show restraint—it had been freed by the highest legislative authority of any limitations on its actions. Since everyone at that time was—at least publicly—united in condemning the assassin, there was no concern that police officers would ever be called to account for their methods. And indeed, that is how it turned out: Those in charge of the police terror against Königsbronn and all the other places where Elser had lived never appeared before a court. They were able to enjoy their pensions in peace, while the long-tormented Elser clan received no restitution for their treatment.

Soon after the arrest, the people of Königsbronn began to feel the derision directed at them. Years later, in 1959, as a journalist was tracking down memories of Elser in Königsbronn, he was disappointed. People who had been squeezed for information twenty years before and were quick to tell anecdotes at the time now wanted nothing to do with Elser; his name was taboo. They knew nothing, couldn't remember anything, or just dismissed the interviewer. The generation that Elser had wanted to save from this Second World War had marched across all of Europe with the German armies—and with them marched many from Königsbronn. Now their motto was: "Forget about it!"

When the journalist who was researching Elser went to his old school, the school's caretaker told him his master sergeant's response when he said he was from Königsbronn. "Aha, from Königsbronn," the sergeant said. "Assassinville. Ten pushups!" Dozens of others from Königsbronn must have had similar experiences.

The trauma began the moment Elser's identity was known; everyone from Königsbronn who was interrogated, arrested, or harassed was warned not to reveal even the slightest detail about what had been said and done—or the punishment would be severe. Everyone understood what that meant: Dachau.

Maria Schmauder's father in Schnaitheim was arrested and subjected to a lengthy interrogation, only because Elser had indicated that he had listened to foreign radio stations at their place—even though such activity was not banned until September 1, 1939. Soon thereafter, on a daily basis, one of the Schmauders was picked up by the Gestapo and taken to Heidenheim for interrogation. The questions could have been handled all at once, but it was more important to humiliate people as all the neighbors watched them being picked up for repeated questioning.

In Berlin, after seeing her brother, head shaved, badly beaten, Maria Hirth had a nervous breakdown. Eleven years later in Stuttgart, as witnesses were being questioned in the course of a Munich investigation, she declared: "It still causes me suffering." An attempt to receive compensation for her suffering and years of unemployment was unsuccessful. Afterward, she never wanted to hear of the matter again, and up until her death in 1999 the subject was not discussed.

Maria and her husband Karl received the harshest treatment. In their case, as with others, the Gestapo didn't conduct just one thorough search of their house—they returned repeatedly, as if they thought incriminating evidence might suddenly appear out of nowhere. Karl was kept in Berlin longer than the others—until mid-December—but he was soon arrested again in Stuttgart, on December 22. In the meantime, their son Franz was forced into an orphanage. The Hirths were not freed until February 20, 1940, and tainted by their relation to Elser, they were unable to find any work for a long period of time. For many years, Maria was unable to work.

Elser's sister Anna Lober testified in 1950 that "after the downfall," many newspaper people had come, wanting to find out something about Georg. "We refused and turned the people away because we preferred not to see anything else about this in the newspapers; my mother always became so upset when she read anything about it in the paper."

At that time, the family did not know what had happened to Georg. At some point, there was no further news of him in Dachau. Around 1940, a Gestapo man came to Georg's mother to tell her that her son was in a concentration camp and that she could write to him. She was to address any mail to Reich Security Headquarters. She wrote only once, received no answer, and then lost all hope. "There's no point in writing," she said. In her letter, upon the advice of the Protestant pastor of Königsbronn, she wrote only of very personal matters. She was crippled by a general feeling of anxiety, as she explained in 1950: "I immediately got suspicious and thought that I might get caught up in this too and that they would come get me if I said anything wrong in the letter. I am still convinced that they were just trying to set a trap for me and that my son never got that letter."

The Elser family had difficulty coming to terms with Georg's assassination attempt. As late as 1950, his mother continued to place the blame on others: "I don't think my son would come up with anything like that on his own. I think it's likelier that there was somebody behind it who put the idea into his head." Asked where she had gotten this idea, she responded, "That's just what I think—somebody was behind my son."

That same year, Georg's sister Friederike Kraft recalled after her return from Berlin how the people in the area reacted: "It wasn't a good time for us once we got back to Schnaitheim, because people saw us only in connection with this one issue. For a long time, I didn't go out among people, and the people in Heidenheim, where my husband was working at the Voith company, acted like they wanted to throw him out."

Georg's brother Leonhard Elser, on the other hand, said in 1959 that people were neutral toward the family and that everything had slowly been forgotten. However, Elser's best friend Eugen Rau—the only person to whom Elser gave any indication about the planned assassination, which he did shortly before leaving for Munich—had a different view. In 1988, Rau recalled the principal complaint of people in Königsbronn: "We can't have friends like this, who might get us sent to the gallows!" But no one from Königsbronn went to the gallows. The quarry owner Georg Vollmer was put into a concentration camp because of his negligence in dealing with explosive materials.

Their relationships with Elser also had a lasting effect on two women who had been romantically involved with him at one point. Mathilde Niedermann of Konstanz, the mother of his son Manfred Bühl, broke off the relationship with Elser in 1930 after an argument. He did not want her to have the child, tried twice to arrange an abortion in Switzerland, and paid her little or no alimony. The court in Konstanz later garnished about half his salary, leading him to seek self-employment so he could avoid paying. Understandably, Mathilde Niedermann was bitter at Georg Elser and ashamed that her child was born out of wedlock. She concealed the identity of the father until Manfred was "enlightened" on the street one day by another boy. Later on, Manfred came across the passport photo of a man in his mother's jewelry case; it was Elser. When he asked who it was, his mother ripped up the photograph.

Mathilde Niedermann later married, and thus her son was legitimized. Her husband died in the war, and she married a second time. Despite all this, "Assassinville" remained a burden for her throughout her life. When the magazine *Stern* tracked her down in 1959, she resisted talking about the matter, expressing the wish that the magazine "shouldn't stir everything up again, with the risk of endangering her son." She begged them not to list her name or her son's name. She wanted only to be called "Hilde from St. Gebhardstrasse." She had not talked with her son in detail about his father until he was eighteen. Later on, Manfred Bühl began to delve into the subject of his dead father. The first time he spoke about him was to a small group in Meersburg in 1995. Two years later, six months before his death, Manfred spoke at the dedication of the Georg-Elser-Platz in Munich. Clearly, even the second generation was able to free itself from the grasp of "Assassinville" only after much time had passed.

In 1939, Mathilde Niedermann was interrogated over a period of several nights. She said the interrogations took a great toll on her. She was not, however, able to comment on Georg's political orientation; she considered him to be "completely uninterested in politics." This was odd, because in Konstanz Elser had become friendly with Communists. Fear of the Gestapo, the tactic of denying everything, and the general tendency in the fifties to suppress certain aspects of the past all appear to have had a significant influence on Mathilde Niedermann.

According to Elsa Härlen, another woman involved with Elser, he "led a double life and completely separated his political life from his private life." After Elser's arrest, the local people at first would not speak with Härlen either. But that changed over time. "When it was clear that the war would be lost, and especially in the period immediately following the war," she suddenly had more friends than ever, she said. People tried to bring her ration stamps for groceries, but she turned them down. She told her story in 1959 to a journalist in an interview that lasted for four hours. She didn't want any restitution, she said, because the government of the Federal Republic had not caused her any loss; it was "those gypsies that were there before"— by which she meant the Nazi regime—who had brought harm to her, and she couldn't blame that on the current government.

The Munich locksmith Max Niederhofer, one of Elser's unwitting accomplices, was also not treated gently by the Gestapo. He was detained at Gestapo headquarters in Munich for two weeks, bound, and beaten. Since he had produced metal parts for the explosive device, he was considered highly dangerous. For a long time afterward he had to report in to the Gestapo at nine o'clock every morning; the fact that he had been born in London alarmed the Gestapo greatly.

Two other businesses located on Elser's home turf came under close scrutiny by the Gestapo: the Waldenmaier Company in Heidenehim and the Vollmer Quarry in Königsbronn. At Waldenmaier, Elser had obtained some explosive material and detonators, and it was from Vollmer that he got the majority of the explosive material. Both companies were suspected of not only assisting Elser, but possibly of acting on behalf of foreign agents. On November 15, 1939, shortly after midnight, businessman Erhard Waldenmaier was rousted out of bed and arrested. The Gestapo set up an office at the company and over a period of six months conducted interrogations of numerous employees. In 1940, Waldenmaier joined the Nazi Party in an effort to provide cover for himself.

It struck the Gestapo as very suspicious that Frau Waldenmaier maintained contact with a woman in England whose father was a professor of Hebrew, then teaching in the United States. This constituted an ideal bit of evidence for their conspiracy theory—in the eyes of the Gestapo, these foreigners were agents of the British Secret Service. Even before the assassination attempt, communications that the Waldenmaiers conducted with anyone abroad were being monitored. During the interrogations, the Gestapo brought in many transcripts of letters they had intercepted.

Erhard Waldenmaier was not only the owner of an important arms manufacturing company; from 1934 until the end of the war he was also a contractor for the *Abwehrstelle* (district military intelligence office), charged with overseeing "military production." He reported to the *Abwehrstelle* in Ulm. When the Gestapo began its investigation at his facility in November 1939, the *Abwehr* summoned Waldenmaier to Ulm.

During the night—in one of the standard games played during the Nazi era—the munitions commander and his *Abwehr* officers advised him what and what not to say to the Gestapo. In their zeal, the Gestapo also wanted to know whether the increase in arms production at Waldenmaier might be due to orders from abroad. In reality, though, Hitler was responsible for the arms buildup.

Once quarry owner Georg Vollmer had been locked away in the concentration camp at Welzheim, Waldenmaier feared a similar fate. As recorded in his denazification file in November 1945, he described his feeling of despair at the time: "For hours on end I was deathly afraid, and I intended to take my own life." The head Gestapo officer announced to Waldenmaier that after England was conquered he and Elser would be put on trial. Then comes a sentence that stands out starkly, the kind of statement not made in 1945, when dozens of supposed eyewitnesses and some historians were spouting Nazi legends. Back in 1940, the Gestapo man had assured Waldenmaier: "In spite of repeated torture, Elser had stuck to his story that he had carried out the attack, in order to save the working people and the entire world from war." Then in 1945, the businessman whom Elser had unwillingly placed in grave danger stuck by Elser: "Elser, who believed he had to do away with Hitler for the good of the German people and the world, is now being portrayed in the press as an SS man and SS leader." This voice from Heidenheim was soon drowned out.

But then the situation started improving for Waldenmaier. Thanks to his advocates in the *Abwehr*, he was awarded the War Service Cross Second Class in November 1940 for his company's arms production, and in September 1944, when the end was in sight, he received the War Service Cross First Class. He made significant contributions to the Nazi Party Motor Corps and the Winter Assistance Drive of the Party's

Welfare Organization, was put on the city council in 1944, and with an annual income of 40,000 marks, he clearly profited from the war.

It was the death of a Polish slave laborer that cost Waldenmaier his life. The man had been employed by Waldenmaier, who turned him over to the Nazis at their request. The man was killed by the Nazis, and after the war the Poles blamed his death on Waldenmaier. In October 1946, an American court extradited Waldenmaier to Poland, where he died in a Polish prison on September 20, 1947.

Affected worst by the events was quarry owner Georg Vollmer from Königsbronn. On November 15, 1939, he was arrested along with his sixteen-year-old son Ernst, as well as the bookkeeper and the chief explosives expert. Vollmer had further enraged the Gestapo by removing Elser's name from the payroll list right after the first arrests were made in Königsbronn—the Gestapo caught the deception right away. Vollmer was an *Alter Kämpfer,* a Party member, and, since 1931, *Ortsgruppenleiter*, the top Nazi in the community. He did not establish a regimented rule, but acted more as a patriarch, and after 1933 he was no longer particularly supportive of the Party. In 1937 he was removed because of rivalry with the district leader in Heidenheim. This provided fuel for the fable that he had been part of the resistance.

Most of the explosive material in Elser's bomb had come from Vollmer's operation; for that reason the Gestapo subjected the Vollmer employees to severe beatings during their interrogations of them. In 1947 Vollmer wrote to the *Spruchkammer*, the body in charge of denazification proceedings, "During the interrogations I was beaten. I was kept for four weeks in complete darkness, given only watery soup and bread, and was repeatedly bound. Over and over they screamed in my face that all of my life I had been a Communist and a traitor to the Fatherland, that I was indirectly responsible for the attack, that I should be shot and all of my relatives eradicated."

After Vollmer was released in 1941, he saw his wife suffer a total collapse. "They tormented my wife so that she completely lost her mind. After my return from the concentration camp, she would get up at night and roam around the house in the crazed conviction that the officers [the Gestapo] were coming to get me again. Six months later she had wasted away to skin and bones and died of acute appendicitis."

While Vollmer was still in the concentration camp, his wife managed, under great duress, to pull off two coups. Thanks to old Party connections in Berlin she was able to gain access to an adjutant for Rudolf Hess. As a result, her husband, whom Himmler had sentenced to twenty years in a concentration camp, was released on April 19, 1941, along with the bookkeeper and the explosives expert.

The second coup had ramifications that extend up to the present. In an attempt to wipe out once and for all the devastating accusation that her husband had given Elser access to explosives, she made up a remarkable story about a Zurich music dealer named Kuch, who was from Königsbronn. This man, she said, was the instigator they had all been looking for—with a group of three Communists he had put Elser up to the assassination attempt.

XII

Elser's Youth and Working Years in Königsbronn

ALL DURING THEIR investigations, the Gestapo focused on establishing the extent to which Elser's heredity might have predetermined the assassination attempt, as if a propensity for assassination could be inherited. Right from the beginning, however, Georg Elser showed none of the tendencies that the Gestapo found significant: He didn't drink, a trait that attracted attention in the Bürgerbräukeller; he had never had a venereal disease; and he didn't associate with Jews. Most important, there were no members of the clergy among his relations.

There were, however, throughout Elser's family history, numerous illegitimate children, but this was fairly common in Germany at the time. Contraception was not accessible to many living in rural areas, and marriage was often put off until people could afford a dowry and a place to live. Georg Elser's illegitimate son Manfred was by no means an anomaly in his family history.

His maternal grandmother, Karolina Müller, had been illegitimate. On December 29, 1879, she bore a daughter by the name of

Maria—Georg's mother. Nine days later she disappeared from her childbed. Her child remained with the father and Karolina was never heard from again. The child's father first took his daughter to a children's home and did not return for her until he had married into the family of a carriage maker in Hermaringen, a village south of Heidenheim.

Grandfather Elser was also illegitimate. He took over the family farm in Ochsenberg, near Königsbronn, where he generally enjoyed a good reputation. During a fight at a wedding he hit a wedding guest on the head with a beer mug, for which he spent two months in jail. This incident hardly qualifies as evidence of a hereditary defect. In the end, he died of food poisoning from eating a sausage—a real Swabian, he couldn't bear to throw away food, even spoiled food.

Georg's father, Ludwig Elser, was born in 1872 in Ochsenberg, had eighteen siblings, and was a good student in elementary school. When his eldest child Georg was conceived in 1902, Ludwig was a wagoner at a mill in Hermaringen. Georg's mother Maria worked in the same village at her parents' farm and helped out there in the household. Georg was born on January 4, 1903, in Hermaringen.

After getting married in 1904, Georg's parents moved to Königsbronn, a community north of Heidenheim. There Ludwig ran a hauling business—at first with two horses, then later on with four—and he dealt in wood. With the help of an inheritance, he was able to build up a farm. However, it was Maria who had to manage the farm, even though they had small children—the father paid little attention to it.

Georg's relationship with his father was very difficult for him, but that relationship was of no interest to the Gestapo, even though it was marked by extreme rage and brutality. Georg's long-standing and deeply rooted aversion to the Nazis had its basis in his experiences with his father. In the interrogation in Berlin, Elser was questioned extensively about his father. This part of the transcript, like most passages in the record, had to be laboriously patched together from many side questions. For his part, Elser felt no need to criticize his father. The questions touched a sore spot inside him: his depressing family life, which forever remained traumatic for him.

During the interrogation in Berlin, Georg tried at first to conceal, or at least play down, the difficult relationship he had had with his

The Elser family in front of their house in Königsbronn in 1910. From left: unidentified girl holding Ludwig Elser, who died in 1915; Maria; Georg; Friederike; and their mother Maria, holding Anna Elser.

father. Only persistent grilling succeeded in dragging the unpleasant memories out of him:

> Not every day, but very often, my father came home quite late. As far as I know, he was frequently at a pub. My mother told us children that my father beat her often—however, I never saw this. Whether my father just hit her with his hand, or maybe with a chair, a lamp, or something else, I can't say. Sometimes when my father came home at night, he would get us out of bed for some reason—to help him take off his boots, for example. And I can't remember, but I don't believe that he ever beat us at night when he was drunk. The only time my father ever beat me—and this happened fairly often—was when I had been up to mischief. And my mother beat me too—every once in a while, but not often.

After a family quarrel over the house on Wiesenstrasse in Königsbronn, which was purchased in 1938, and in which Georg felt he had been cheated out of his rights, he became estranged from his mother and almost all his siblings. And it was this circumstance that gave rise to the legend of Georg the loner. His father was the only family member with whom his relations later improved. This was

Georg Elser's father Ludwig at his wood storage site in Königsbronn, around 1920.

in part because his father was living in a summer house out on the Flachsberg and was suffering greatly, as the Gestapo attested in their outline of the family history: "Because of a rheumatic illness that he has had for years, both his legs are almost paralyzed. He appears to be suffering greatly; only when it is absolutely necessary, he is able to get around with the help of two canes."

A photograph taken around 1920 shows Ludwig Elser at his wood storage site in Königsbronn. Standing in front of some large woodpiles is a short, stocky man—all the Elsers were small. During this time Georg had to constantly help his father, who, it must be said, did not have a real knack for the wood business. He was abrupt, ill-tempered, ambitious, and easily provoked. At wood auctions he would arrive with a few beers under his belt, so competitors—sometimes as a joke, other times on purpose—took advantage of him by pushing his bids higher than he could justify from a business perspective. At the end of the auction, Elser looked like the winner, but then incurred losses upon selling that ate away at the family estate. Situations like this may well have provoked his drinking and taking out his rage on his family.

In 1910, when Georg was seven years old, Maria had finally had enough and took her children to her parents' wagon shop in

Hermaringen. A week later, Ludwig's sister managed to work out a reconciliation, and Maria and the children returned. Georg's early experiences with his father's violence probably gave rise to his strong sense of justice, which was a major motivating factor in his anti-Nazi views.

It was widely known in the community that the parents' marriage was a disaster. In 1959, as a journalist was tracking down Elser's background in Königsbronn, he met Anton Egetemaier, a tailor and mailman who had been in the zither club with Elser in the 1930s. According to Egetemaier, Elser's father was "extremely hot-tempered, inconsiderate, and violent. . . . At the slightest provocation he would fly into a rage, grab the nearest thing to use as a club, and then wale away indiscriminately at the whole family. This likely included his wife." In 1950, Maria said nothing about the grim family circumstances, but she lavished praise on Georg in a belated effort at reconciliation with her eldest son, who had been driven away. "Georg was an obedient boy and gave us no trouble. He was fairly quiet—almost too quiet, we thought."

As the eldest, Georg was in every way the most severely affected. Since the next of his siblings were girls, he was the only one who had to work in the wood business, as well as the farm that his mother ran. He didn't even get an allowance for his labor—yet his father found money to squander in the taverns.

In addition, Georg had to be "nursemaid" to his younger siblings. As was often the case with farm families, Georg was able to do his homework only after he had finished his chores. His parents had no interest in his schoolwork—they never even asked about his grades. Later, during the interrogation in Berlin, Georg Elser recalled that such treatment had made learning "rather difficult" for him. The only way he could develop his talents was autodidactically.

In school, things were not quite as difficult for Georg as they were at home, but he liked only the subjects that he did well in—penmanship, arithmetic, and drawing. There was no shortage of beatings at school—but Georg was simply inured to them. "I didn't get any more beatings than the others, and I only got them when I hadn't done my homework properly." And since he had to work on the farm, this was frequently the case. Most of the teachers, Elser recalled, were fair—for him an important factor in judging people's character. In the interrogation in Berlin he said of his first teacher: "As far as I know, he administered beatings only when they were called for."

It was a different story with his teacher in the fourth and fifth grades, who "would sometimes just beat everybody in the whole class." But such behavior was the exception, even back in those days. It was during this very period that Elser was rewarded on two occasions—even though it was in a typically modest Swabian way: One time, he received a notebook for a drawing he had done, and another time he got ten pfennigs for his good performance in arithmetic.

Maria's only respite—and only comfort—was in attending Bible study on Sunday afternoons, which took place at the Protestant Church. The Bible study harkened back to the days of Württemberg Pietism, but was not a Pietist "lesson" as such. This may have had an influence on Georg because as he became more nervous during his preparations for the bomb attack, he sought solace in reciting the Lord's Prayer in a quiet church, regardless of the denomination. Throughout his life, his only other comfort lay in his handicraft and in music.

Someone who could identify with Georg Elser's traumatic childhood was his girlfriend Elsa Härlen. She had been through a marriage similar to that of Elser's mother: Her husband was a drunkard, worked only sporadically, and then drank up the money. She called her marriage her "martyrdom." Georg Elser was able to pour out his heart to her, as Elsa Härlen recalled twenty years later. He had never had a real home; his father frequently drank away the family income, and Georg, as the eldest, had to look after his mother and his siblings. "He must have had a dreadful childhood," Elsa concluded. Elsa enjoyed baking pastries, which Georg ate with particular gusto, having never had anything of the sort at home. "My mother didn't even have the money to buy half a pound of sugar once in a while," he said.

At the start of World War I, Elser's father was ordered to Ulm as a driver for the construction work on the fortress. Toward the end of each year during the war, the Elsers suffered from hunger. A certain portion of their farm production had to be given up, and they were allowed to keep only a small amount for themselves, which had to last them for the entire following year. For Georg Elser, the war constituted a dramatic and portentous turning point, even though he was not drafted into service. Later on, the Gestapo had difficulty understanding why someone like Elser, who had not been a soldier, would try to prevent war.

Because of his family, which was on the social fringe in Königsbronn, and because of his troubled life, Georg Elser did not exactly enjoy great popularity among his young peers. But his best friend Eugen Rau sat next to him at school from the first grade on and played an influential role in Georg's first choice of occupation; he also lived next door to him on Wiesenstrasse, where the family's second house was located. During the interrogation in Berlin, in which Elser strove to divert the suspicion of the Gestapo away from everyone he knew, he pulled off a clever move. Rau could consider himself fortunate that Elser downgraded their friendship, calling it no longer very close, and then craftily named Hans Scheerer, who had emigrated to America and not been heard from again, as his only friend. Elser was successful in concealing the names of other friends, such as the Communist Josef Schurr.

In 1917, Elser finished seventh grade, the final year of elementary school. While waiting to start an apprenticeship in the fall, he worked at his father's wood business and on his mother's farm; he received room and board, but no wages. His thriftiness, which was to stand him in good stead during the preparations for the assassination attempt, took on a quality of stinginess, as Robert Sapper, his foreman in Königsbronn, later remarked. Elser didn't know the meaning of spare time. The first chance he got to develop his own skills outside the family came later on, at Lake Constance.

On the advice of Eugen Rau, Elser started an apprenticeship as a lathe operator at the Königsbronn Iron Works, one of the oldest industrial plants in Württemberg. The deciding factor for Elser in choosing this occupation over the objections of his father was that Eugen was working at the same plant. Elser considered it worthy of note that he had not received a beating from his father for this decision. His father advised against it, but his mother supported him. Ludwig wanted the boy to continue working at home—as unpaid help, to be sure. Then he managed to get Georg to turn over all of his wages as an apprentice.

Only when Georg wanted to buy something specific did he receive any money—and then it was the precise amount he needed for the purchase.

At the trade school in Heidenheim, Elser was quite successful, receiving one of three commendations given in his class. He clearly possessed technical talent. His pride in his work, which he displayed even at Gestapo headquarters on Prinz-Albrecht-Strasse, had its origins here. He also acquired basic skills in metalworking, which were to be of use to him during the construction of his explosive device.

In the lathe shop, Elser soon developed fevers and headaches. The dirty conditions were affecting his health. After a year and a half, he had to quit and seek out a new trade. Following his inclination, he went into woodworking. He had become familiar with this trade in his neighborhood back home. When he used to go after work to pick up sawdust and wood shavings for the farm, he would stay and watch the work going on at the woodworking shop and began to like it more and more. On March 15, 1919, he became an apprentice to the master woodworker Robert Sapper. It was a small shop—besides the boss, the staff consisted of a journeyman and three apprentices.

During the interrogation at State Security Headquarters, when Elser was asked about his apprenticeship, he spoke more freely. At the beginning of his apprenticeship he made simple things: He built boxes, stools, and footstools; he cut out the wood, planed it, and assembled the pieces. Even at this stage the work appealed to him, and he was clearly very talented. The tasks became more difficult, and by the end of his apprenticeship he was able to produce large and complex pieces of furniture completely on his own. During this period he also occasionally worked in the construction branch, but the work was generally dirty and he didn't care for it. He was more interested in the more challenging work of furniture making, and liked to call himself a *Kunstschreiner*, an "artist in woodworking." His weekly salary in the first year of his apprenticeship was one mark, in the second year two marks, and in the third year three or four marks. It was enough so that he could now buy himself clothes as well as tools for use on his own projects. Elser's tool collection was his lifeblood, his pride and joy—and in 1939 in Stuttgart, it was to become the undoing of his sister Maria Hirth.

At home as well, Elser demonstrated his skill and industriousness. In what was probably his first attempt to build a room, he converted a cellar into a living space.

Georg Elser as a young man.

Elser finished the Heidenheim Trade School at the top of his class. Now at least his parents could be satisfied with him. Since the apprenticeship with Sapper paid so little, he soon gave notice and moved on to Aalen to work in the Rieder Furniture Factory (now the Hotel Antik). His boss Sapper did not want to let him go—this skilled craftsman was irreplaceable. Even as an apprentice he had worked overtime when it was necessary. After he gave notice a second time, Elser simply didn't return to work. Independence and determination were trademarks of Elser's character throughout his life.

Elser then worked in Aalen until the fall of 1923. Soon thereafter, inflation plunged him into the first crisis of his working life. The precipitous fall of the currency diminished his pay week by week at first, then hour by hour. With the amount in today's pay packet, one could barely manage to buy a loaf of bread tomorrow. So Elser decided to give notice and return to working in his father's wood business and on his mother's farm—as before, in exchange for room and board and without any allowance.

In the summer of 1924, Elser found a new job in Heidenheim with the furniture manufacturer Matthias Müller, another small shop with four or five journeymen and one or two apprentices. The company produced custom-made furniture for the home. For the most part, Elser built kitchen cabinets and wardrobes. He was able to carry out these projects from start to finish, working completely alone, as was his wont. Elser's independence, of which he was very proud, was being threatened by the advent of modern furniture factories with their mass production. Individual craftsmen like Elser were able to survive mainly in rural areas because of the proximity to their customers as well as lower wages. Elser's self-reliance was a key factor that differentiated him from others who opposed Hitler. The idea that one man could eliminate Hitler on his own apparently did not occur to the members of the military resistance.

At the beginning of 1925 Elser gave notice once again. Like Elser's previous boss, Matthias Müller also didn't want to let him go. Elser left the company without permission and went back to working at home. But he couldn't stick it out there for long: "I really wanted to get away and get more training in my trade." His mother reflected after the war: "As far as his occupation was concerned, Georg was very ambitious; he wanted to get ahead and continue learning." His lifestyle, she said, was very respectable—he didn't smoke and he didn't drink. Georg's aversion to alcohol certainly traced back to his grim experiences with his father.

Georg Elser had other objectives: he wanted to get away from the misery of his parents' fighting, the constant control over his life and his wages, and the obligation as the eldest to always be at the family's beck and call. "He never wanted to have anything to do with girls while he was living here in Königsbronn," his mother claimed, and unknowingly touched on a sore spot. As a twenty-two-year-old, Georg surely felt that the situation had to change, but he saw no opportunity for romantic experimentation under the watchful eye of his mother. Upon his return from Konstanz seven years later, he fell in love with a woman who was still married and, like his mother, deeply troubled. When he took the woman to his room, his mother threw him out of the house.

XIII

A Freer Life at Lake Constance

GEORG ELSER, BRANDED by posterity as an eccentric and a loner, struggled for weeks at the beginning of 1925 with his desire "to get away." But he didn't know where to go. On one of his Sunday walks with Eugen Rau, he met a woodworker at the Zum Hirsch tavern in the neighboring town of Oberkochen. The man had himself gone away and recommended his old employer, the Wachter Company, a small woodworking shop in Bernried near the Swabian town of Tettnang.

After applying for a position by mail, Elser received approval to begin work on March 15, 1925. He took the train to Tettnang, then walked two hours to get to Bernried, a small spread-out community consisting of only a few houses.

The Wachter Company is still in business today, run by the grandson of the owner back in Elser's day. At that time the equipment at the shop was very simple. Everything was still done by hand, somewhat to Elser's dismay. The only machine was a circular saw, which the master had built himself. There wasn't even a workbench—the pieces had to be planed by hand. Since Georg was the only employee, he was taken into the family. He had a room in the attic and took his meals with the family. Room and board were free, and he received a weekly wage of eight to twelve marks. All in all, it wasn't bad compensation, but Elser felt very isolated. After six weeks, he gave his notice. The owner was reluctant to let him go.

At the beginning of May, Elser simply took off into the wild blue yonder, with no new job in sight. For the first time in his life, he was out traveling on his own. He took his time, first hiking along Lake Constance, perhaps through Kressbronn and Langenargen, but in any case headed for Friedrichshafen. It took him a week to cover this stretch of about fifteen miles. Although his mother knew him only as a hard worker who spent many Sundays at home working in his shop, he now discovered personal freedom and the pleasure of idleness. For a work-obsessed Swabian, this represented a subversion of the traditional values. The shackles of the repression and constant fighting that had marked his life started to loosen.

He didn't need to ask for money along the way, and with his savings he was able to stay at inns. He always asked around about work, but had no success. Through the employment office in Friedrichshafen he found a position as a woodworker at Dornier Metal Works in the neighboring community of Manzell. It's hard to imagine a more dramatic technological shift for that time: from simple carpentry executed by hand to a modern airplane industry expanding by leaps and bounds and producing one sensational product after another.

At his plant, which had been founded only recently in 1923, Claude Dornier produced a series of flying boats called "The Whale." Everything was still in a pioneer stage. In 1925 alone—during Elser's time there—the new seaplane set twenty-five world records. International air travel, which was still in its infancy, depended largely on Dornier planes, primarily "The Whale." Although the flying boat was constructed of metal, the propellers were fashioned out of wood. Since the work required great precision, it was right up Elser's alley. Perhaps it was here that his well-known "check-o-mania," which people were to make fun of later on, got its real start. The wood was glued together in layers, cut out roughly with a circular saw, and then planed with painstaking patience to the prescribed curved shape. The work was not boring, because the propellers varied in shape, the number of blades, the kinds of layers, and in diameter. And in this modern plant, the compensation was appropriately high. With piecework and much overtime, Elser earned more money than ever before.

However, he was still not satisfied with his personal circumstances. Since Lake Constance attracted many vacationers in the summer, he was not able to find a room in Friedrichshafen and had to take a room at an inn in Kluftern, which was located near the rail line between Friedrichshafen and Markdorf. At Dornier, he became friends with Leo Dannecker, who played the clarinet and wanted to join a music organization in Konstanz. This idea appealed to Elser, who had enjoyed playing music since his school days. The two of them found work as cabinetmakers with a clock manufacturer in Konstanz and gave notice at the much more promising Dornier Works.

It was the practice of the clock factory in Konstanz to purchase clockworks in the Black Forest, then build individual cases for them. Using this method, they produced mantel clocks, wall clocks, and grandfather clocks. But during the Depression, when unemployment was so high, orders from customers fell off. The clock factory was located on the left bank of the Rhine, at Fischenzstrasse 1, in a spacious factory building in the part of town known as Paradies. On the ground floor there was a chemical and pharmaceutical factory called Medico. The clock factory had its operations on the second floor.

The first room Elser rented in Konstanz was in the old part of town at Inselgasse 15 on the third floor of the rear building, in the apartment of Bruno Braster, a painter. The front building was an old patrician villa with four floors, listed in older documents as the "Haus zum Blaufuss." Elser shared the room with a friend named Fiebig, a Communist who also worked at the clock factory. In 1928, Fiebig convinced him to join the *Rote Frontkämpferbund* (Red Front Fighters League), an organization of the German Communist Party that was banned in 1929. After his friend died in 1930, Elser moved to St. Gebhardstrasse in Petershausen, a part of town located on the right bank of the Rhine. His girlfriend Mathilde Niedermann lived at number 4 on the same street. He later rented a room from his girlfriend's sister-in-law at Fürstenbergstrasse 1, where he stayed until early 1932.

As they did while he was in Friedrichshafen, Elser's family maintained ties with him. His mother in particular continued to look after him: Georg sent his laundry home to be washed and mended. Two of his siblings came to visit him in Konstanz: His sister Anna spent Pentecost of 1928 or 1929 with him, and his brother Leonhard stopped by during a bicycle tour with friends in 1929.

The greater personal freedom Elser found in Konstanz came at the price of more insecurity in his job situation. From August 1925 until early 1930, Elser worked at the same clock factory making clock cases. During that time, he was placed on leave for six months on three separate occasions. The entire clock industry remained in constant crisis, and the company changed hands several times. In 1920 it was called the Winterhalder Home Clock Factory; in 1925 it became the Constantia Clock Factory, owned by Rudolf Metzner and Georg Fuchs; then in 1926–27 it went into bankruptcy. For a period of six months Elser had no work, even though he regularly inquired at the employment office as well as furniture manufacturers and cabinetmakers. In 1928, the company reopened as Schuckmann & Co. Clock Factory, and Elser was rehired.

By the beginning of 1929, Schuckmann was in difficulty, and he offered the entire facility to the city of Konstanz for 90,000 marks. The city considered this price too high, so Schuckmann tried to sell off individual parts for ten marks per square meter. But the company could not be saved, and in desperation the boss set fire to the place. The police immediately saw arson as the cause of the fire. Once again, all the workers were dismissed. The story of this small company can serve to illustrate how things were during the years of the Great Depression.

Through the employment office in Kreuzlingen Elser found an attractive position in the nearby Swiss village of Bottighofen. So he went to work in Switzerland for the first time, at an hourly wage of 1.30 franks, which at the time was 1.04 marks. He was very content there; however, within six months the work ran out at this small business as well, where Elser was the only employee. He was let go.

Elser got through these periods of unemployment but became more serious as a result, as some of his siblings noticed after his return. He survived on unemployment benefits and his savings without having to depend on anyone. By 1927 he had saved enough that he was able to spend 140 marks to buy himself a new bicycle, a symbol of affluence on a modest scale. For his own enjoyment, he built small artistic pieces such as jewelry boxes and sewing boxes, often decorated with fine marquetry. He gave most of these to his girlfriends.

Beginning in May 1929, Elser would ride his bicycle every day to the Schönholzer woodworking shop in Bottighofen. It was a short trip of three miles—no more than twenty minutes by bicycle. At the customs office in Kreuzlingen he showed the customary red card used for local cross-border traffic. At that time border control was fairly loose. The customs officers on both sides were unconcerned when locals smuggled small quantities of coffee, sugar, cocoa, and tea. Looking back on these innocent times, Elser felt that he knew the border area between the customs offices in Kreuzlingen and Emmishofen quite well. The fact that he could not imagine the changes brought on by the beginning of the war in 1939 became his undoing on November 8, 1939.

In Konstanz, Georg Elser was able to broaden himself and become more independent. He acquired skills in clock making and produced cases for sophisticated clocks. Later on in Königsbronn he used these skills to establish a small business. His assassination plans were to hinge upon these very skills.

Elser would not achieve greater personal independence until he could escape the watchful eye of his mother. His contacts with women did not come about as quickly as the Elser literature heretofore would have us believe. At first he might venture a kiss after an evening spent practicing at the Konstanz zither club or an evening at the Kreuzlingen temperance club. Then word would have it that he was "going" with yet another girl. Even the Berlin Gestapo was sufficiently titillated by the subject in 1939 that they created a separate chapter in their reports entitled "Sex life." Appropriately, it was followed by the chapter entitled "Religious life."

The first time that Georg Elser slept with a woman he was twenty-two years old. This was probably around the beginning of his time in Konstanz. His first experiences were so brief and superficial that he could not recall the last names of the two young women involved. The Kripo summarized Elser's romantic encounters with bureaucratic crispness: "During my stay in Konstanz, I first had sexual intercourse with a certain Brunhilde, whose last name I cannot recall. . . . After Brunhilde, there was a certain Anna, then Mathilde Niedermann, then Hilda Lang; then later on in Königsbronn there was my land-lady, whose name was Härlen." It cannot be said for certain that Elser changed girlfriends frequently. It was likely just some envious people who in their thoughtlessness subsequently made him out to be the Casanova of the Ostalb.

Love brought with it confusion for Elser. An outing with his girl-friend Mathilde Niedermann to the island of Mainau in Lake Constance was captured in a photograph from the year 1929. Mathilde, quite the lady in her elegant shoes, is seated on a large stone; Georg is standing behind her with a smile on his face, a handkerchief rak-ishly tucked into the pocket of his jacket. Standing next to them is Leonhard Elser, ten years younger than Georg and visiting his older brother at the time. It was probably summer. In December of 1929, Mathilde Niedermann, who was working as a waitress, became pregnant. By the time she became aware of it, it was already too late for an abortion, which in Switzerland was permitted up until the third month. Georg Elser didn't want the child. So following up on announcements found in newspapers, the two of them went to Switzerland and tried to find help in Weinfeldern (in Thurgau) and Geneva. On both occasions they were turned down because it had been longer than three months. When Elser first heard the results in Geneva, he didn't believe Mathilde Niedermann and had the doctor explain everything to him again in minute detail. Their mutual trust was destroyed.

It was only with great reluctance that Elser paid child support for his son Manfred, who was born September 13, 1930. Time and again he had to be warned by the youth welfare office, until finally a large part of his wages were garnished. This drove him to seek greater independence,

Georg Elser with his girlfriend Mathilde Niedermann and his brother Leonhard on the island of Mainau in 1929.

Georg Elser's son Manfred and his mother Mathilde Niedermann (Bühl), around 1939.

so in Königsbronn he started working for himself more, taking on jobs from private individuals in order to avoid the child-support payments. Mathilde Niedermann held this against him for the rest of her life.

In the meantime Georg sought comfort in Konstanz with Hilda Lang, a seamstress who lived at Hussenstrasse 9. From 1923 until 1936, she had a position as a cutter with Pius Wieler and Sons in Kreuzlingen; she was a very capable and popular worker, who had the resilience to weather the crises of those times.

Elser first met Hilda at the Kreuzlingen Free Temperance Union, a close-knit group also frequented by many people from Konstanz. He was at times so close to the Lang family that he occasionally attended church—a Catholic church—with Hilda. The relationship continued until the summer of 1932, and the two visited each other often when Elser was living in Meersburg, until a cry for help from his mother called him back to Königsbronn.

During the interrogations in Berlin, Elser concealed this part of his life at Lake Constance. He must have enjoyed the temperance group; the evening social gatherings fulfilled a need for him. And once during a brief visit from his sister Anna, he was pleased to show her the café where he occasionally enjoyed the luxury of a cup of coffee. Fundamentally, Georg was very modest and yet at the same time very tenacious, capable of enormous sacrifice in pursuit of a greater goal. At the temperance group, Elser particularly liked being the rooster in the henhouse. The organization had about thirty members, both working class and middle class, as the Swiss police determined. After questioning the Swiss members in 1939, the Swiss police summarized their findings: "Elser was a member for a year and a half during the period 1929–30. At that time Elser carried on a relationship with Hilda Lang of Konstanz, who was also a member of the same temperance union." Then comes a statement that doesn't quite fit the typical image of Elser: "Elser was considered a dapper young fellow and was quite popular." Nothing here of the eccentric, nothing of the slightly grubby craftsman in Munich, nothing of the man plagued by depression.

For the most part, Elser seems to have been serious about both Mathilde Niedermann and Hilda Lang. He took each of them to Königsbronn and introduced them to his family, primarily to his mother, who twenty years later recalled that he had never spoken of marriage. A concerned mother does not forget a detail like this.

Another highlight of his experiences in Switzerland was surely the sense of freedom in the work environment at the Schönholzer woodworking shop in Bottighofen. Indeed, he had this same sense about Switzerland in general and felt ever more drawn to it as circumstances under Hitler weighed ever more heavily upon him. From May 1929 until the fall of that year, Elser rode his bicycle across that border every workday to the shop, where besides master Schönholzer and his son, he was the only employee. He was well acquainted with the work. He focused primarily on home furnishings. With his flexible approach to his work schedule, Elser was not only ahead of his time, he was also revealing a degree of self-confidence not typical for one of his proletarian origins—at the very time that he was becoming more involved with the Communist crowd. If Elser saw himself as a socialist, as he surely did, he was nonetheless also an individualist with a desire for independence and self-reliance and had a great need for freedom. This nonproletarian relationship to his work manifested itself in other positions that he held.

A love for music became an important factor in Elser's maturation process. He had played the flute and the accordion since his school days without benefit of instruction, simply by ear. Later on, when he had finished school, he played only the accordion, performing at small parties. In 1924 in the town of Ochsenberg, located near Königsbronn, he once accompanied dancing lessons on his accordion, but later on he sold the instrument.

In 1926 Elser became acquainted with the Oberrheintal Traditional Dress Club. He joined the group and from a member named Dassler, also a woodworker, he purchased a concert zither for twenty marks. Elser wanted to learn to play the instrument properly, and spared no expense in doing so. He first took a few private lessons from a music teacher at one mark fifty per lesson, then continued his lessons with the chairman of the organization for two marks a lesson. After more than two dozen lessons, he quit—it was a question of money, he said. The recurring periods of unemployment forced him to watch his money carefully.

The weekly meetings of the club took place on Saturdays at the inn Zum Kratzer, which was located at Salmannsweilergasse 13 in the old part of Konstanz near the fish market. Here they practiced music and dancing. When the society offered an evening of entertainment, family members came as well. Elser had no difficulties establishing contacts. Occasionally, when accompanying one of the girls home, he would give her a kiss. The Gestapo was disappointed that they could not extrapolate such encounters into new love affairs.

In 1930, Elser experienced a low point in his life at Lake Constance: For the third time, he became unemployed. In the same year, Herr Rothmund of Meersburg, former owner of the Oberrhein Clock Factory on Fischenzstrasse in Konstanz, started up a new company manufacturing clocks. Early in 1930 he opened the operation in Meersburg in the facility of the master glazier Wilhelm Matthes at Stettener Strasse 2. Rothmund concentrated on mantel clocks and kitchen clocks and had a workforce of eight. Some of them, including Elser, commuted daily by ferry across Lake Constance. Once again he was paid according to the scale of the woodworkers' union. In May of 1932 the company went bankrupt. Instead of his back pay, Elser received several clock mechanisms as a settlement; these provided the basis later on for his private business in Königsbronn. He was later to incorporate two of the devices into his work at the Bürgerbräukeller.

Once again Elser had to look for work. He would have been left completely outside the socioeconomic fabric if it had not been for his connections and his self-reliance; even so, he managed to eke out only a minimal existence. In order to cut back on expenses such as the ferry and room rent, he moved to Meersburg, where he bartered furniture construction or repair work for room and board. It was a modest lifestyle, but one to which he had become accustomed at home. He found the first such arrangement for eating, sleeping, and working with the Dreher family on Kunkelgasse, located behind the town hall.

Sooner or later, this formula for getting by would have to play out. At some point Elser would exhaust his circle of friends and he would receive no more orders. The Drehers recommended Elser to a widow named Becker who lived above the Matthes' glazier shop. There were small jobs to do such as repairing and building tables. Food and drink were always provided by the customer. He moved on to three other families who were acquaintances of the Drehers. After the assassination attempt, these families were dragged to the Gestapo and interrogated for weeks and even months. According to the oral record, two of those interrogated were so mistreated that they suffered from the experience for a long time afterward.

It is clear that Elser had a close relationship with the Dreher family. From this period a photograph survives that shows a different Elser from the one known to us through clichés. In the picture, taken at Stadtgraben 5 (a former Catholic rectory, which is now a historic site), there are nine people standing in front of the barn door. On the far left is a Herr Holz and on the far right, his wife. Second from the left is Herr Dreher, next to him his wife. Fourth, sixth, and seventh from the left are three Dutch women who happened to be staying there at the time. Second from the right is the farmhand Josef Kopp, who later became a servant at the Hotel Seehof. In the middle of this cheerful assembly is the future assassin: a harmless man with a smile on his face and a large black shock of hair hanging down the right side of his face—a carefree, rakish hairstyle, one no longer tolerated in the

Georg Elser (center), Meersburg, 1932.

Third Reich and associated with artistic circles, the youth movement, or swing-era young people.

Here at rye-threshing time, which usually took place early in the year, people are taking a break; Elser is holding a flail in his hand. It is cool, and the visitors are wearing coats. Elser appears neither shy nor eccentric—the Dutch woman to his left casually rests her arm upon his. He seems rather gentle—at first glance a pleasant-looking person.

The Drehers were monarchists—in this Catholic area around Lake Constance there were still many people with this view. For the father of the family, the Grand Duke of Baden was the only real authority; for the mother, who was originally from Bavaria, it was the Prince Regent Luitpold. Nevertheless, Elser was taken in by them and got along quite well with them—this comity does not seem to fit the image of an eccentric or a fanatic. Both Drehers, however, found Elser too progressive. So it appears that Elser took part in political discussions when the occasion arose.

During the Depression Elser's life fell apart. He had no job, no social connections, no permanent place to live. He only did work that was "off the books" and was dependent on occasional orders for items he could build. He was living from hand to mouth. He seemed to have lost his interest in handicrafts and had no hope of setting up his own workshop. Then a cry for help from his mother reached him in Meersburg. The message was that his father was drinking up the money and that Georg needed to come home immediately to his family to try to keep him from wiping them out completely.

Georg Elser had no other choice, but the return to Königsbronn was very hard on him. It meant going back to the stifling and narrow-minded world that he had fled seven years before. However, the years at Lake Constance had liberated him and helped shape his identity, both personally and politically. This period was to remain as an ideal for him. Waving like a shadow over all his wishes now was the flag of a country to which he passionately wanted to emigrate, yet never could—Switzerland.

XIV

Back to Königsbronn

Dᴜʀɪɴɢ ᴛʜᴇ Bᴇʀʟɪɴ interrogation, Elser spoke more openly of the family drama than of other matters that would have implicated outsiders. Here he felt no need to suppress anything. In May of 1932, he said, his mother had written to tell him:

> . . . that my father was drinking more and more and that he was selling one plot of land after another just to pay the debts that he ran up with his wood dealings and his drinking. By getting me to come home my mother expected to see my father's behavior improve. . . . My mother and my brother [Leonhard] were very happy to have me back at home. My father was indifferent. I soon learned that my parents had run up large debts because of my father's wood business—I can't recall the amount of the debts. My father incurred these debts primarily because he would bid too high for wood at auctions and then have to sell it at a loss. I found out from my uncle Eugen Elser in Königsbronn that my father was always under the influence of alcohol at wood auctions, and that was why he always paid such high prices.

As he had in the past, the good-natured Georg found himself exploited, this time by his mother; yet he never received any thanks. He was not able to get anywhere with his stubborn father. He fell back into his no-cash life, helping his mother on the farm and his father at the wood business, where he smoothed and trimmed off pieces of wood. His only source of pleasure was a small woodworking

134

Georg Elser with his younger brother Leonhard, 1933 or 1934.

shop that he managed to set up at the house, in which he could build furniture on order, as he had done in Meersburg.

The sacrifice he made by returning was for naught. His father started drinking even more heavily and sold land to pay off his obligations. The family was living off what it could harvest. And as he had done throughout Georg's childhood, his father would come home drunk and create a scene, cursing his wife, Georg, and Leonhard, saying it was their fault that everything was falling apart. In only one way he did seem to have improved: the aging man, who was now sixty and clearly becoming weaker, no longer abused anyone or tore up the furniture, which his sons would then have to repair.

Such a situation might well have provided a strapping young working-class fellow reason enough to straighten out the intergenerational relationship in a physical way, but Georg was too good-natured to ever punch his father. Georg's girlfriend Elsa Härlen would later tell the Gestapo that this man, the assassin, was in every way a friendly and helpful person who could never do anything to hurt anyone.

After an absence of seven years, Elser returned to Königsbronn with the basic views of a Communist. Elser's friend Anton Egetemaier, who played in the zither group with him, later recounted that Elser had never been openly political nor engaged in political discussions, but had brought back from Konstanz "a very firm political view"—translation: a clear and uncompromising enmity toward the Nazi regime.

During the Berlin interrogation Elser admitted that, although he had not been a member of the KPD (Communist Party of Germany), he had always voted Communist in order to do something for the interests of the common worker. He had also always been a member of the Woodworkers Union, which was considered a left-wing organization. So it is not surprising that at a meeting in Königsbronn he made the acquaintance of Josef Schurr, a Communist from Schnaitheim. What is surprising is that a letter to the editor by Schurr, which appeared in a newspaper in Ulm in 1947, was overlooked by Elser researchers. Even if it contained several errors stemming from faulty recollection—a common occurrence in many such sources—the basic political message of the letter is surely accurate.

At the meeting, which was held sometime before 1933, Elser revealed to Schurr, whom he did not know, that he was an ardent anti-Nazi. Elser, who since his return had become more closed off, was rarely this outspoken. Both of these men were practical people, not public speakers, and they wanted to do something. Assuming that Schurr's recollection was not influenced by information acquired later, the opposition that Elser expressed could be described as almost brutal. Carefully working out a motivation was not Schurr's strong suit, and he has been criticized by many historians for this.

Schurr recalled a determined Elser: "He was always extremely interested in some act of violence against Hitler and his cronies. He always called Hitler a 'gypsy'—one just had to look at his criminal face. We spent a lot of time talking about what could be done and what absolutely had to be done. Elser and I managed to strike a few blows against the Nazis, and they never suspected us."

What did Schurr mean by "a few blows"? Did they destroy the Party's display cases containing the anti-Semitic paper *Der Stürmer*? Did they burn a flag, break windows at a Nazi's house, or play a trick on the local Nazi official Georg Vollmer? It is assumed that Elser did not produce and distribute leaflets—the classic form of Communist protest. In a rural environment, this kind of action would not have made a great deal of sense.

Their friendship was interrupted when, like many other Communists, Schurr was arrested early in 1933 and incarcerated for five months at the Heuberg concentration camp located near Stetten am Kalten Mark in the Schwäbisch Alb region. When Schurr was released, he got a job at the Waldenmaier armament factory, where he was kept under surveillance. It was probably not a coincidence that in 1937 Elser got a job at the same company and started gathering materials for his time bomb.

After Hitler assumed power, it became almost obligatory to listen to his radio addresses. At the sound of his voice, Elser would get up and leave the tavern. He refused to listen at home as well. Elser was not the type to listen to his enemy and analyze his words in order to combat him. He was opposed to him for good reasons and felt no need to reveal them to anyone. He simply did not want to hear all this agitation and scolding, and would leave without saying a word. He was by no means alone in his views; however, it was soon forgotten that such opposition had existed.

Elser's recalcitrance was also evident when it came to saluting the swastika flag. People on the street were required to publicly acknowledge their allegiance to the regime. In 1933 in the town of Giengen in the Brenz valley, there was an incident involving the SA. When a pedestrian passed by an SA parade and failed to salute the flag, an SA man jumped out of ranks and punched him in the face. The man who had been struck trusted in the justice system and hired an attorney known for his anti-Nazi views to defend him in the municipal court in Heidenheim. His acquittal rested on a key statement by his attorney: "There is no law stating that the *Blutfahne* must be saluted."

An occurrence witnessed by Egetemaier on May 1, 1938, demonstrated Elser's scorn for the Nazi regime more blatantly. He and Elser were standing near the Weisses Rössle, the most popular inn in Königsbronn, when a procession of brown shirts passed by the inn carrying the *Blutfahne*. According to Egetemaier, everybody on the street saluted except for Elser. When Egetemaier warned Elser that he had to salute the flag, Elser answered bluntly in Swabian dialect, "Nope, just kiss my ass!" Then he turned around, looked down the street in another direction, and starting whistling a tune. Elser's attitude, which he did not care to discuss, was: "I'd rather be shot than move a muscle for the Nazis." And that was that.

At elections during the Third Reich, Elser was also uncompromising. Once, when his girlfriend Elsa Härlen asked him if he was going to vote, he replied tersely, "No." She tried to urge him to vote, "because of the townspeople." But Elser was indifferent to such considerations. He was displeased that she was going to vote, but he did not try to stop her.

Elsa Härlen had similar experiences with Elser when it came to campaigns for the Nazi Party. Elser was very consistent in his statements. "He always said he was for something or against it, but he didn't like discussions. One time when the SA was collecting money in order to buy uniforms, I said I didn't like this way of raising money. And then Elser said: 'Either you're for it and give them something, or you're against it and you don't.'"

In the working-class environment of the upper Brenz valley, Elser's attitude was not so unusual. In Itzelberg, a village near Königsbronn, as well as in Schnaitheim, the KPD received the most votes in the Reichtag election of November 1932. In the district of Heidenheim, there were more votes recorded for the Communists than the national average, but the Nazis got more votes as well. In Schnaitheim the Nazis lagged far behind in fourth place. The situation was different in Königsbronn, where the quarry owner Georg Vollmer as local Nazi leader wielded his patriarchal scepter. Here the party of the swastika led in elections even before 1933.

Georg Vollmer had been a Party member since 1931. He immediately became the local Party boss and was the de facto head of the municipality; however, he had since ceased any effort to build the Party. Those in the community who held differing views—and he of course knew them—were simply left in peace. In this rural area the political climate was not as heated as it was in the big cities. During the 1934 election, a slip of paper was found in a ballot box with the following bit of folk poetry: "Give Hitler the boot/And beat Röhm, the fruit." A poll worker claimed it was the handwriting of the Communist Christian Konrad, who resided in Eichhalde. Konrad was generally considered to be a Communist, even though he had never been a party member. As people were trying to decide what to do with the note, Party leader Vollmer came by and put it in his pocket, saying he would take care of it—then promptly ignored it. This type of thing was typical in rural areas. People were among their own, and political strife seemed unnecessary. It wouldn't do to squeal on a member of the community. It was in such an atmosphere that Elser was able to hold his own and continue his criticism of the Nazi regime unscathed.

At the beginning of 1933, Elser joined the Königsbronn zither club, an organization that had been started in 1927. In the Berlin interrogation, he cited his family circumstances as his main reason for joining: "With music I was hoping to find relief from the situation at home." The club had eight to twelve members, many of whom were related. Hans Elser, who was at the time only twelve years old, recalled that Georg often came to their house and remembered him as "a very accessible, helpful, and affable person" who seemed "completely apolitical." Many people said that Georg Elser was simply neither an agitator nor one who talked politics. Any political deliberations he engaged in he seemed to have engaged in alone.

Faced with the increasing manipulation of cultural life by the Nazis, Elser took refuge in music and dancing. Rehearsals were held on Friday or Saturday evening in a side room at the Hecht tavern. Occasionally, dances and concerts were held in a dance hall. In 1934, Konkordia, a glee club with many members, wanted to provide dance music but was lacking a bass. At that point Elser decided to add bass to the list of instruments he could play, so he bought a bass with his own money and started taking lessons. He also became quite accomplished at *Schuhplatteln*, a kind of Bavarian clog dancing.

Elser found yet another way to escape his grim family life by joining a hiking club. The cultural machine had insinuated itself into the club's motto "Strength through joy", but otherwise there was no evidence of political indoctrination in the organization. It was here in 1933 that he met Elsa Härlen, who by 1936 was to become the love of his short life. There is a group photo taken in the Wental, a beautiful dry valley located in the uplands of the Alb near Steinheim and one of the most popular spots for outings in the area, which shows Elser wearing knickerbockers and standing behind his sweetheart Elsa. He still favored this style of trousers when he was living in Munich, and the investigative branch of the Gestapo made use of this detail in its wanted poster.

The Weisses Rössle in Königsbronn, the most popular place in town during Elser's time.

Georg Elser's work situation was now even more erratic than it was in Konstanz. He moved between the independence offered by his small shop and a regular job in a woodworking shop. This irregularity was brought on by the alimony requirements imposed on him in

Konstanz. Whenever he started working at a regular job, the child welfare office soon found out about it from the employment office and moved to seize a large portion of his wages.

When he worked on his own, Elser was extremely conscientious. Paul Bässler of the Stuttgart Gestapo recalled from his investigation: "As a craftsman, he [Elser] produced first-class work. He would prefer to take a loss than have anyone say that his work was not satisfactory. For the most part, he created small boxes as well as grandfather clocks or cases for them." He produced generally the same items that he had developed in Meersburg.

If orders were slow coming in, Elser would work for a while at Eugen Grupp's woodworking shop in Königsbronn. The first time he worked from July through November 1934, another time from June through September 1935. However, as soon as the child welfare office showed up, Elser would go back to working for himself, sometimes as a subcontractor for his boss. Wages during the Nazi era were of course modest at best, as Elser subsequently recounted in detail to the Gestapo, even after being subjected to brutal treatment. His hourly wage had fallen to fifty-five pfennigs, half of what it had been in Bottighofen—giving him yet another reason to see Switzerland as the promised land. Being thus relegated to the fringes of economic life provided Elser with his most potent criticism of Hitler's government.

When Hitler began to step up arms production for the Wehrmacht, Elser was also affected—Master Grupp received a large order for desks for the Wehrmacht. Since Grupp needed extra help because of the tight deadlines, he rehired Elser, who then left after only six months. He had two reasons for leaving: The pay was too low, and he was tired of having the boss interfere in his work. Elser had distinct pride in his work, and even as an employee he insisted on working independently. There were possibly also questions of ethics and economy involved in his decision to leave. The shop had to deliver desks to the Wehrmacht by a specific date, and the work did not need to be so meticulous. But Elser insisted on delivering top-quality work— meaning of course more expensive work—even to the military.

The continued decline of Elser's father hastened the final breakup of the family. (In a grotesque turn of events, the Elsers would be reunited briefly in November 1939 by the Gestapo, as they were being taken to Stuttgart as prisoners.) Toward the end of 1935, the father had to sell his entire estate to his principal creditor, a cattle dealer from Königsbronn named Maurer. The indebtedness was so great that, despite an appraised value of 10,000 or 11,000 marks, the property brought only 6500 marks. The only parcel remaining in the hands of the family was a fruit orchard on the Flachsberg. There Georg took a shed and converted it into a permanent cottage where his father lived. Gradually the old man lost the ability to walk, so Georg had to take his meals to him. It was here, on the outskirts of town, that Elser would later on carry out tests of his explosive devices.

The orchard and the shed stand out as sad symbols of a family in ruins. This last bit of property became a refuge for what remained of the Elser estate and at the same time the practice field for a bold assassination attempt that, with a bit of luck, might have saved Europe from a mad dictator.

From the sale of the old property, Elser's mother received 2,000 marks for herself. With the balance, Elser's father settled his debts—and continued drinking. He was allowed by the new owner to have a room in his former house; Elser's mother moved in with daughter Friederike in Schnaitheim; and brother Leonhard went into the Reich labor service. This time at least, Georg had it a little better. He became a lodger with the Härlens, so that he was closer to Elsa. In the basement of the house, he once again set up his own shop and worked on his own. He attempted to cover his rent by bartering his skills, building chairs and a cupboard for the kitchen. But Elsa's husband put a stop to this as soon as he began to suspect that the two were having an affair.

Another rift in the Elser family occurred in 1938 when his parents purchased half of a double house on Wiesenstrasse with what money they had left. Georg was present at the notary's office and observed that not everything was entered into the record that had been agreed upon. Appearing as owners were his father, his mother, and Leonhard, who in the meantime had gotten married—each with a one-third interest in the property. Apparently, Georg had been promised part ownership, but in the notary's office this agreement was disregarded. Elser felt that he had been expelled from the family, and his sense of justice had been deeply violated. For nearly his entire life he had contributed the most to sustaining the family. For years he had worked for them for nothing. Now he was not even given the right to a place to live. Since almost everyone in the family stuck together in this matter, Georg Elser abruptly severed his relationships with all of them except his sister Maria in Stuttgart. In so doing, he provided another source for the tenacious legend of Elser the eccentric. One by one the bridges behind him were being burned. He was distancing himself from his surroundings and had nothing more to lose. Before him now lay only Munich, the scene of the assassination attempt, and Switzerland, the land of refuge.

Against the backdrop of these constantly worsening circumstances, there was no chance for his love with Elsa Härlen to blossom. At first things looked positive; Elsa was relieved that Georg was completely different from her violent and drunken husband. In the six years that she knew Georg Elser, she did not feel that he had behaved badly even once. She considered him "decent, modest, quiet—even taciturn—frugal, very skilled and hard-working." In all matters he would pour out his heart to her—all matters, that is, except politics. He wanted her to take care of him like a mother; she was his "motherly sweetheart."

After a few months, Elsa Härlen's husband threw Elser out. The marriage was dissolved around the end of 1938. The commonly held view was that Georg Elser was at fault; the men in the community did not speak of Elsa's suffering. His musician friend Egetemaier offered him a room. But the illicit love affair was now the talk of the town. When Egetemaier saw Elsa leaving Georg's room around four in the morning, he told him, "Georg, this is going too far—not in my house." Egetemaier was doubtless concerned about the procurement statute, under which toleration of illegal relations could be prosecuted as procurement. The same scenario played out again later; when Georg tried to take Elsa to his room at his parents' house, his mother stepped in and threw him out of the house. The only option he had left was a storage room at the Schmauders' place in Schnaitheim, where he lived almost as a member of the family.

In his memoirs, Egetemaier continued to embellish the myth of Elser as a Casanova. His love for Elsa had put him "on the wrong path," he wrote. Regarding women, he had been "very impulsive." "Like music, women were his hobby and his passion." In Königsbronn and vicinity, however, no one to date has produced names for all these conquests.

Once Elsa was divorced, Georg visited her at her parents' house in Göppingen-Jebenhausen. Her father was impressed with Elser's technical skills and offered to pay for him to study interior design. Elser turned him down, saying that he was put off by the prospect of such a cozy situation.

XV

Assassination: The Decision

O<small>N</small> N<small>OVEMBER</small> 20, 1939, the second day of his interrogation in Berlin, Elser states: "I reached my decision regarding this action in the fall of 1938." The next day, during the most intense part of the interrogation, Elser is made to lay out in detail the process by which he made this decision. In contrast to his reticence about discussing his background or acquaintances, his responses about the assassination plot are more detailed, firm, and accurate, and he makes no effort to conceal his views about the fundamental dissatisfaction of the working class with the regime. For the first time, we gain insight into his political thinking, which up until this point he has kept to himself. Even in the brutal environment of Reich Security Headquarters, after being tortured several times, Elser remains steadfast—his family would say stubborn—in his rejection of the Nazi regime.

In Elser's testimony he makes it clear that his decision had been thoroughly considered:

The dissatisfaction among the workers that I had observed since 1933 and the war that I had seen as inevitable since the fall of 1938 occupied my thoughts constantly. Whether it was before or after the September

crisis of 1938 I can't say. On my own, I began to contemplate how one
could improve the conditions of the working class and avoid war. I was not
encouraged by anyone to do this, nor was I influenced by anyone regarding
this matter.

His mention of the "September crisis of 1938" refers to Hitler's
threat of war against Czechoslovakia, which was resolved when, in
the Munich Pact of September 29, 1938, the Western powers handed
him the areas comprising the Sudetenland. In actuality, the Nazi
press had been waging a hate campaign against its neighbor since
June 3, 1938.

Elser states two goals, but the first one, to "improve the conditions of the working class," has vanished in the commonly held
perception of Elser. Only the second goal, to "avoid war," has, after
years of resistance, made its way into the popular consciousness. The
pacifist determined to carry out an assassination was accepted; the
champion of workers' rights was consciously ignored.

The deliberations regarding the need for the assassination,
which are laid out in detail in the transcript, make it appear likely
that his decision was made before September 1938. An item in the
records of the arms manufacturer Waldenmaier seems to indicate
that Elser had been contemplating the assassination for quite a
while. In the summer of 1937, apparently at his own request, Elser
is transferred to the shipping department, where he is in contact
with detonators and explosive material. It is his responsibility to
check shipments for completeness as they come in. He remains in
this position until March of 1939, and it is here that he has the
opportunity to get hold of a detonator. A detonator would be out of
place in a woodworking shop.

At Waldenmaier, Elser also learns something about a special
division in which powder pellets are pressed into explosive plates
and detonators for projectiles are produced. Highly attentive and
yet seeming completely harmless, he moves about the arms factory
with its thousand employees like a fish in water. He shows interest
in everything, asking many questions and having many procedures
explained to him. In his first job in the fettling shop, for example, he

notices a cart out in the yard loaded with rough-cast parts for detonators. Even though Waldenmaier is an official arms supplier, the carelessness of its factory inspectors works to Elser's advantage. But to
the factory owner, the downtrodden workers hardly seem to present
any potential for danger. It is not until the fall of 1938 in the atmosphere of mounting war hysteria that records are kept on detonators
and detonator parts. Elser is so adept at feigning a purely technical
interest in things that he even finds someone to explain to him how to
assemble a detonator.

The conditions at the factory are ideal for a quiet, circumspect
assassin. In early September 1938, a shipment of twenty rough
detonators comes his way in a package from the firm Rheinmetall
Borsig A.G. Werk in Düsseldorf. While checking the contents, Elser
keeps one of the items for himself and writes up a claim slip: "19
steel detonators of chrome-nickel, heat-treated steel . . . one item
missing." This went undetected in part because Waldenmaier was
completely preoccupied with expansion plans for his arms factory.
He also had little understanding of monitoring procedures and no
reason to suspect his workers. Even when he moved Elser into the
shipping department—a sensitive area from a security perspective—
Waldenmaier didn't bother to have the Gestapo run a background
check on him. With typical brazenness, Elser carried the claim ticket
for the detonator with him as he attempted to cross the border in
Konstanz.

On September 8, Waldenmaier files a claim regarding the missing item. Rheinmetall Borsig answers on September 14 "that it is not
possible that an item could have disappeared from the shipment if the
shipping container arrived in sealed condition." The container had not
been damaged. But Elser did not come under suspicion until much
later, when detonator parts were found in his clothing after he tried to
cross the border into Switzerland.

The incubation period for the decision on the assassination
attempt might have begun as early as fall 1936 when he left his position as a cabinetmaker with Grupp because of the low pay of fifty-
five pfennigs an hour. He admitted to his interrogators that he could
have easily found a better-paying job as a cabinetmaker, but even so,

he took the job working in the dirty conditions of the fettling shop, making only fifty-eight to sixty-two pfennigs an hour. Previously, he would have rejected such work with indignation.

In Berlin Elser explains to the Gestapo, "I had no interest in making more money; I was just looking for work that I enjoyed." He added: "If I had earned any more, it wouldn't have done me any good because any wages over 24 RM [Reichsmark] a week would have been docked for payment of alimony."

According to Josef Schurr's letter to the editor of 1947, he and Elser had met up again in 1937 when they were both employed at Waldenmaier. Schurr noted that Elser's politics had not changed: "I immediately started to feel him out to find out to what extent he had remained committed to his antifascist position. To my amazement, I saw that Elser had become even more radical in the fight against Hitler's fascism than he had been in years past. We renewed our mutual commitment with a pledge: 'May Hitler die a horrible death— and soon!' "

Elser dates what they did next (perhaps in an effort to protect Schurr) to two years later, when he was living at the Schmauders' place in Schnaitheim. As Schurr wrote in his letter: "We frequently got together at my apartment [Heckenstrasse 9 in Schnaitheim] to learn the truth about what was going on in the world over the radio." Foreign stations were always "a source of strength" for them, he wrote.

At the time when Elser started working at Waldenmaier, reports of increasing levels of dissatisfaction and fear of war were becoming more frequent. The main reason was the worsening civil war in Spain, in which Hitler, Mussolini, and Stalin had become involved. Restrictions regarding materials necessary for arms production were put in place. The radio stations in Moscow and Strasbourg were casting doubts on Hitler's willingness to seek peace, doubts that Elser saw confirmed in 1938.

More clearly than those in the military opposition, who appeared content with each new victory that Hitler chalked up, Elser observed that Hitler was provoking war. After the Munich Pact, Hitler insisted hypocritically that the Sudeten areas would be his last territorial demand. However, because Elser was able to witness firsthand the rapid increase in arms production at Waldenmaier, he never believed Hitler's claims that he wanted peace.

During the interrogations in Berlin, the Gestapo employed an ideological strategy in an effort to get at Elser's motives for the attack. But as victims of their own ideology, they used as points of departure religion, faith, and *Weltanschauung* and were thus not able to understand Elser, who was a calculating, intelligent workman. On this level he was much more modern than his adversaries. His motivation lay not in an ideology; rather, it was to be found in people's living conditions and in the entirely predictable collective catastrophe brought on by Hitler's politics of war.

Elser's motives and his rejection of the Nazi regime become most evident on the third day of interrogation. The chapter entitled "To the point" in the printed record takes up five pages, representing about two hours of interrogation. Elser begins with a bombshell the likes of which the Nazi leadership rarely got to hear. Under other circumstances, the man being interrogated would have immediately been beaten to a pulp. But Elser was shielded for two reasons: First, Hitler and Himmler were interested in the criminal aspects of his case, and second, the Gestapo commissars were gaining increasing respect for this impressive assassin from such humble origins.

Elser begins with an economic assessment commonly voiced by the working-class opposition at the time: "In my opinion, conditions for workers since the national revolution have in many ways gotten worse." Only here does Elser allow himself to be forced into using the otherwise detested expression "national revolution"; otherwise he holds fast to his condemnation, going quickly into considerable detail: "For instance, I saw that wages kept decreasing and the deductions kept increasing. . . . While I was working at the clock factory in Konstanz in 1929, I was earning on average 50 RM a week; at the time the deductions for taxes, health care, unemployment, and disability came to only about 5 RM. Today the deductions on a weekly salary of 25 RM amount to that." And then there were the significant wage reductions. In 1929 a carpenter earned between 1.00 and 1.05

marks an hour, now it was sixty-eight pfennigs (Elser had worked at Grupp for less). He cites conversations with workers from other trades—all of whom confirmed the worsening wages. He reports on the dissatisfaction he observed in all the communities where he had lived. By this testimony, Elser was clearly not the isolated loner—a mischaracterization that was an apparent attempt to remove his name from the history of the Resistance.

Another element that fuels Elser's radicalism is his commitment to independence. He is a socialist, but a liberal one—not one in favor of strict regimentation. In his view, the working class at the time is "under some coercion." Elser points out that a worker may not change jobs at will—and he views this as a fundamental right, one that he has often exercised. He notes that workers' children are being alienated from their parents by the Hitler Youth, and that workers are losing their religious freedom. Elser says that the Nazis' assault on the churches is abhorrent. Even though he is not a churchgoer, he feels that people should have the freedom to choose in the matter of religion as well.

Observing such widespread dissatisfaction leads Elser to draw a radical conclusion, one that undermines the very basis of the Nazi system: "During this period I have become convinced that, because of all these things, workers are outraged at the government." And he observed this negative attitude everywhere he went: in factories, in taverns, on trains. In the course of his descriptions we learn about the places in which his political views took shape.

Finally, Elser makes a remark that is a logical conclusion stemming from his observation of the poor morale among workers: "In the fall of 1938, from everything I observed, working people generally assumed that war was inevitable." He comments that even though things had calmed down after the Munich Pact, he had gained a different perspective on the situation. On this point Elser shows himself to have had better foresight than the entire military opposition, which intended to topple Hitler in the fall of 1938 but canceled plans when Hitler prevailed against England and France in Munich. In Elser's view, Hitler was just beginning to become dangerous.

His view sounds like an article of faith, his first in the course of this interrogation: "Last year [1938] at this time, I had already come to the conclusion that the Munich Pact wouldn't be the end of it and that Germany would make more demands on other countries and continue to take over other countries, so that war would be inevitable." He went on to say that listening to foreign radio broadcasts had strengthened his convictions.

In his next statement, Elser makes clear the point alluded to at the beginning of the chapter: "The dissatisfaction I had observed among the workers since 1933 and the war I had considered inevitable since the fall of 1938 occupied my thoughts constantly." Here at last we learn what it was that preoccupied the taciturn Elser. But he does not just speak of the fear of war as most others do; he plainly wants to "avoid war."

Point by point Elser continues; he is ready to articulate his political views, having spent many solitary hours refining them: "My observations led me to the conclusion that conditions in Germany could only be improved by removing the current leadership." He is immediately asked who the leadership is. Heretofore Elser has been circumspect regarding ideological questions, but he is well aware of who his target is: "By leadership I meant the 'uppermost authorities'. . . " Again the Gestapo fires a question, not letting him off the hook, and he is forced to add: ". . . by this I mean Hitler, Göring, and Goebbels. Through my deliberations I came to the conclusion that, by removing these three men, other men would come to power who would not make unacceptable demands of foreign countries, 'who would not want to involve another country', and who would be concerned about improving social conditions for the workers."

Expansionist-style nationalism, which has influenced broad segments of the opposition among the military and the bourgeoisie, leaves Elser unmoved. He has no interest in foreign countries. The commissars find his exhortations to cease further conquests so shocking and embarrassing that they place them in quotation marks. With comments as dangerous as these their police jargon is of no use; they are unable to translate them into standard Party terminology, thus rendering them less inflammatory.

Elser's pragmatism extends to politics as well. He assumed that the Nazis would not relinquish power after the assassination and did not believe that he could destroy National Socialism on his own. His goals were more modest: "I was simply of the opinion that removing these three men could bring about a modification of the political objectives." In contrast to the military-bourgeois opposition, Elser did not give much thought to the composition of a new government.

Now Elser draws his conclusion—the decision to act: "Once the idea of removing the leadership had come up, I couldn't get it out of my head, and in the fall of 1938—this was before November 1938—I had reached the decision, for all the reasons I've stated, to undertake removing the leadership myself."

In the interrogation the Gestapo had failed in its effort to portray Elser as an unstable henchman with no thoughts of his own, who was under the control of foreign powers. In spite of the gawking spectators, usually heavily armed chaps whose final argument was war and extermination, Elser managed to maintain his dignity as an independent thinker.

On the previous day, the police officers had tried to shake Elser's basic religious beliefs. They encountered a devout Swabian Protestant who had been raised by a sternly religious mother but whose father did not think much of religion. He had retained a belief in traditional religious values, which bolstered his conviction that by eliminating a mass murderer he was doing good. What could be considered good in this situation was very apparent to him: "I wanted to prevent even greater bloodshed through my act."

When the commissars asked him whether he understood his act to be a sin in the Protestant sense, he answered decisively, since he had asked himself this question a hundred times: "In a deeper sense, no." Holding up to him the eight victims of his attack had no impact—Elser felt confident in the moral and religious superiority of his position.

Scarcely anyone could have formulated a more moving tribute to the morality of Elser's position than Arthur Nebe did to Gisevius around Christmas 1939: "You know what Elser's problem was? This

man of the people loved ordinary people; he laid out for me passionately and in simple sentences how, for the masses in all countries, war
means hunger, misery, and the death of millions. Not a 'pacifist' in
the usual sense, his reasoning was quite simplistic: Hitler is war—and
if he goes, there will be peace . . ."

XVI

The Preparations

THE MATERIALS NEEDED for an assassination attempt were not all that difficult to come by if one was determined. Elser did not allow himself to get caught up in the widespread fear of the police state, and nowhere did he encounter security checks. This general lack of concern was to some extent justified, because the regime knew it could count on its citizens. For a people for whom obedience to authority was a chief virtue, assassination was unthinkable.

Elser's first thoughts concerning a favorable occasion for an attack tended in the direction of some kind of rally, but he changed his mind when he read a newspaper report announcing that Hitler would speak on November 8, 1938, at the Munich Bürgerbräukeller, as he did every year. All the woodworker had to do was get on a train, travel to Munich, and mingle among the masses of brown-shirted pilgrims. With no difficulty, he made his way right into the inner sanctum of the Nazis; the train ticket cost eleven or twelve marks, his room for the night—one mark. The initial inspection of the assassination site was just that simple.

Elser's objective of preventing Hitler from unleashing a war took precedence over everything else—his professional pride, his modest savings, his family relations, his friendships, even his love affairs. From now on Elser had only one goal—and he kept it secret from everyone. His feeling of righteousness is well documented; everywhere he went he used his real name. This kind of behavior does not bolster the theories that he was a henchman for the Nazis or for a foreign power.

Starting in the summer of 1937, Elser worked at Waldenmaier in the shipping department of the main division responsible for the materials that were to be of great significance to him. It is not likely that Elser came to work there by chance, as he tried to claim; he must have played a role in gaining this position. When there was something he wanted, he had an irresistible way of pleading, almost like a child, until he got it. His Munich landlady Rosa Lehmann had watched in amazement as Elser cajoled the craftsmen in the neighborhood into letting him use their shops.

In the shipping department, samples of detonators and detonator parts were received, which Elser, after checking the shipment, was to send on to individual specialists. At his post Elser learned everything he needed to know without having to take anyone into his confidence, and he had the authority to go at any time to any department of special interest to him. Without arousing suspicion, he could wait for an opportunity to gain access to key materials.

The first thing Elser did was travel to Munich on November 8, 1938. At that time, Maurice Bavaud of Switzerland was lurking around town, looking for a chance to eliminate Hitler with a pistol. Here too, security was lax. Even as a French-speaking Swiss citizen who knew barely a word of German, Bavaud was able to get to the platform at the Feldherrnhalle. But the sea of flags and the many arms raised in salute as the hordes marched by prevented his assassination attempt. He would in any event have had little chance; the small-caliber (6.35 mm.) so-called "lady's pistol" he had purchased in Basel was effective at a distance of at most three yards.

As Georg Elser proceeded to Munich, he did not have a preconceived plan; he wanted to adapt his approach to the circumstances he observed at the site. When he arrived at the Bürgerbräukeller, he was at first unable to register anything but the hysterical enthusiasm of the crowd. Hitler's histrionics, later used to explain people's susceptibility to mass psychosis, had no effect on Elser. For Elser, Hitler did not, as he did for many Germans, represent the expression of their secret desires. For Elser, Hitler was an absolute catastrophe that had to be removed. Elser was not waiting for a savior to rescue the German people from humiliation; he wanted to liberate the Germans and the peoples of Europe—and liberate them permanently—from this deadly menace. In the midst of pseudo-religious fanaticism, Elser remained the rational technician with a keen eye, seeking out vulnerable spots at this cult landmark.

Arriving around 8:15 p.m. at the intersection of Rosenheimer Strasse and Hochstrasse near the Bürgerbräukeller, Elser found the street barricaded. He waited among the crowds on the street until 10:30 p.m. without getting a glimpse of Hitler and concluded that this would not be a good spot. Once the street was reopened, he moved on to the Bürgerbräukeller and found everything open. He passed through the main entrance and proceeded through the cloakroom directly into the hall. There were a few people inside, but no one asked him what he was doing there. He walked around the room and observed that the speaker's platform was against the wall in the middle of the hall, not by the front wall. He made note of any important features, but did not work out his assassination strategy until later on, when he was back at home.

Part of the strategy involved making contact with the staff. His strength was always his simple, straightforward approach to people, a trait that made the Gestapo nervous. His best disguise was his natural guilelessness, which was immediately apparent. He walked through the cloakroom into the Bräustübl of the establishment and ordered a late supper. It was 11:00 p.m., but on a special day like this, anything was possible. Soon a fellow Swabian, the manager of the slaughter-house, sat down at his table and the only thing he noticed about the future assassin was that he drank very little beer.

The next day, November 9, 1938, was a holiday. Elser returned to the Bürgerbräukeller in order to observe the organization and execution of the traditional march to the Feldherrnhalle. This time he at least got to see Hitler drive up. Afterward he walked around town for a while, then returned to Königsbronn. If he had stayed another day, he would have gotten to see the city after the Kristallnacht pogrom instigated by Goebbels.

Georg Elser was a thorough man, for whom ideas took a long time to form, but once formed remained firmly rooted. In this case, it took only two or three days for him to realize that the Bürgerbräukeller was the only possible location for an assassination attempt, but he needed another few months to work out how it was to be executed. During the Berlin interrogation Elser gave a good description of his mental work habits: "In the course of the next few weeks I slowly worked it out in my head that it would be best to pack explosives into this particular pillar behind the speaker's platform and then by means of some kind of device cause the explosives to ignite at the right time."

In April 1939, Elser worked for a short time at the Vollmer Quarry in Königsbronn and there he learned from explosives expert Georg Kolb that the explosive material should be placed as close to the floor as possible. However, the base of the column in the hall was not an option, since Elser might have been easily discovered at his nocturnal labors. So Elser chose the bottom of the column on the gallery—and in the process assured a far greater effect during the explosion. During all of his careful contemplation at home, Elser also came to the conclusion that he would need a timed detonator.

From the very outset he calculated the effects: flying debris striking people on and around the speaker's platform, the ceiling caving in. When the commissars coyly asked him if he had been aware of who was seated around the speaker's platform, Elser, unfazed, responded: "No. But I knew that Hitler was going to speak and assumed that the leadership would be sitting closest to him."

Before his visit to Munich, Elser's parents had gotten back together and moved into their half of the double house on Wiesenstrasse. Georg refused to vacate the room to which he felt entitled, and paid no rent even though his mother desperately needed the money. But he now needed the money even more—for his months of arduous work in the Bürgerbräukeller.

From this point on, he started gaining the reputation of being heartless, stingy, and inconsiderate. And he indeed became stranger. But it was not until his assassination plans began taking shape that out of the great need for secrecy he started to take on the personality that people generally ascribed to him after the war: He became an eccentric, but only vis-à-vis the world from which he had to absolutely shield himself, for security reasons. From the very beginning he took into consideration the likelihood of gossip and Gestapo snooping.

He put three locks on his wooden suitcase and built two secret compartments into it, then he constructed an ingenious double bottom for it. He always carried the keys to the suitcase with him. He installed two new locks on the door to his room and never allowed anyone inside. He continued to work at his project but knew that he could no longer afford to carry on such dangerous activities in the workshop at the house. Eventually his parents called in the village authorities, and while Elser was at work, Officer Michael Aigner opened the room with a master key. There they found clockworks, tubes, and springs lying on the table—just things for tinkering, nothing dangerous. Twenty years later, Aigner would boastfully proclaim that these were "parts of the bomb." Obviously, Aigner would have turned Elser over to the Gestapo if he had had the faintest suspicion.

After the trip to Munich, Elser increased the pace of his preparations. By the end of 1938 he was already thinking of making his escape through Konstanz. On a trip there, he found conditions between the Kreuzlingen customs office and the Emmishofer customs office unchanged. He started selling off everything he no longer needed, including his bass. By the time of his departure, his savings amounted to a total of between 350 and 400 marks, a substantial sum for the time. According to the calculations of the Kripo as well, one would have been able to get by for three months on this amount, assuming a lifestyle as frugal as Elser's.

Elser took advantage of his position at Waldenmaier, acquiring, over a period of five months, 250 compressed pellets of powder. In his conscientious manner, he recalled the size: "Such a sheet of compressed powder was 9 mm. (3/8") thick and had a diameter of 19 mm. (3/4")." The disappearance was not noticed because in this area, too, there were no checks. And Elser exploited his advantage—with an apparently clear conscience and steely nerves he would stroll through the special area and take something, as he described it, "inconspicuously and quickly." Later on, this black powder would rain down in the Bürgerbräukeller as thick black dust and become the first evidence to allay Nebe's fears that this might have been the work of the German military opposition "fooling around" with English explosives.

Elser's camouflage act slowly became almost comically grotesque— by feigning "normal" behavior he was able to avoid all suspicion.

He would pack the pilfered discs of explosives in paper and store them in his wardrobe, which he locked, and then cover everything with clothes—quadruple security, since the room was also locked.

As soon as the explosive device took shape in Elser's head, he started having misgivings about the dimensions. He was afraid the apparatus might exceed the maximum size possible for the chamber at the Bürgerbräukeller. In March 1939, he gave notice at Waldenmaier.

Now he was free, and on April 4, 1939, he traveled to Munich a second time, in order to take measurements of the column in the Bürgerbräukeller. Twice he walked around the hall without being stopped, taking measurements with a measuring stick and writing them in a notebook, just as a craftsman does when planning a job. His contact with the staff increased, and every day he had a meal or something to drink there. Right away Elser made the acquaintance of an errand boy and, by giving him a written promise of fifty marks, made him promise to help him get his job when the boy was called up for military duty. With the same camera he used to photograph the column, he took a snapshot of three of the waitresses. Allowing himself time to become part of the scene, Elser didn't return home until April 12.

Early in 1939, the situation at his parents' place was getting worse. Georg was supposed to move out in order to make room for his brother and his wife, but he didn't want to. When Elsa visited him around the end of February 1939, and he took her up to his room, his mother threw him out of the house. The only place he could go was Schnaitheim, where he had established close ties with the Schmauder family, whose address was Benzstrasse 18. In his disarmingly unselfish way, he had continued to help these people remodel their place after he got off work at Waldenmaier—rather sociable behavior for an "eccentric." He would pitch in wherever he was needed, whether it was digging or carpentry. At ten-thirty in the evening, he would take the last train back to Königsbronn.

Even though he had been evicted from one home, Elser was nonetheless capable of creating a new one for himself by making himself useful. The official registration of his residence did not occur until

May 4, 1939, and the address given was Benzstrasse 16. Prior to that he camped out for a while in the shed out on the Flachsberg with his father, with whom his relationship had improved since he was thrown out.

For his assistance with the Schmauders' remodeling project, Georg Elser received free lodging and laundry. He seemed content to have a storage room to sleep in, located in their daughter's house next door at Benzstrasse 16. After fetching his tools, he placed his wooden suitcase with the materials for the assassination attempt next to his bed. From that point on he would not be separated from his "bomb trunk." He remained at Benzstrasse exactly three months. It was the most intensive period of his preparations for the assassination attempt.

Since his return from Munich, Elser knew that he needed to acquire much more explosive material. Furthermore, he did not yet have a clear picture of the detonating device. He began to hang around at Vollmer's quarry in Itzelberg, making himself useful in various operations and helping out here and there. When asked by the boss what he was doing there, he answered in his disarming manner that he was unemployed and bored. Needing workers at that moment, Vollmer hired him on the spot. His work consisted of loading up the debris onto trolleys after an explosion. On the job, Elser would stay as close as possible to the area where Kolb was setting up an explosion. He was observant: "Kolb always brought more explosive from the concrete hut than was needed for the blast." So some was always left lying around, and Elser made note of where it was. Since controls were nonexistent at the quarry too, he was able to get hold of several explosive cans over a period of time. When leaving for the day he would take them out in his knapsack, which he always had with him.

But things were moving too slowly for Elser. So he would accompany the explosives expert to where the supplies of explosive were stored—at the entrance to the quarry, just to the left of the old main building in a concrete hut, which is no longer there. It was five feet deep and three feet wide. Elser decided to "pay a visit" to the supply depot at night, as he phrased it to the Gestapo. Probably in an attempt to protect the quarry owner, he claimed that he returned at night with a bunch of old keys. In reality, however, the hut was in such

The house in Heidenheim-Schnaitheim, in which Elser began designing his explosive device. In a workshop attached to the house, he carried out his first tests with gun shells and firing caps.

unbelievable disarray that the boss got a year and a half in the Welzheim concentration camp for it. If the key to the iron exterior door couldn't be found, it was just yanked open, and the wooden interior door could no longer be locked.

The crew of the Vollmer Quarry in Königsbronn, around 1930. Fourth from left in the first row is owner Georg Vollmer; second from left is explosives expert Kolb.

Later on, as the Kripo and the Gestapo learned of these conditions, they just shook their heads in disbelief—such lack of security at the company of a former local Nazi leader! To round out this scene, it turns out that the bookkeeper kept no books on the purchase and use of the explosives despite the regulations requiring it. The local police officer Aigner (who had been so diligent in investigating Elser) was part of the picture: It was his job to monitor the records of the explosive materials, but he never made even one attempt to do so. The quarry owner pushed responsibility off on the explosives expert. So Himmler sent the owner and his two employees away to the Welzheim concentration camp for a year and a half, while the policeman went free.

Given the easy access to the explosives, Elser made frequent nocturnal "visits" to the quarry, obtaining over sixty cartridges of the industrial explosive Donarit 3. He then found detonator caps in the hut. Even though he needed only two or three, he carried off a container of 125 of them.

In a sewing machine shop in Heidenheim, Elser bought rifle ammunition. In order to acquire the necessary knowledge of explosive techniques, he purchased "a booklet designed for the training of Pioneers," according to the Gestapo. Ironically, under Hitler it was possible, with some determination, to obtain all the materials and information necessary to carry out a professional assassination. In the militarized society everything necessary was made available. After Stauffenberg's failed attempt, Nebe would maintain to his friend Gisevius that any Pioneer could have positioned the explosive better than Stauffenberg did. Elser's little "Pioneer" booklet would have made it clear. In the meantime, Elser was working on his detonation device, at first in his head and in sketches, then with experiments using wood blocks. He mounted three blocks on a board, drilled holes through them, stretched a spring across them, and used a nail as a firing pin to strike the firing cap of a rifle shell. The powder ignited and caused the blasting caps to explode. While the Schmauders were away, Elser conducted his first detonation experiment down in his workshop and was amazed at how well it worked, even knocking some plaster off the ceiling. When the owners noticed the results afterward, Elser just commented on the poor work of the plasterers.

From this point on, Elser's preferred testing site was his parents' fruit orchard on the Flachsberg. Here as well, he demonstrated what great control he had—although an amateur at this sort of activity, he knew exactly what he could get away with. Even though his father, unable to walk, was living in the remodeled garden shed, Elser conducted four test explosions close by which caused a terrific bang. His father could hear the noise, but he had long since quit caring about anything. Nearby, an uncle of Elser's heard the explosions while working in a field with two horses. It was July 1939. Upon hearing the bang, the horses reared up, and he almost lost control of them; then he saw Georg looking out from the shed. When he asked him that evening about the noise, Elser told him: "I'm trying something out. When it's finished, you'll find out about it." When the uncle left to go home, he noticed an object on the table in the shed that looked like "some kind of clock that had gotten too big." Attached to it was a cable that ran out into the yard. Elser tossed the smashed wood blocks from the tests into the bin of wood scraps in his workshop at the Schmauders' place. This was where the Stuttgart Gestapo found them six months later along with his first design sketches.

This phase of the construction—the detonation—is the only one that Elser executed first through experiments; all other problems he worked out with sketches. His pride in his methods is still evident during his interrogations by the Gestapo. His next challenge was to transfer the preset detonation point from a clock to an ignition mechanism. In mid-May 1939, an accident Elser had at the quarry provided him with the time needed for the execution of his drawings. Having suffered a broken leg, he was put on sick leave for two months. Lying on a couch in the kitchen at the Schmauders' place, he would listen to foreign radio stations and work on sketches of his explosive device. He would take the most useful ones and hide them under the false bottom in his suitcase.

From the beginning, Elser was adept at reining in the curiosity around him with his little white lie about an "invention," thereby achieving his desired objectives of secrecy and respect. In March 1939, he started preparing for the move to Munich. He had planned for the eventuality that the Waldenmaier Company might not release him, and so he placed a personal ad in a Munich newspaper seeking marriage to "a young lady or widow with apartment." His intention was to take a response to the ad to the employment office and present it as proof that he was moving to Munich and getting married. He in fact received two responses, but since he found that he could move to Munich anyway, the marriage ruse was no longer necessary.

The Schmauders in Schnaitheim were in the best position to observe Elser closely during these final three months before his move to Munich. Elser was, according to a report given by Berta Schmauder: "very handy, he helped them carry the furniture into the new addition; he was helpful, modest, pleasant, reliable, and punctual. He was extremely hard-working. They [the Schmauders] could not recall ever seeing him just sitting around. They also could not recall seeing him eating. Around noon he would just say, 'I'm going out now—I'll be right back.' Then he disappeared and came back a little while later. They assumed that he ate in a pub."

Karoline Schmauder was also struck by something else: "During this period he [Elser] always seemed to be thinking about something, and it often happened that if you were sitting next to him and asked him a question he wouldn't even hear it and didn't answer. He was always complaining about headaches back then, too, which had to be caused by all that thinking."

This perceptive observation made the connection between his concentration on the assassination and his isolation, which was essential to his purpose. Around the beginning of August Elser became ill, exhibiting psychosomatic symptoms resulting from the continued tension. The things that he could not discuss with anyone he had to work out in his head, and it was clearly taking its toll on him.

Under such conditions Elser's relationship with Elsa Härlen had no chance. Elsa moved in with her parents in Jebenhausen and worked in Esslingen. The two visited each other from time to time, but Elsa found that he sometimes seemed strange to her. Something was going on inside him that was bothering him, but he wouldn't talk about it. When she confronted him, asking why a skilled craftsman would go to work in a quarry, Elser told her he was only doing it temporarily because he had to go to Munich.

During his last visit in Stuttgart in early 1939, he took one last photograph of Elsa, which he would keep on his table in the concentration camp at Sachsenhausen. Twenty years later she recalled him fondly: "He wasn't tall, just medium height, but he had pretty black hair and artistic hands that were smaller than mine. He took my hands in his, then hugged me and said, 'Else, wait for me—be faithful to me! I have to do something, I can't tell you what, but it will turn out well and it has to be done. I want to marry you when it's all over, and then we'll leave and go to Switzerland!' Then he sobbed openly and couldn't say another word."

In Munich, Elser was so absorbed by his work on the assassination that he did not maintain contact with Elsa. In her love letters she asked him where he was working and how much he was making, and remarked bitterly that he wouldn't answer her questions. So in December 1939, she married another man, who soon became a casualty of the war that Elser had wanted to prevent.

When Georg Elser moved to Munich, he took his wooden suitcase with the explosives and the detonator parts on the train with him. He had his boxes of tools and clothes shipped separately. On August 4, he rode his bicycle to Königsbronn to visit his father and say good-bye. On the way, his friend Eugen Rau saw him and called him over. After the usual small talk, Elser blurted out to him in dialect: "Times ain't gonna get better in Germany, the future ain't gonna be no better till this government gets blowed sky high. And I'm tellin' ya, I'm gonna do it—I am," to which Eugen answered, "Hey, Georg, you can't do that!" Georg then said: "Just you don't tell nobody, okay!" Similarly, Josef Schurr recalled Georg's parting words: "[I would] soon read his name in the papers if his plan succeeded. . . . But he asked me not to repeat that remark."

XVII

Night Work in the Bürgerbräukeller

O<small>N</small> A<small>UGUST</small> 5, 1939, Georg Elser arrives at the main train station in Munich with his huge wooden suitcase full of explosives. It's a bit like a scene from the theater of the absurd. The assassin takes the lethal case down from the baggage net and lugs it past unsuspecting passengers. He has a baggage handler take him in his small delivery van to the room he has rented from Joseph Baumann, a tax official; it is located on the second floor of Blumenstrasse 19, south of Marienplatz. It is a pleasant, almost luxurious furnished room, large but unsuitable for Elser's purposes; he won't be able to do any work on his construction there or make sketches—the furniture is too elegant. The rent is soon too much for him—35 marks a month for rent and 20 marks for breakfast—and he must save his money. So he soon looks for cheaper, simpler lodgings in which he will be undisturbed; but when he moves, he leaves on good terms with the Baumanns. He looks in on Frau Baumann from time to time and, in keeping with his custom, offers to barter odd jobs for a meal.

First, Elser has to wait until his other suitcases arrive with his tools and clothes. He varies his cover story for being in Munich: He says he is taking a master's course in woodworking and working on an invention. The people here want to know more, but Elser keeps quiet. The first difficulties arise when he starts staying out overnight, catching up on his sleep during the day on the sofa. Explaining this change in his habits requires all his acting skills: Since he is working on his invention, he says, he has to spend the night outdoors on a bench. This is an odd excuse, since it would no longer have worked once winter came. The image of the eccentric takes root, but at least Elser achieves peace and quiet. And he is always handy, helping out here and there; he is quiet and friendly and pays his rent in advance.

Within a few weeks the shadows of war catch up with Elser. On August 28, the first food ration stamps are issued; at first bread, flour, and potatoes are exempted. The explanation given for the rationing is that the Poles are mobilizing, but there will surely be no war. There is no word about German preparations for war, but the first draft notices start to appear in mailboxes. Women storm the shops. Soon they will have to get training in areas important to a war effort, such as antigas defense and medical service. Economizing on food becomes a high priority, and low-budget recipes are in demand. With the start of the war in Poland on September 1, 1939, there are mandatory blackouts. Foreign radio stations are now called "enemy stations"; from this point on listening to them is considered "sedition" and a punishable offense. On the same day, Hitler signs the decree approving euthanasia. After this, he will sign no further orders to kill. Two days later, the first air-raid trenches start cropping up—they are useless but provide work. One particular measure hits the people of Munich especially hard: a ten-pfennig war tax on beer. By comparison, a workman's meal at the Bürgerbräukeller costs sixty pfennigs.

There are some in Munich who are not taken in by all the war activities. In the district called Berg am Laim behind the East train station, at Schweppermannstrasse 9, the Communist locksmith and building superintendent Karl Zimmet produces leaflets—an approach Elser never considered. In an August leaflet Zimmet issues a call to action: Anyone wanting to protect himself and others from war "must protest this abominable war and do everything possible to prevent it. Anyone opposing the warmonger Hitler and his

Nazi system is part of the struggle to stop the war. Anyone fighting against Hitler's criminal war is fighting for Germany." It is powerful language, but without any practical consequences. How should one protest? How can one express opposition without immediately landing in Dachau? Besides, things like this don't bother Hitler and his military machine in the slightest. The calls for action in flyers like this are of no use.

It works to Elser's advantage that he is not a Moscow-style Communist Party member; on August 23, 1939, Stalin and Hitler sign their nonaggression pact, and Poland is divided. Until Hitler's attack on the Soviet Union, the Communists are politically crippled. For this reason alone they were never able to identify with Elser's attack, even after much time had passed; they chose to maintain their silence regarding the woodworker at the Bürgerbräukeller.

For the next few weeks Elser strolls through the Munich district of Maxvorstadt. On Türkenstrasse he finds a cheap room. He is probably unaware, and likely doesn't even notice, that this street lies in the midst of a particularly "brown" area, which voted predominately National Socialist even before 1933. Today, standing as a small symbol of history's revenge is a Georg-Elser-Platz, located between Türkenstrasse 68 and 68a—a diminutive square, but still recognizable.

At Türkenstrasse 94, Elser sees a note hanging from the doorbell on the street: "Cheap lodging. Inquire at Lehmann, 3rd floor." He makes a good impression: He seems quiet and modest; he asks about the price and is satisfied with the rate of four marks per week, 17.50 per month. It is really only half a room, more of a storage room between the kitchen and the front door to the apartment, but this doesn't bother him. This tiny space, measuring seven feet by sixteen feet, later on will be converted into a bathroom, with a view of the rear courtyard.

Georg Elser arrives with several suitcases and boxes, which he is allowed to store in the cellar. He keeps only the suitcase with the explosives with him, but he has to put it out in the hall because there is not enough space in his room for it. The room is big enough only for a small wardrobe, a desk, and a bed. One Sunday morning the Lehmanns return home unexpectedly early. Elser has just opened his assassin's suitcase and is looking through his sketches; startled, he throws them back into the suitcase and slams it shut.

He is a bit strange, almost spooky, this "inventor and artist in woodworking," as he had introduced himself. Alfons Lehmann, a paper hanger and upholsterer, calls him their "private creep" because he moves around so quietly that they don't hear him. Elser is withdrawn and doesn't talk much. His being away at night doesn't seem to bother them. Then he stays in bed during the day. He manages to keep them placated by always paying his rent in advance. He has no visitors, and certainly no women visitors. He is not allowed to lock his room—Rosa Lehmann wants to clean and make the bed. He keeps all his boxes and suitcases locked. Soon Elser will need a workshop and the assistance of craftsmen.

On the night of the eighth or ninth of August 1939, he gets down to work for the first time in the Bürgerbräukeller. With his love of order he soon establishes a specific routine. As he did at the pubs in Heidenheim, he has a favorite table here in the Bürgerbräustübl, at which he has supper sometime after eight: It is the middle table, where he is always waited on by a waitress named Berta. He usually orders the simplest meal for sixty pfennigs and has one beer with it— he is not a big eater and a noticeably moderate drinker.

Around ten he pays, then strolls through the cloakroom into the hall, which is not locked. He checks the room to be sure that no one is there by carefully walking to the other end of the hall; only then does he climb up to the gallery. He quickly disappears into a storage space, which is behind a folding screen. The only things stored here are cardboard boxes, for who knows what purpose. Fortunately, there is also a chair there, on which Elser can doze for a while after three or four hours of highly concentrated night labors.

Elser appears so much to belong there that he is never stopped by anyone. Soon enough, the staff consider him one of the regulars. After war begins, there is no emergency light in the hall because of the blackouts, so Elser must use a flashlight covered with a blue handkerchief to dim its light. Soon a team of medics occupies a side room—Munich is expecting air attacks. But this group just makes coffee in the morning next to the podium where the band usually plays during special functions.

Shortly before the hall closes for the night, the cigarette girl feeds the cats that roam the hall. This poses no problem for Elser—unlike the night watchman's dog. But Elser knows how to win the trust of the dog—he brings him a piece of meat from his dinner every night. It's an extravagance that pays off and demonstrates Elser's ability to think ahead strategically. One night, the watchman sends his dog across the gallery. Recognizing Elser's scent, the dog is happy and doesn't bark; the watchman has to call him back from the dark area several times, and he comes slowly, wagging his tail. The night watchman just wants his peace and quiet, and prefers to make nothing of this behavior.

Another danger presents itself in August. Early one morning, an employee of the beer hall comes to the storage space unexpectedly to get a box; he sees Elser, but then disappears without saying anything. In a flash Elser recognizes the danger, goes out, and sits down at a table, pretending to write—Elser, who rarely wrote a letter. The employee returns with the manager, who questions Elser. Elser has already thought up an excuse: He says he has a boil on his thigh and wanted to squeeze it in there. All right then, why not in the lavatory? Elser's answer: He can't bring himself to—it's too embarrassing. And now, he says, he's writing a letter. He manages to pull it off and is just sent out into the courtyard, where he orders a coffee. Fortunately, he is not banned from the establishment. And now the boss knows him, too.

The hall is locked up for the night sometime between 10:30 and 11:30 p.m.; the key turning in the lock three times is clearly audible. Up until that time locals use the hall as a shortcut between Rosenheimer Strasse and Kellerstrasse. Elser waits awhile to see if anyone is hiding there, perhaps a pair of lovers or a vagrant. Only when he is absolutely certain that no one is there does he go up onto the gallery to the column located behind the speaker's platform and get to work.

In the morning, too, after the hall is opened sometime between 7:00 and 8:00, he stays hidden for a time. Later on in Berlin he will state to the Gestapo for the record the simple principle behind his camouflage: "When I was leaving the hall, I made sure not to appear cautious—so that I wouldn't arouse any suspicions." Elser is an absolute master at feigning natural behavior.

In the initial phase of his nocturnal labors Elser creates a door in the wood paneling on the column, close to the bottom. Here the woodworker is in his element. First he loosens the wood strip on the baseboard, then he saws off the upper molding on the paneling. Now he can saw a board in the base of the column at the bottom of the paneling in such a way that the cuts are not visible when the molding is replaced. From the piece of paneling he sawed out, Elser fashions a door using hinges not visible from the outside, then installs a bolt that can only be opened by inserting a pocketknife into a slot.

According to the Gestapo, Elser gave a vivid description of the process: "It took me about three nights to build the door. But then I was able to get right down to work as soon as I opened the door, and after I was done working for the night, all I had to do was close the door in order to conceal the fact that there was any activity going on in the pillar. Even if somebody had examined the pillar closely during the day, he would not have noticed any difference at all."

So one-tenth of his nocturnal activity is spent on creating the door. When he starts to dig out a bomb chamber in the column, Elser at first uses a chisel, but it makes too much noise. In the empty room—which has the best acoustics of any hall in Munich—the banging becomes cause for alarm. So he opts for a hand drill with a chisel bit. On three occasions, as the hole becomes deeper, he has a metalworker by the name of M. Solleder, with a shop at Türkenstrasse 59, weld an extension onto the bit. He opens up side cavities using a special chisel. He is able to get everything he needs for his work with ease from local shops or craftsmen. Over the course of time he has dealings with more than a dozen small businesses. No one suspects what he is actually planning. Once when he is in the workshop of the woodworker Johann Brög, located at Türkenstrasse 59, a girl, seeing the box of gears in front of him and growing curious, asks him what they're for. Elser answers meaningfully: "They's gonna be a patent, little girl, they's gonna be a patent."

Georg Elser progresses slowly. He has to use all his strength to press the drill into the brick and bore hole after hole. He is an artisan of delicate build, not a laborer. He wraps the tools in rags in order to minimize the sound. But when he breaks out a piece of masonry, he has to wait for some kind of noise from outside, usually the flushing of toilets, which occurs automatically every ten minutes.

Every night he is on edge, listening intently, worrying that someone might hear. By the dim light of his flashlight (he has to change the batteries frequently), Elser spends night after night kneeling because he has placed the bomb chamber as close as possible to the floor of the gallery. Given the dimensions of the opening—70 cm. by 90 cm. (27 1/2" x 35 1/2")—it is an exhausting undertaking. After two months, he develops pus-filled sores on his knees, forcing him to seek medical treatment and then several days in bed. Because of the difficulties, it takes Elser until the end of October to finish hollowing out the chamber.

Georg Elser's reproduction of his explosive device.
Right: Side view showing the two clock mechanisms.
Left: Side view showing the sleigh, which drives three nails into firing caps of cartridges.
The powder charges in the cartridges cause the explosion.

He scrapes out the debris using a special tool, collects it on a small carpet in front of the hole, then hides it in one of the boxes in the storage room on the gallery. Every few days he shows up with a small suitcase, transfers the debris into it, and then walks down to the Isar River with it. Before he finishes his night shift he meticulously sweeps up the remaining dust from the floor. Elser is an exceptionally conscientious workman, who truly thinks of everything.

After three or four hours of this night work, Elser is exhausted and spends the rest of the night dozing on his chair. In the course of three months he spends thirty to thirty-five nights working in this way, generally coming in at three-day intervals.

During the day, after Elser has gotten some sleep, he gets down to developing his explosive device. One of the first things he does is modify the clocks. The bomb case will have to wait until he finishes boring out the chamber. At first he considers connecting the clock to the detonator using an automobile turn indicator and a battery. Then he installs a wooden cog in the clock. The hour hand strikes a tooth on the cog every twelve hours and moves the cog one-twelfth of a rotation further. With this arrangement, Elser can set his ignition mechanism no more than 144 hours in advance—six full days. The Gestapo was surprised by this system.

When the cog is struck, a lever in the clock is moved. This lever was intended in the clock mechanism to activate the striking of the clock; after Elser's conversion, it sets a gear in motion that winds a wire soldered onto a small drum. This wire releases a ratchet lever, pulls away a spring under tension, and frees a sleigh, which is a molded block of iron with three nails implanted into it. These strike the igniters of live gun shells from which the shot has been removed, setting off firing caps that cause the blasting caps to penetrate into the explosive containers, finally triggering the detonation.

But Elser still has technical concerns—his "checkomania" reasserts itself. Lacking sufficient confidence in one clock, he installs a second one. He also thinks of the possibility that someone sitting near the column during the day might hear the clocks ticking inside it. He therefore insulates the interior of the wooden bomb case with a layer of cork. Elser cannot carry out such detailed construction without workshops and the help of experienced craftsmen. His land-lady, Rosa Lehmann, observed how he won over the craftsmen: "He drove all the craftsmen in the neighborhood crazy. He needed to do something in every shop—at the locksmith or the carpenter or the mechanic. He could beg like a little child."

If it suits his purpose, Elser can overcome his penchant for privacy and become chatty. If need be he can be downright gregari-ous. The strongest ties develop between him and master woodworker Brög. He has been in his good graces since helping him with the con-struction of a large heavy wardrobe for no pay. Brög couldn't afford an assistant, so in exchange Elser was allowed to work in the shop and even use the adjoining supply room to sleep in. At Brög's own suggestion, he provided Elser with a key; Elser was able to spend the night there after he vacated his room at the Lehmanns at the begin-ning of November.

On November 1 and November 2, Elser is at last able to fill the chamber with explosive. Conscientious as he is, he makes sure to pack every corner with dynamite. At home during the day he tests the accuracy of his clocks several times. On November 3, he arrives at the hall carrying his clocks wrapped in newspaper under his arm—and finds the hall locked for the first time. He can't go to the supply room at Brög's place because the street access is bolted. So Elser has to spend this night in the courtyard of the brewery among beer kegs, a scene that foreshadows his role as an outcast. The cold gnaws at his dwindling strength.

He makes his next attempt on November 4—the hall is open and there is a dance, as Elser already knows. He buys a ticket and has no problem making his way up to the gallery with his clocks. He sits down at a table and watches the people dancing. At closing time, he disappears into the storage room—then he gets his second shock: His ignition apparatus is too big to fit into the bomb chamber. Elser has only three nights left and he becomes even more nervous. For-tunately, the difference is not great; he saws off the corners of the wooden case and files them down.

On November 5 there is another dance. Elser again waits up on the gallery. This time the case fits. Elser inserts the wire, tightens it, and starts the clocks. This is the longest night for him so far—he does not finish until 6:00 a.m. Since November 1, he has been slowly folding his tents. Having already given notice, he vacates his room; he sleeps during the day in Brög's supply room, and sends a box containing clothes and tools to his sister Maria in Stuttgart.

His final meeting with master Brög, who without his knowledge has been Elser's best helper, is the crowning event in this theater of the absurd. Two affable craftsmen who have unselfishly assisted each other say good-bye. Each nods to the other and expresses his warmest thanks for his cooperation and support.

Elser neglected his connections to Königsbronn during the three months in Munich. He insisted on receiving Elsa's letters from Esslingen at general delivery so that she would not find out his address. He no longer wrote to his family. On his last trip to Munich on November 7, he wanted to stop by Königsbronn only to say good-bye to his father, who had become very frail. There was no time for anything else.

The constant tension in Munich, having to keep everything—all his thoughts and worries—bottled up, made Elser even more nervous. This tendency had already begun in Schnaitheim when he was living at the Schmauders' place. He recalled his childhood, when his mother had prayed with him. Since the beginning of 1939, as he told the Gestapo during the interrogation, he would frequently seek out a church—silent prayer did him some good, he said. "It wasn't until this year that I once again started going to church a lot—maybe thirty times since the beginning of the year. Lately on weekdays, I have been going to a Catholic church to say the Lord's Prayer if there wasn't a Protestant church close by. In my opinion, it doesn't matter whether you do it in a Protestant church or a Catholic church. I'll admit that there was some connection between my plan, which was always on my mind, and going to church frequently and praying frequently—I definitely wouldn't have prayed so much if it hadn't been for the action I had been planning and preparing for. And it's true that I always felt a little calmer after praying."

While Elser's clocks were ticking on the gallery of the Bürgerbräukeller, the military opposition was tearing its hair out trying to figure out how Hitler's next war could be stopped. But the opposition couldn't act—more and more new considerations kept it paralyzed. Hitler assumed there would be a rebellion or an assassination attempt. Yet he did not have much respect for his top military leaders; he had often witnessed how quickly they knuckled under when he yelled at them. Since the Polish campaign, the General Staff was aware of the brutality with which Hitler conducted war, and they suspected his motives: the extermination of the Polish Jews, clerics, and intellectuals. And so it would continue. The high-ranking German military officers who didn't dare to eliminate Hitler then sacrificed entire divisions without compunction. Elser, by contrast, had made his decision: one instead of many millions.

XVIII

In the Concentration Camp at Sachsenhausen

B EFORE THE INTERROGATION in Berlin, which took place November 19–23, 1939, Elser was repeatedly tortured. As a prisoner at the Wittelsbacher Palais in Munich, he had been brutally beaten on Himmler's orders. After November 23, the punishment became truly systematic. In Berlin, as one of the Gestapo's most important detainees, Elser was certainly kept in the cellar at Prinz-Albrecht-Strasse 8. Sooner or later almost everyone who had made a name and reputation for himself in the resistance movement was imprisoned there, from Canaris to Bonhoeffer. The only one generally overlooked by posterity was the little woodworker from the Ostalb.

On direct orders from Hitler and Himmler, all the torture sessions centered on the question of instigators. It is entirely possible, and could hardly be held against him, that under great duress Elser occasionally fabricated the existence of instigators. When Elsa Härlen was brought face to face with him in Berlin, she watched as Georg was forced to state that he was following the orders of foreign agents when he was working at Waldenmaier in Heidenheim.

Claims of another scenario dreamed up by Elser can be traced to Walter Schellenberg, former head of the domestic intelligence division at the SD, "Elser explained that two unknown persons had assisted him in the preparation of the attack and promised that they would arrange to get him safely out of the country." What came next might clearly have been made up by SS secret service man Schellenberg. According to him, the day after the SD commando group responsible for the Venlo abduction received a commendation, he was summoned to Hitler at the Reich Chancellery. Beforehand, he asked Gestapo Müller about the status of the investigation. Müller's response:

I just can't get anywhere with this guy; he's completely bullheaded and always sticks to his original story—that he hates Hitler, who put his brother in a concentration camp because he was a Communist. Then he claims that tinkering around with this infernal bomb was fun for him and that he always kept an image of Hitler's maimed body in his mind. . . . He says these two unknown men delivered the explosives and the detonators to him at a Munich café. It may well be that Strasser and his Black Front have a hand in this.

The Gestapo figured out all on its own that these two stories were not compatible. Müller went on: "So far I've always been able to break every one of these types that I've taken on. If this guy had been treated to my beatings earlier on, he never would have thought up this nonsense." In a subsequent discussion, Hitler issued an order to Heydrich: "I would like to know what kind of man this Elser is. We must be able to classify him somehow. Report back to me on this. And furthermore, use all means to get this criminal to talk. Have him hypnotized, give him drugs; make use of everything of this nature our scientists have tried. I want to know who the instigators are. I want to know who is behind this."

A few days later, Schellenberg heard from Gestapo Müller that three doctors had worked on Elser for twenty-four hours and injected him with "sizable quantities of Pervertin," but that he continued to say the same thing. Müller had a workshop set up for Elser at Prinz-Albrecht-Strasse and ordered him to reconstruct the explosive device.

Elser accomplished this task in a short time, then installed the device into a wooden pillar. The Gestapo and the SS could not conceal their enthusiasm: "A masterpiece!" Heydrich and Schellenberg visited Elser in his workshop. When Schellenberg saw Elser for the first time, he said:

Police photo of Elser with a shaved head.

He was a small, slight man, somewhat pale, with bright eyes and a high forehead—a type that one finds occasionally among skilled craftsmen. He spoke pure Swabian dialect, and he seemed shy and reserved—a bit frightened. He responded to questioning only with reluctance, but he opened up when he was praised for his craftsmanship. Then he would comment on his reconstructed model in detail and with great enthusiasm.

But Elser still stuck to his story about the two unknown men at the Munich café.

The same day, Gestapo Müller summoned four noted hypnotists. Only one was able to put Elser into a trance, but the hardheaded prisoner stuck to what he had already said. A hypnotist rendered a report reflecting the role of psychology in the service of the regime, stating that Elser was a "fanatic," a "sectarian loner with the obsessive notion that he had to avenge his brother," and that he also had a pathological desire for recognition—a need for some extraordinary technical achievement." The conclusion of the report might be accurate; Elser had made similar statements before the attack. According to the psychologist, Elser had the "drive to achieve fame by eliminating Hitler and simultaneously liberating Germany from 'the evil of Hitler.'"

At first Elser remained at the headquarters of Reich Security. Hitler issued the order to hold Elser, along with the two British Secret Service men, for a show trial after the war. This unlocks the secret of why Elser was given preferential treatment as a special prisoner at the concentration camp. Elser's reproduction of the explosive device was held in high regard by the Gestapo, who adopted it into their field manuals for training purposes. Elser indeed achieved recognition as an inventor, albeit among his archenemies.

According to a secret message passed by an inmate of the concentration camp at Sachsenhausen to Secret Service man Best, it was rumored that Elser was kept imprisoned on the top floor of Gestapo headquarters in Berlin until January or February of 1941.

Nebe was one of the last to see the prisoner in 1941, as reported by Gisevius:

> In the courtyard of the Gestapo building, a prisoner suddenly came running at him so fast that the guards couldn't keep up. He couldn't believe his eyes: It was the Munich assassin. He had heard nothing more about him and assumed that he was no longer alive. With tears in his eyes, Nebe told me at the time of the haunting encounter with a tormented creature. Elser was just a shell of his former self because they had tried to squeeze information out of him by feeding him very salty herring and exposing him to heat, and then depriving him of liquids. They wouldn't let up—they wanted him to confess to some kind of connection, however vague, to Otto Strasser. The artisan remained steadfast. Almost like an innocent child or the kind of person one sometimes finds among sect members, he told Nebe of his torment, not begging for mercy, not even complaining—it was more like an outburst of joy at seeing once again the only person who had treated him humanely since his arrest.

The standard program of Gestapo torture included turning up the heat full blast, giving subjects only salted herring to eat, and depriving them of liquids. The procedures surely also included such routine measures as waking a prisoner and interrogating him, never turning off the light and shining it directly in his face, threatening him with additional torture, destroying the last vestiges of hope by describing various kinds of execution, and so on.

Even before Elser was placed in a cell block in the concentration camp at Sachsenhausen, rumors about him circulated among a public burdened with disinformation. German society in its confusion tried to find someone to blame for anything out of the norm. Their speculation could never be proved, but neither could it be refuted. Anyone reporting a rumor was therefore at first assumed to be right. Of course, rumors were prohibited, but they continued to flourish— there was simply too much need for clarification and hope. In the concentration camp at Dachau, the confusion was so rampant that many inmates thought even the assassination attempt of July 20, 1944, had been staged by the SS.

The origin, development, and spread of rumors about Elser are as tangled and impenetrable as a dense jungle. An early published attempt appeared in the *St. Galler Tagblatt* of November 24, 1939, according to which Elser was a Communist, was sent to a concentration camp in 1936, and was part of Strasser's Black Front. Judging by the remaining content, which contained details of the assassination attempt, one is led to conjecture that the source of the information was within the headquarters of the Gestapo. From here there were direct connections to the "Political Department" of a concentration camp, the Gestapo office responsible for maintaining the political files of all prisoners. Prisoners who worked in this "Political Department" were held in the highest regard in the information marketplace at the camp. Those in control here were frequently Communist prisoners, who were also responsible for passing on rumors about the Gestapo.

Probably the oldest version of all the rumors about Elser circulating in the concentration camps goes back to Ernst Eggert, a trusty in the prison cells of the concentration camp at Sachsenhausen. Eggert heralded his remarks as a "great scoop" with the heading: "The assassin at the Munich Hofbräuhaus" (citing the wrong beer hall as the location of the attack). At first Eggert was struck by the suspiciously civil reception Elser received at the concentration camp:

I am completely convinced that the attack on Hitler in Munich was staged, purely for propaganda purposes. One day we have big excitement at the prison cells—the senior officer as well as Commandant Lorenz [actually *Loritz*] appeared and issued orders to prepare a large room—and make it the best one we had. They put cloths on the tables, and vases with flowers. They provided a radio.

This is followed by a description of the prison conditions prescribed for Elser, the main parts of which are probably accurate:

The door was never locked, and there was an SS man stationed in his room—the guard was changed every two hours. Three times a day he [Elser] was allowed to move around outdoors, and he had all kinds of other privileges—he could smoke without restriction and he was provided with excellent food, the same as the food served to the commandant. Every day there were potatoes, meat, sauces, vegetables, stewed fruit. The assassin was given classy treatment—he was handled with kid gloves.

Every line exudes envy—an understandable reaction, given the hellish conditions in the prison cells. As if there had been objections to his remarks, Eggert adds: "I firmly believe, after what I have seen and heard, that I am justified in saying that the attack was staged—because nobody would treat a real assassin in this manner. If this t[hing] hadn't been staged, they would have put him in chains and made short work of him."

It is not until this point that Eggert describes the conspiratorial path that led him to his discoveries:

When he [Elser] was let out of his cell, I [had to] leave the corridor and go to my cell, but I wasn't locked in. I suspected something and said to myself something's not right here—so I waited until I caught sight of him. But I still didn't quite have a handle on what was going on. But then one day I got hold of a magazine, and guess what I saw in it—a picture of the Munich assassin with his name under it, Georg Elser. At the prison they called him Schorsch. Then it dawned on me. So I started feeling out the SS in the cell block and got confirmation that he was the assassin. The SS was outraged that the assassin would receive such treatment. If the camp directors had known my secret, they would have shot me on the spot.

Given this kind of jealousy, the seemingly preferential treatment granted Elser worked to his disadvantage. From that point on, no political prisoner wanted to talk to Elser—a daunting undertaking in any event since there was at all times a double guard in his cell and another posted outside the door. The magazine Eggert referred to was the November 1939 issue of the SS publication *Das Schwarze Korps*.

It was left in the small library at the prison and was much sought after by the prisoners. Anyone looking at the article and the photographs only through the lens of envy failed to notice that in actuality the SS was bitterly attacking Elser. There was no hint that the Nazis were behind any of this.

Amidst the jealousy, it was overlooked that Elser was missing one vital element of survival: the solidarity of the prisoners. He was denied the assistance and the encouragement that prisoners could provide each other. The justification lay in the logic of the political prisoner: Anyone protected by the Nazis had to be their crony. The legend of Elser the Nazi spread like wildfire among the prisoners who set the political tone. Among the many Catholic clerics who were imprisoned in Sachsenhausen and Dachau, however, hardly any subscribed to this discriminatory gossip.

Emilio Büge, a prisoner who wrote for the "Political Department," wrote in his secret notes, which he was able to smuggle out: "Elser, the 'assassin' at the Munich Bürgerbräukeller (1940), is comfy and happy in a cell here in the bunker, where he has every possible privilege. He has tools and wood available, so he can putter around and build things—not a likely situation for a guy who was out to kill the Führer."

Martin Niemöller, a special inmate in the camp prison, heard a rumor as early as 1940 in the latrine that Elser was an SS man and that Hitler and Himmler had ordered the attack. At that point, Elser was not even in the prison. Once Elser did arrive, he was greeted with condescension and mistrust. In the camp, truth could no longer be distinguished from fiction—gossip was infectious. The Communist prisoner Rudolf Wunderlich remained in solitary confinement at the prison for ten months and heard nothing about Elser during that time; he was nevertheless certain that Elser was only "the presumed Munich assassin." As a camp messenger, Wunderlich had access almost everywhere and was therefore an ideal disseminator of such "new information." And perhaps the camp administrators were content to have the attack in the Bürgerbräukeller ascribed to their organization.

The Communist prisoners played the same game with Herschel Grynszpan, who attempted an assassination in Paris in 1938. As Wunderlich wrote: "Could it be that he [Grynszpan] carried out the attempt on the orders of the Nazis, perhaps so that he could launch something against France?" Proof of this: Grynszpan is said to have had it easy in the camp prison. And in fact he was occasionally allowed to work as a trusty, his head was not shaved and he got to keep his civilian clothes. But privileges like these were also enjoyed by political prisoners who were given functions in the camp.

It is assumed that Elser was moved to the concentration camp at Sachsenhausen at the beginning of 1941. As was usually the case with a prominent special prisoner like this one, Elser was transferred at night in a black Gestapo limousine, which drove through the gate and then went right to the small camp where the prisoner was handed over. On orders from the highest levels, three cells were specially arranged for Elser—cells 11–13 on wing B. Today, the walls of the entire cell block are still standing, but access to them is gained from the front left. To get to the walls of Elser's cells, one must go through wing A (the only wing still standing), then on to the other cell walls, which are outdoors to the front and the right. The basic layout of a cell was 2.5 m. x 3.75 m. (8.2 ft. x 12.3 ft.), or an area of 9.35 sq.m. (100.6 sq.ft.).

With three cells from which the dividing walls had been removed, Elser appeared to be better off than most of the others. But he actually lived in only one cell—the second one contained his workbench and wood, and the third was outfitted with cots for two SS guards who were relieved at twelve-hour intervals. And as in every other cell, the light was kept on all night.

He could be awakened at any time, just like any other prisoner in the cell block. The walls were thin, so the inmates always knew what was going on even if they couldn't see it. Their sense of hearing became so acute that they could distinguish every sound and knew what was going to happen next. In the yard in front of the cell block, prisoners tied to posts were tortured until their long, tormented cries sounded like those of animals. The SS would handcuff a prisoner with his hands behind his back, then, with a pole thrust between his arms, lift him by his hands until his toes barely touched the ground. The screams of pain, which probably diminished only as death approached, penetrated every cell. Anyone who was released alive after an hour or more was nothing but "a quivering heap, a human being broken in body and spirit," as the Bavarian prisoner Weiss-Rüthel remarked after watching a friend so treated.

In this interior courtyard, a wooden horse was used for beatings. The prisoner was shackled, then beaten on the buttocks with a bullwhip twenty-five times—the prisoner was required to count the lashes himself. Because of the screams, all the inmates felt somehow that they were participants in the process—especially when they were forced to give the cynical shout "Let's head for the festival!"

From the shouts of the SS crew, inmates knew when a prisoner had been placed in a "standing cell," where he would be kept on bread and water in darkness for at least three days and could neither stand nor sit. When there were executions in the interior courtyard, the prisoners could hear the gunshots. They could recognize the footsteps of prisoners by the sound of their wooden clogs and those of the SS men by the sound of the iron taps on their boots. But if the guards in the cell block wanted to catch prisoners (whose cell doors were kept open) while they were engaging in prohibited activities, they crept up

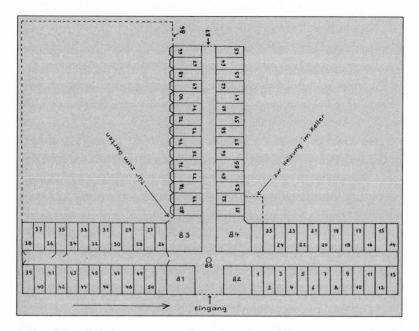

Plan of the cell block in the concentration camp at Sachsenhausen. Cells 11–13 were occupied by Elser and his guards.

wearing socks. When the prisoners heard the command "Clear out!" they had to get out of the corridors—someone else was to be taken away unseen to some unknown destination.

If they heard pop music over the loudspeakers, all the prisoners cringed—they knew people were being shot to death in the factory yard next door.

In 1942, the SS murdered 12,000 Soviet prisoners of war here. The stench from portable crematoria penetrated from the camp all the way to Oranienburg. Around this time, ninety-two Dutch hostages were murdered in the same manner. Amid great hubbub, they had arrived the previous day at the camp prison, where they had been crammed into several cells.

If there was a strong stench of corpses on the clothes of the trusties, everyone knew that they had just come from duty at the crematorium. Death was present at all times. Elser had to assume that he could be taken out at any time and eliminated. In the midst of this death camp, his privileges could not be seen as assurance that he would live. The conditions at this special prison, in which Elser too got to hear all the horrors of the concentration camp, were notorious. As Wunderlich wrote: "Every inmate at Sachsenhausen dreaded the cell block."

In 1942, the Jehovah's Witness Paul Wauer was a barber in the cell block. Accompanied by an SS man, Elser got a shave from this man every day. Wauer did not know who this diminutive prisoner was until he learned it from a trusty. He too got hold of the SS magazine with Elser's photograph, but he did not let himself be drawn into the political discrimination against Elser. Wauer attested that during this time, Himmler was in Elser's cell once. It must have been 1943, and the conversation lasted about an hour.

In December 1942, the People's Court moved to initiate proceedings against Elser, but the case was never opened. When Elser's father died on August 11, 1942, the Ministry of Justice ordered "the estate of the enemy of the people" seized, by which it meant Georg Elser's share of the inheritance. The Elsers had to pay this amount to Gestapo headquarters.

In 1964–1965, former SS man Walter Usslepp gave a detailed account of Elser's living conditions. This account is credible, unlike the myths that he drew from the rumor mills of the concentration camp. He was a member of Elser's special guard during the period 1942–44. According to Usslep, the furnishings in Elser's cell included a large cupboard and a lectern he had built himself, on which lay his zither. By the bed there was a small nightstand with a receiver for "official" radio stations on it and next to it, in a wooden frame, the picture of a woman he called his bride—it must have been Elsa Härlen. Below the windows, which contained flowerboxes, there was another cupboard.

Georg Elser was a heavy smoker, and he received an allowance of 120 cigarettes a week. Although he was supplied with a good diet and double portions of food, Elser had always been a poor eater. He was known to pass on much of his food to the guards, which contributed to his physical decline. In 1943–44 he weighed at most 115 pounds. On Saturdays, prisoners were allowed to shower and sheets were changed. Elser wore blue metal worker's trousers and sport shirts. He never received mail or visitors. Reveille was at 6:00 a.m., and then the regular prisoners emptied their slop buckets and went to wash up. Afterwards the special prisoners were taken to the washroom one by one. Breakfast was at 7:00 a.m. Elser was never interrogated while Usslepps was on duty.

The SS permitted Elser to construct a zither, which he played with enthusiasm, yet with melancholy. By the end of his term at Sachsenhausen, he had built three or four zithers. He also built a table for pocket billiards, which he liked to play with his guards. He was often irritable and subject to mood swings. One time, to calm him down, the commandant sent him a woman from the brothel barracks, a prisoner from the concentration camp at Ravensbrück—Elser flew into a rage and sent her away.

With time a familiar tone developed between the SS guards and the amiable prisoner. They all used the familiar "du" with him and called him "Schorsch," until his name simply became "Little Schorsch." Niemöller, with his elitist obsession for labels, believed he recognized political complicity in this kind of behavior. In fact, Elser remained mistrustful despite all the overtures. Anytime he left the cell to go outdoors or to the toilet, he would turn the place upside down on his return, looking for hidden microphones. Five or six months passed before he revealed to his guard, Walter Usslepp, who was strictly forbidden to talk about the attack, that he was the Munich assassin. This was in mid-1942.

From that point on, Usslepp's recollections take on a Münch-hausen character, blending actual events recalled with rumors from the camp. He claims Elser told him that he had carried out the attack on orders from Hitler and Himmler and that he was a member of the general SS. According to Usslepp, Elser claimed that one day he had received a commission from Reich Security Headquarters to carry out a special mission and that Himmler himself had once come to Königs-bronn regarding this matter. Toward the end of his account, Usslepp becomes almost kooky, reporting that during the final week, Elser had difficulty gaining access to the Bürgerbräukeller because of the Gestapo guards in the place. As a reward for his work, Elser was sup-posed to receive a house and a state pension. These two elements recur in other rumors about Elser, probably reflecting the hopes of the low-level guards themselves. Finally, in Usslepp's version, Elser decided to go to Switzerland because he mistrusted Hitler. All such claims of Els-er's purported involvement with the SS have long since been refuted.

Usslepp, who considered himself Elser's "real confidante" and even called himself the "executor of his estate," claimed that in 1943–44 he mapped out a plan of escape with him. He was going to simply take Elser, who weighed very little, and stuff him into a garbage bag with wood shavings and just take him out of the camp right past the SS guard. But Elser, he says, finally backed out of the plan because he felt he would not be able to count on any assistance once out-side. Even if he had such fantasies about escaping and idly chatted about them on occasion, there was never any chance that they could succeed. Moreover, it is simply not believable that an SS man like Usslepp would risk his life for an assassin. Perhaps there is behind all of this some information planted by the Gestapo in order to test Elser.

In 1944, Elser had a map hanging on the wall of his cell on which he followed the progression of the front by moving little flags. In the process, he compared the announcements from the BBC in London with those of German radio. He clung to life to the very end. But he had been so ravaged by his imprisonment that he no longer possessed the same unshakable will as before. At first he would rejoice when the Allies advanced, but then he would get depressed because he knew full well that he would be executed first: "Even if it means my own death, at least I know that Hitler will not outlive me by much." During air raids he refused to proceed to the bunker—he had nothing more to lose. He preferred to get up on his nightstand and watch the bombers in the sky and the glow from the fires in Berlin.

While Usslepp could at least be considered a reliable source regarding Elser's living conditions, the British Secret Service agent Sigismund Payne Best was simply a wild-eyed fantast. Even though by his own admission he never spoke with Elser, he nonetheless claimed to have found out from him everything about his life. He claimed that Elser, who rarely wrote anything, wrote secret messages over a period of twelve months and smuggled them to him—even though such activity was strictly prohibited. Why then did Best, who after the war prided himself on the diary he kept while in captivity, keep none of these messages—or at least copy them down?

Best was terrible at spinning tales. He simply repeated everything fed to him by the Gestapo. According to him, Elser's biography went as follows: He was born in Munich, lost his parents in the First World War, was raised by an uncle, printed and distributed Communist leaflets in Munich in 1937, was arrested as "antisocial" in a police raid and taken to Dachau, and was ordered by the camp commander in 1939 to carry out the bombing at the Bürgerbräukeller in order to liquidate a group of traitors in Hitler's inner circle.

As early as Venlo, it was clear that Best was a dilettante at his trade. Here he claims that on the one hand Elser built a timing mechanism into the bomb, yet on the other hand that he laid an electric cable in the cellar—which of course nobody noticed. He goes on to say that Elser, after his arrest at the border, was promised 40,000 Swiss francs if he would state at a trial that he had been in contact with Otto Strasser and the British Secret Service. His story makes no sense from beginning to end.

The last living witness from Elser's time in the camp prison was Franz Josef Fischer, who was born in Czechoslovakia in 1916 and lived in Gruibingen on the Schwäbisch Alb. In 1931, Fischer became actively involved in the Czech resistance against the Nazis in the neighboring area of Silesia and was opposed to the Sudeten German Henlein Party. In 1938, when the Germans marched in, he refused to serve in the German Wehrmacht and was placed in Gestapo custody for two years, where he was severely mistreated. After being acquitted by the People's Court in Leipzig in April of 1940, he was sent to the concentration camp at Sachsenhausen. By March 1943, he was working as a supervisor in the clothing stores for the SS at a field warehouse in Berlin-Lichterfelde. After a bombardment, this office was scheduled to be moved to Schlackenwerth Castle near Karlsbad, and Himmler had to decide whether the Sudeten German Fischer should be transferred along with it. So Fischer was moved to Himmler's SS business office, located in Berlin-Lichterfelde at Unter den Eichen 126. While he was waiting in an alcove in the corridor, he noticed a bushy-headed man whom he didn't know. The man was called in first, but was soon ejected with a kick in the rear by Himmler.

Before Fischer's turn came up, the two had a chance to speak. The stranger said: "Don't you know me? I'm the one they say is an assassin. I just wanted to avoid a great disaster—even more killing. So I said the leadership's got to go." At that point Fischer realized that this was Elser. Elser was well known in the Resistance; his actions served as encouragement. Then after Fischer too had been thrown out, the conversation resumed for another half hour. Elser said: "I'm alone and I did everything by myself—the arrest at the border was just bad luck. They all talk a lot about me, but none of them know anything." Fischer was liberated from the concentration camp at Theresienstadt in 1945.

During a devastating bombardment of Berlin on February 3, 1945, the headquarters building of Reich Security was also severely damaged, and Elser's time at Sachsenhausen came to an end. Those arrested in connection with the events of July 20 had to be moved to the south. The Gestapo control center created one of its backup locations in the Bavarian town of Hof. Himmler had already given the order to evacuate Sachsenhausen on February 1. On February 6, 1945, news arrived in the concentration camp at Dachau, where a

Franz-Josef Fischer, who spoke briefly with Elser in Berlin in 1943.

typhus epidemic had been raging since November 1944, that 10,000
prisoners from Sachsenhausen were on their way to Dachau. Presumably around this time Elser was picked up by a Gestapo car.

XIX

The End in Dachau

In EARLY FEBRUARY 1945, Elser, accompanied by four SS men, entered the concentration camp at Dachau. The SS man responsible for the bunker, Edgar Stiller, carried Elser's zither in a wooden case. It was very cold and Elser was wearing an overcoat. Upon his arrival security measures were tightened—Elser, the SS men grumbled to the other inmates, was "a very special prisoner." Soon everyone learned that he was Hitler's personal prisoner.

The concentration camp at Dachau was in the process of being closed down and was in catastrophic condition. For months concentration camps located further to the east had been evacuating their occupants to Dachau. The trains, which were frequently carrying Jewish prisoners, arrived with thousands of corpses on board. When the boxcars remained stationary for several days, the stench of death permeated the entire area.

As the war progressed, the makeup of the SS forces changed. The younger SS men, who were the bane of the prisoners, went to the front; the older generations taking their places were more concerned about saving their own skins, so they tried to get along with the prisoners. The clever ones were already thinking about trying to get a denazification certificate, called a "Persilschein."

Waves of typhus had swept through the camp, so the crematorium could no longer keep up with the piles of corpses. The SS people scarcely dared to leave their building. More and more, the inmates were left to fend for themselves.

The bunker in Dachau was immense in size—Dachau served as the model for all the other camps. It was a one-story building, 643 long by 31 feet wide. In the center section, measuring forty-five feet by forty-five feet, there were four rooms: a guard room, an admission room, a medical examination room, and the interrogation room of the "Political Department." In the two wings located to the left and right of the center section, there were approximately 140 cells, each 9' 6" by 7' 3", an area of sixty-nine square feet—significantly smaller than at Sachsenhausen. The special political prisoners were housed in the front part of the left wing; the section for the SS prisoners was located behind an iron door. The right wing was reserved for members of the clergy, who were separated from the other prisoners and provided with their own exit into the prison yard.

The Munich SS official Franz Xaver Lechner was charged with guarding Elser. Lechner had been wounded in the war and his right arm was paralyzed. His thoughts were more about Mozart than the world of terror perpetrated by an SS now on the verge of disappearing. Lechner had wanted to attend the Munich Conservatory while serving in the military. With some pride he declared in 1959 that a quite distinguished group had been assembled in the camp prison: "I had two SS generals, a recipient of the *Blutorden*, a *Reichshauptamtsleiter*, two high-level SS judges, the entire Rumanian Iron Guard, scientists, artists, and inventors." In addition, there was a Greek Orthodox archbishop, the former Dutch minister of war, the Italian partisan General Sante Garibaldi (a grandson of the famous Italian liberation fighter), a count and his daughter, the abbot of a monastery, Pastor Niemöller, and other clergymen.

When Elser was brought in, Lechner was on duty. According to Lechner, "Elser was unimpressive, bedraggled, emaciated—a wreck. . . . He was decidedly unresponsive. He showed interest in nothing. A human wreck." Orders on how to deal with Elser came by telephone from the commandant's office in the guard house at the camp entrance. Elser was to occupy cell 6, his name was not to be entered into the register, and he was to be guarded day and night. Under no circumstances was he to be allowed to come into contact with other prisoners. No one else was to be allowed even to see him.

From this point on, there was an SS man on a stool sitting outside Elser's cell, and there were two guards in his cell at all times. Soon Elser was moved to cells 2 and 3, and three days later, as a privilege, he was provided with a workbench, tools, and wood, with which he would occupy himself when he wasn't lying apathetically on his bed.

Elsa's photograph had disappeared. Plagued by extreme nervousness, Elser had become a chain smoker, and he alone received a special daily allowance of forty cigarettes. And with his poor appetite, he continued to go downhill.

Elser liked to carve figures, and in the evenings he enjoyed playing his zither. Even Lechner, the discerning devotee of classical music, found the sound very pleasant. In Munich, Lechner purchased a collection of Viennese songs for zither. Elser was ecstatic upon finding his favorite song from Sachsenhausen among them. The song became Elser's main consolation: "In my heart I carry a bit of old Vienna, a bit of bliss from those days past." Even though Elser had never been to Vienna, tears came to his eyes and his voice choked up when he played the song for the first time.

"My days are numbered—I've known this for a long time," Elser frequently told Lechner. Once Elser asked him bluntly, "You know the score here. What's better—gassing, hanging, or being shot in the back of the head?" Astonished, Lechner tried to calm the prisoner, but Elser wouldn't have it: "I know better—I'm not going to live much longer." One last time Elser was subjected to an interrogation, in which he was repeatedly asked whether he acted alone. Each time he would say the same thing he had always said: "I acted completely alone." He had not been in Lechner's charge long enough for the rumors from the SS and the political prisoners to make their way in. He stated that the only person to assist him was an old man who helped him find workshops and ran errands for him. He was pleased to learn that the Gestapo still had not been able to track him down.

According to SS man Lechner, Elser revealed to him his motive for the attack:

I had to do it because, for his whole life, Hitler has meant the downfall of Germany. You know, Herr Lechner, don't think that I'm some kind of dyed-in-the-wool Communist—I'm not. I have some sympathy for Ernst Thälmann, but getting rid of Hitler just became an obsession of mine. I knew I was taking a great risk, but I never thought I could be caught. But, as you can see, I'm sitting here in front of you—I got caught, and now I have to pay for it. I would have preferred it if they had executed me right away.

Lechner noted that Elser's hands were trembling.

Around the beginning of March the prisoners heard the thunder of the American artillery drawing closer. Rather than being elated by this development, Elser said to Lechner, "I don't regret what I did—it wouldn't make any difference anyway. I believed I was accomplishing an important task. I didn't succeed, and now I have to pay the consequences. I'm afraid of these consequences; day and night I wonder what kind of death I will suffer."

Lechner's impressions of Elser revealed his sense of superiority over his prisoner. He described Elser as "the simplest and most primitive special prisoner. . . . Elser was a harmless, simple man—almost simpleminded. One certainly cannot ascribe great intelligence to him." Lechner was careful not to condemn those whom he had observed committing murder in Dachau. It is likely that he did not want to risk offending anyone who might come into favor once again.

Even in his final days, Elser remained true to himself: "I at least have the satisfaction, even if it is no longer really satisfaction, of knowing that each and every one of them will be hanged!" This was only partially true. While the Americans executed the twenty-eight most notorious mass murderers after the Dachau trials of 1945, the Soviets spared the life of every murderous thug in the hope of being able to win over the war generation politically.

The relatively cordial attitude in the camp toward the unknown special prisoner changed when Pastor Niemöller heard of his presence. The only thing the pastor had seen on Elser was the photograph in the 1939 SS magazine. The final proof of the prisoner's identity for him was the workbench. Niemöller, a special prisoner and internationally respected man of the cloth, became the self-appointed judge of this helpless man without ever having spoken a word with him. Niemöller informed the other clergymen, all of whom were Catholics, about Elser's identity (he called him "Eller"). The clergymen elected to call him by the code name "The Zither Player."

When Elser's prediction that he would not leave captivity alive became known, the enmity toward him among his fellow prisoners began to abate. Elser made a pitiable impression upon Dr. Michael Höck, director of the Catholic Seminary in Freising and a Gestapo prisoner since 1941, and this impression helped to break down the prejudice against him. Höck conferred with Johann Neuhäusler, who before his arrest was a cathedral canon in Munich. The clergymen would then "pluck up their courage," as they put it, and persuade an SS officer to take "an Easter package to Elser containing Easter eggs, flatbread, etc." It was Easter week, on Maundy Thursday—April 5, 1945. Elser wept with joy that there were still people thinking about him.

The time of Hitler and his assassin was coming to a close. After March 11, Hitler did not leave his bunker in the courtyard of the Reich Chancellery. On April 2, he dictated his political will and testament to Bormann. One last time, his deranged logic manifested itself as he proclaimed that victory would be more certain even as the situation became more dire: "The more we have to suffer, the more striking will be the resurgence of the eternal Reich!" Hitler believed that people would be forever grateful to him for exterminating the Jews in Germany and central Europe.

Three days later on April 5, after an audience with Hitler, Himmler issued the order to Ernst Kaltenbrunner, chief of the SD, that he was to decide the fate of the special prisoners. At the very center of this group of victims was Georg Elser. Gestapo Müller signed the order of execution the same day and handed it to SS man Wilhelm Gogalla to take with him as he traveled south to Dachau. The dispatch was labeled "express letter," but the trip took four full days.

The express letter was addressed to the commandant of the concentration camp at Dachau. It established the procedure for transferring the prominent special prisoners to the facility, ordered good treatment of others, and specified that Secret Service men Best and Stevens were to have no contact with each other—which was nothing new. But in the case of Elser, who was referred to throughout as "Eller," there were special instructions emanating from the "highest level," meaning of course Hitler, the one whose name could not be spoken. The instructions read:

> During one of the next terrorist attacks on Munich or the area around Dachau [this was standard jargon for bombing raids], "Eller" was apparently fatally injured. It is my order that, when such a situation arises, "Eller" be liquidated in a completely inconspicuous manner. I further order that extreme caution be taken to inform as few individuals as possible and that these be sworn to absolute confidence. . . . After this communication is read and understood, I order that it be destroyed.

Elser was considered among the most dangerous of the prisoners still alive. Hitler had not forgotten him; after almost six years, the blow from the Bürgerbräu attack had still not lost its effect on him.

SS officer Gogalla, a butcher by trade, started off in a truck with a Gestapo escort, taking special prisoners from Buchenwald with him and then stopping in Flossenbürg where, along with an execution order, he dropped off Canaris, Bonhoeffer, and others who were then hanged on the morning of his departure on April 9. At the makeshift concentration camp at Schönfeld, Gogalla picked up the Englishman Best and the Russian Kokorin. He arrived at Dachau around nine in the evening.

Gogalla handed over the sealed order to the commandant, who opened it and relayed it to the man in charge of the bunker, Edgar Stiller. The insidious bureaucracy of SS operations functioned until the bitter end. The "Political Department" placed its stamp in the upper left-hand corner, noting the admission date, 4/9/1945, and the day book number. In early May in South Tyrol, Best would succeed in spiriting this letter out of Stiller's briefcase, managing to do so before the liberation and before Stiller could destroy it.

From the commandant's office at the camp came a call for SS officer Ludwig Rottmaier, giving the order: "Schorsch to the gate!"

That evening Elser was having his favorite meal, semolina pudding with cherry compote, which, given his almost chronic stomach problems, agreed with him best. Rottmaier proceeded from the guard cell to Elser's cell, where he called him out of his cell, telling him that he had to report for interrogation. But Elser hadn't been interrogated in years. Why now, when the end of the war was so near and one would sooner expect orders to evacuate the camp? That same evening his two cells were reassigned to the French special prisoner Léon Blum and his wife.

Wearing a coat but no hat, Georg Elser walked out into the corridor, where he saw Dr. Lothar Rohde in the cell across from his. He exchanged a glance with him, from which Rohde concluded Elser was expecting the end. He simply left without showing emotion or offering any resistance. Such things were futile in the camps.

An SS officer named Fritz, who was a recent arrival from Buchenwald and known for his brutality, led Elser to the guard house at the camp entrance. Elser might have believed that there was still hope for him until he was taken down the final path, past the electric fence to the end of the camp, and then across the brook to the Old Crematory.

What happened to Elser between the two crematoriums has never been determined. In the account of the assassination attempt, Elser's murderer is not identified. The crematorium was, like the bunker, completely isolated from the rest of the camp, and it was pitch black that night. The only people allowed to go there were those who had duties to perform. Thus there were hardly any witnesses.

The crematorium lay on the other side of the large wall, in the middle of a small park with beautiful old trees. Beginning in March 1943, regular executions were conducted here by shooting the victims in the back of the head. A special setup was constructed for the executions. In front of a backstop for bullets, there was a wooden grating placed over a trench. Many prisoners knew of this murder facility— they could hear the gunshots in the camp. Previously, Jewish prisoners had done the cremation work. A former prisoner named Ziegler reported the following: "The men on the work detail before me were all Jews, and according to Mahl, Bongartz forced all of them to hang themselves." The hangings at the crematorium were handled primarily by a prisoner named Mahl who functioned as an overseer. The Gestapo used the duty rooms to conduct interrogations, which were accompanied by torture—if they had been carried out in the general camp area, the screams of the subjects would have attracted too much attention.

At the crematorium there was an eight-man work detail under overseer Mahl. The man in charge of the crematorium was SS Oberscharführer Theodor Heinrich Bongartz. Beginning in 1950, in an extensive investigation carried out by District Court Munich II, all individuals who could be contacted were questioned. The one who should have been most familiar with the circumstances of Elser's death was the prisoner Mahl, a Nazi from Karlsruhe who had been found guilty of embezzlement at Party headquarters. After serving his time in jail, he was transferred to Dachau. As overseer at the crematorium he volunteered, against the advice of the prisoner functionaries, to be the hangman—for increased bread and schnapps rations.

After the war, Mahl appeared along with thirty-seven SS men before an American military court in the first Dachau trial, and in December 1945 was sentenced to death. His sentence was then reduced to ten years in prison, and in 1952, he was released from the fortress at Landsberg am Lech "on account of good behavior."

While still in prison, Mahl was questioned as a witness and indicated that one night he and the prisoners at the crematorium had been ordered not to leave the building. The work detail was housed in the back rooms at the crematorium. Mahl said that he later heard one or two gunshots outside. Around 11:00 p.m., he was called by Bongartz to come with two men and pick up a body. Bongartz was standing about fifty yards away and in the darkness could only be recognized by his voice. The work detail could see only the beam of a flashlight. Mahl ordered the two prisoners to get on with it. Shortly afterward, three or four SS men walked through the small gate into the camp. Mahl could not recognize who they were. He and his two men met Bongartz next to a body. Bongartz gave the order to cremate the body immediately. In contrast to the usual practice, the clothes were not removed from the body. The dead man was a little taller than 5' 6", of slight build, with no beard or signs of balding. The next day Mahl had to remove the blood from the grass.

Apparently Mahl was ignorant of what was going on. He had no idea who the dead man was. Only after the prompting of the inves-

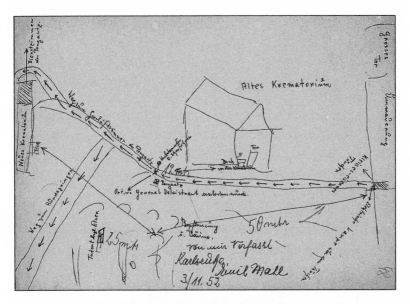

Execution site of Georg Elser and French General Delestraint on a sketch made by former prisoner Emil Mahl on November 3, 1952.

tigating judge Dr. Nikolaus Naaf did he conclude that it must have been Elser, because only two prisoners had been shot to death in the past several days, and the execution of Charles Delestraint, a French general of the resistance, took place during the day.

A year later, in July 1952, Mahl was calling himself an antifascist in hopes of receiving restitution for his imprisonment. He wrote to the Munich District Court for Reparations asking that, "without exception, all details and all murders be cleared up and substantiated." He stated that he would address any discrepancies: "Yes, at my appearance I am prepared to make clear to all nations the crimes of the SS, along with all details." In the style typical of the antifascists of the time, he cited his reasons:

In declaring my readiness to testify, I do so only because, as a former prisoner, I feel a close connection to my comrades, living and dead, and know that I am not guilty of anything. The world should and must know of every murder and the location of the remains. What is more, all should know what means were used to send these comrades to their deaths. For no grass should be allowed to grow over this heinious [sic] spot, out of respect for the memory of our ded [sic] comrades in suffering.

Mahl even proposed that he give them a tour of the camp.

During the questioning by the court he became even more brazen, making the grand declaration that everything reported about Dachau thus far had been based "on deceit and deception," and that he could pinpoint where every single murder in Dachau had been carried out, with one or two exceptions. Nevertheless, Dr. Naaf took the trouble to continue questioning Mahl in Karlsruhe for two days.

On the evening in question, according to this testimony, Bongartz ordered the work detail not to leave the crematorium. When they heard shots, they were to come immediately with a stretcher. Assigned to this task were the prisoners August Ziegler from Mannheim and Franz Geiger from Augsburg.

Around 11:00 p.m. the three men heard gunfire. They took the stretcher and moved in the direction of the flashlight, which appeared to be about eighty feet outside the door to the new crematorium in the park. At the scene there was a dead man lying face down on the ground. Mahl's conviction was that Bongartz had committed the murder alone. "I can confirm with a clear conscience and absolute certainty that in my experience as an overseer, it was Bongartz who personally committed all such murders on the premises of the crematorium. He has many crimes to answer for, and in my opinion he was a completely ruthless criminal." At the end, Mahl recalled that with Elser the only wound visible was a gunshot wound in the back of the head, and that when the work detail arrived he was already dead. Mahl had not known Elser previously. It was not until he found Elser's picture in a magazine while he was in prison in Landsberg that he recognized the dead man from that night.

In 1951, August Ziegler gave a more precise description. Around Christmas 1944, the number of cremations started increasing—there were 200 to 250 bodies a day, and there were four ovens in operation. Later on the SS started using mass graves in order to save on coke. At the time of Elser's execution, only those who had been hanged or shot were cremated. Shootings took place in the area in front of the new crematorium. The victims had to strip naked and were taken out into the yard to the backstop, where they had to kneel facing the backstop and were shot in the back of the head by Bongartz and occasionally by camp director Ruppert. Sometimes there was a doctor present. Eyewitnesses were strictly forbidden, but curiosity drove the prisoners to come out, as Ziegler admitted: "We were able to watch the shootings from a distance." Then the prisoners had to rush out with the stretcher and carry the dead to the morgue. They had to inform Bongartz if a victim was still alive, and he would finish him off with another shot.

On that evening Ziegler was already asleep. It might have been 10:00 p.m. when Mahl came running in and woke him up; he was in such a rush that he wouldn't even let him put on his shoes and a coat. Outside it was so dark that Ziegler was able to follow Mahl only by shouting back and forth. Bongartz was standing near a flowerbed, with his hands in his pockets and a corpse next to him, lying on its back, as he recalled. Ziegler knew immediately that Bongartz was the only one who could have pulled the trigger. The corpse was still fresh; the blood had not yet started to coagulate. Ziegler's hands and trousers became smeared while transporting it. The dead man was small and of slight build; he was wearing good clothing but no hat; his head was shaved. He was cremated the next day.

After lengthy inquiries, the investigating judge of District Court Munich II, Dr. Nikolaus Naaf, concluded on November 8, 1954—the fifteenth anniversary of the assassination attempt—that Elser had been shot to death on April 8, 1945, by Theodor Heinrich Bongartz. His only error was in the date: Bongartz actually fired the fatal shot one day later.

Judging by the general practices at Dachau, it is to be assumed that witnesses at Elser's execution would have included the following

high-level SS officers: camp director Friedrich Ruppert, camp doctor Dr. Hans Eisele, and liaison officer Franz Böttger. All three were
hanged by the Americans in 1945. At that point the execution of
Georg Elser was not taken into consideration because it had not yet
been discovered.

Around 10:00 p.m. on April 9, the special prisoners, who had
been waiting in trucks, were given an exceptionally cordial reception
by the commandant. As Best was being delivered to the cell block that
evening, he was greeted by an old acquaintance from Sachsenhausen,
Jehovah's Witness Paul Wauer, who told him that "Little Schorsch"
had been there. "They just took him out and shot him." Wilhelm Vis-
intainer was a trusty who had earned the nickname "Coal Thief," in
reference to a Nazi propaganda character who hurt the war effort by
wasting power. From him Best learned that Elser had been executed
with a shot to the back of the head. The opinion was widespread that
this shot could have been fired only by Bongartz—he was the only
one who carried a pistol out in that area.

The manner in which Bongartz killed individual prisoners
becomes clearer with the case of French general Delestraint. On this
occasion, unlike others, Mahl, Ziegler, and Geiger were standing just
a few feet away. And it was daytime—April 19, 11:00 a.m. By this
time shootings were no longer customary; evacuation of the camp
was expected at any time. The American army was positioned fifty
miles from Dachau.

Delestraint was led to believe that he was being released, then was
taken to the crematorium. From the gate he walked on alone. Eyewitness Geiger was not far away. The usual higher-level SS officers were
waiting close by. Ruppert cordially greeted the general and shook his
hand. He then instructed him to proceed on to the new crematorium to
pick up his papers. Delestraint had gone no more than fifty feet when
Bongartz slipped out of the old crematorium wearing gym shoes and
started following him, unnoticed. Ziegler saw Bongartz fire, and the
prisoner fell forward face down. Since the victim was still alive at the
crematorium oven, Bongartz shot him in the mouth from the side,
knocking out a gold tooth. This provided Bongartz with yet another
exploit to talk about. He liked to boast that he was the best shot with a

Theodor Bongartz, who shot Georg Elser.

pistol in the camp. It was well known that he always kept his weapon at the ready.

Theodor Heinrich Bongartz, who was born in Krefeld in 1902, was a terror at the crematorium. Having been trained as a plasterer, he worked in his hometown from 1922 until 1930 as a plasterer, and in 1928 he was made a master plasterer. The same year, he joined the SA and four years later, the SS. He then became a stoker and machinist with the army post administration in Krefeld. In 1939, he was transferred to a *Totenkopf* (Death's Head) regiment in Brünn and in 1940 to the commandant's staff of the concentration camp in the town of Dachau, where he lived at Schleissheimer Strasse 121. His first wife committed suicide in 1941—as her reason he cited "melancholy."

According to witnesses, Bongartz was "an exceptionally brutal-looking man." Lechner said that he "had a very sallow complexion and looked dreadful." Periodically, he would also drink heavily and would fire his weapon when drunk. In 1951, a policeman from Dachau submitted a personal description to the court: "About 5' 8", somewhat frail, strikingly erect posture, black hair parted on the left, pale complexion, oval face, heavy black eyebrows, slightly prominent cheekbones, no mustache, no eyeglasses; particular traits: strikingly erect posture, determined stride."

On Saturday April 28, 1945, the SS cleared out—one day after the last of five death marches had left Dachau. Before they did, they dynamited the crematorium, destroyed the standing cells in the cell block, and burned all the files that the prisoners had not managed to spirit away. It was an effort to undo the existence of Hell. A week before, the commandant's office had issued the guards forged military IDs, German army uniforms, and backpacks.

When they began their retreat on April 28, the members of the prisoner work detail were in a horse-drawn wagon with Bongartz; then one by one they started fleeing. Ziegler made it to Munich-Pasing. Bongartz also took off—presumably headed for home in the Lower Rhine area. Along the way, an American patrol stopped him and took him to the P.O.W. camp at Heilbronn-Böckingen. There he died so suddenly—on May 15, 1945—that at first suicide was suspected. But the entry on the list of the dead read "Master sergeant, born 1901"—the tattoo showing his blood type, which was typical for the SS, appears not to have been discovered, and the cause of death is listed as tuberculosis. His strikingly sallow complexion might indicate a different cause of death—hepatitis or cirrhosis of the liver. Bongartz was buried in a grave in the military section of the cemetery at Böckingen: row 17, number 6. To this day it is cared for as a military grave.

SS man Lechner was placed in an internment camp for a year. He had thought ahead about exonerating himself and had Georg Elser write a *"Persilschein"* for him. There was an SS man from Heidenheim, now in prison for his role at Dachau, whose wife established contact with the Elser family in Königsbronn. Her hope was that Elser was still alive and that she could get a letter of commendation. In a flurry of tastelessness and falsification of history, Elser achieved a brief bit of attention. The Englishman Sigismund Payne Best, who had propagated so much nonsense about Elser, suddenly referred to him as "my poor little friend" in a letter written in 1952. It would seem that a dead Elser was the "best" Elser.

XX

The Long Road to Recognition

E LSER'S ATTEMPT ON Hitler's life left two piles of rubble in its wake: the first was in the Bürgerbräukeller, the second was in the minds of the German people. This second pile of mental debris has taken more than thirty years to clear away. The Nazis' *idée fixe* that Elser's attack was a plot between the British Secret Service and Otto Strasser did not survive very long, but it helped fuel the notion that the Nazis could be suspected of virtually anything. In addition to technical considerations, the fact that the assassin had been kept alive so long appeared to speak in favor of this theory. People had become accustomed to the Nazis' practice of executing such an enemy immediately. The logic was simple: Anyone still alive must be an accomplice. In that case, people should have condemned the many co-conspirators who survived the attack of July 20—but that was another story, a much more serious one.

Around the beginning of 1946, Martin Niemöller started the vicious circle of claiming that Elser had been an SS man and the attack an undertaking of the SS leadership itself. He claimed that he alone among the prisoners at Sachsenhausen and Dachau had been a direct witness, stating that he had spoken with Elser. In a series of presentations, Niemöller contended that the attack had been "carried out on Hitler's orders, in order to strengthen the belief among the masses so often stressed in Nazi propaganda that Hitler was protected by Providence." Elser had been an "SS staff sergeant," he claimed, had been treated gently while being arrested at the border two days after the attack, and had enjoyed "advantages" at the concentration camp: "He had a large living area, a radio, a library, and a private workshop at his disposal."

This depiction appeared repeatedly in newspapers and on radio broadcasts, and also reached the Elser family, who had no idea what had happened to Georg. On behalf of her mother, daughter Anna Lober wrote to Niemöller. First she vehemently disputed the claim that Georg had been in the SS. She also wanted to know whether Georg was still alive.

Anna Lober expressed the widespread sense of helplessness that her family as a whole must have felt: "In the Third Reich we were persecuted and imprisoned, the whole family, and now everything is being turned upside down. Who can make out who is telling the truth and who is lying and who has lied? Why did they drag all of us as prisoners all the way to Berlin back then? We innocent people who had no idea about the whole affair?"

Why indeed were the Elsers interrogated and persecuted at the time? Why all the criminal investigation? These are questions that journalists and historians over the next several years did not ask. Writing even more frankly to another contemporary, Niemöller revealed the speculative nature of his claim: "I am convinced that it was Himmler who instigated this."

In his response to Elser's mother, Niemöller trotted out as arguments the camp rumors about Georg Elser. And he admitted that he in fact had spoken to him only one time, briefly. They had not spoken about the attack, he said. Elser just mentioned that his wife—meaning Elsa Härlen—had read Niemöller's book *From U-Boat to Pulpit*.

Anna Lober responded for her mother:

You know, Herr Pastor Niemöller, it creates a great strain on us when all the newspapers and radio stations send out the message to the whole world that my son [was] in the SS until 1939. One newspaper said he was an SS staff sergeant; the others said he was in the SA. None of this is true.

Up until the time of his capture in 1939, he had never been associated with any part of the Hitler regime. The entire village can confirm this.

And Anna went on to say that Dr. Lothar Rohde, Elser's cellmate at Dachau, was also now claiming that Elser himself had admitted to him that he was a member of the SS.

In her mistrust of such witnesses, Anna Lober proved herself quite worthy of her brother: "A man who is no longer alive cannot defend himself. So people can just dump even more suspicions on him." She made short shrift of all the rumormongers: "There are people who make themselves out to be important, yet know nothing at all about this matter."

The Elsers of course received no response from Niemöller. However, when the Munich investigating judge Dr. Naaf questioned him in 1951, Niemöller quickly shifted into reverse and started downplaying the once so popular theory about Elser the SS man and the appearance of Nazi involvement in the attack. In an NDR television broadcast in 1965, all he had to say was that Elser was "a good, honest craftsman." The world of the camp rumors had vanished into thin air.

In 1949, the hearsay from the camp underground found its way into a book by Hans Rothfels, which was considered to be the definitive account of the German opposition to Hitler. The author expressed doubts that Elser could "be counted among the lone fanatics." Interesting that Rothfels did not consider any of the conspirators of the July 20 attack to be a "fanatic." Perhaps his implication was that Elser was lacking the proper breeding and education to carry out such a plan. In short, he was a man without social and political legitimacy.

Hans Rothfels's reasoning was particularly odd: "In the public opinion it had been proved that this was another case of a paid *agent provocateur*, like the one involving van der Lubbe—in all probability they were close to the truth." Rothfels appeared to have already forgotten that four years before then, the National Socialists were the ones who determined public opinion. For dissenting views there was no public forum.

The assessment of the Hitler era by Rothfels was accepted throughout the 1950s and 1960s by other historians such as Allan Bullock, Gerhard Ritter, and Eberhard Zeller. It was not until the appearance of the seminal essay by Anton Hoch and the transcript of the Berlin interrogations, edited by Lothar Gruchmann and released in 1969–70, that this assessment was proved to be false.

More "mental rubble" was created by the journalists who incessantly interviewed the craftsmen in Munich who had unknowingly helped Elser. They were hoping to reveal that at least a few of these craftsmen knew about the bomb. It was not until the 1950s that any serious interviews of contemporary witnesses, including Elser's girlfriends, were undertaken, and they were still tainted by the lingering Nazi conspiracy theory and driven by the popular press and its desire for exposés. Scholars of the period were insufficiently rigorous in confirming their sources.

After the end of the war, as long as interest in the idea of a militant opposition to Hitler persisted, the isolated attack by Elser attracted charlatans. Hans Loritz, commandant of the concentration camp at Sachsenhausen from 1940 to 1942, suddenly claimed that he had carried out the attack on Hitler himself. Naujoks, who was camp leader among the prisoners at Sachsenhausen, described Loritz as "primitive, ruthless, corrupt." The Jehovah's Witness Wauer saw Loritz as a sadist of the first order. So Elser's act of liberation had fallen into the worst possible hands. But Loritz took himself out of the debate by committing suicide on January 31, 1946.

In 1941, while the Königsbronn quarry owner Georg Vollmer was in the concentration camp at Welzheim, his wife tried in desperation to place the blame for the attack on a trio of Communists in league with the music-store owner Kuch. The Stuttgart Gestapo didn't take this subterfuge seriously. Vollmer himself continued embroidering this story when he filed an objection during a denazification hearing. In a letter to Bavarian Radio dated March 17, 1946, he audaciously conjured another version of the tale out of his bag of tricks. Suddenly Vollmer revealed himself as a staunch antifascist, who had seen it all coming after the Reichstag fire of 1933. Since he was such an opponent of the Nazis at that time, it was "not so surprising that Georg Elser . . . would apply for a position at my quarry," he claimed. Vollmer resorts to village gossip: "And he [Elser] was foolish in his relations with women. He surely lived beyond his means and usually associated with people who, like himself, had just a little education.

The people in his circle were not part of the middle class; they were what we call in dialect 'half gentlemen.'" Vollmer then brought up Kuch, the ominous man from Zurich; next he tried to portray Faistelhuber, the man Elser said he was looking for when he was arrested, as the middleman who arranged access to the Bürgerbräukeller for Elser. According to Vollmer, Elser expressed great interest in demolition techniques and said he wanted to find work in this field in Munich, claiming that he would produce something "that the whole world would talk about." Elser was, he stated, "simply a paid tool."

In August 1947 this tale entered a third phase. Now Vollmer tried to show that he had been placed in the concentration camp because of his activities in the resistance, but he had nothing to do with the explosives, he said; that was all the doing of Kolb, the explosives expert. At the hearing before the denazification tribunal in September 1949, Vollmer finally went all out, claiming that Elser had requested explosives from him because "he had a project he wanted to carry out that fall that the entire world would be talking about," but that Elser did not receive the explosives. Elser would then go on to steal the explosives in order to bring Vollmer down politically, he claimed.

A few months later, Vollmer wrote to the court of appeals in Stuttgart saying that Elser "asked me for them [the explosives]—and came into possession of some." So Vollmer came a bit closer to identifying the supplier.

In 1950, Vollmer was interrogated by the Kripo on behalf of the investigating judge in Munich. Kuch, according to Vollmer's latest claims, was involved "only in espionage" and was mixed up with an English resistance group, which in turn had contacts to a German group. The German secret service had gotten onto Kuch's trail. The Propaganda Ministry was in on the assassination attempt, but Hitler knew nothing about it. Faistelhuber had been ordered to keep Elser under surveillance. After crossing the border, Elser was to receive a reward of two million marks. At the end, Vollmer called everything he had patched together a "combination." Or perhaps the work of an amateur detective with a lot of imagination.

This absurd fable reached its conclusion in 1956 when Vollmer requested restitution for his imprisonment in order to gain a tax advantage. Now he risked everything, saying that he had known of Elser's assassination plan and had given him the explosives himself. The state office for reparations expressed its irritation: "So now the plaintiff is making the claim that he aided and abetted in the attack."

On February 23, 1950, the Bavarian Ministry of Justice initiated an investigation of an "unknown party for bomb attack." This soon became an investigation of Edgar Stiller, the former director of the prison at Dachau—for aiding in the murder of Georg Elser. The investigation was conducted by Dr. Naaf, whose thoroughness is evidenced by the five large volumes produced by the investigation. The direction of the investigation changed once more. As Naaf wrote to the criminal police in Konstanz in 1950, the purpose of the investigation was "primarily to establish the historical truth." Naaf soon determined that Elser had acted alone, but in the mind of the public nothing changed.

Around this time, a psychic known to the police in Augsburg announced a revelation he had had: the bomb had been built in Höchst am Main by a Herr Assisi, who had learned "time bomm [sic] manufacture" in England. The man described his vision to the police and included a sketch of the explosive device. He stated that while Hitler was speaking at the Bürgerbräukeller, Assisi was sitting at a table in a large room and the "time bomm [sic] with a small gas bag" was on a chair. First the gas bag bomb in the room exploded, then a second later "the bomm [sic] in the cellar." According to the psychic, Herr Assisi had an errand boy warn Hitler fifteen minutes beforehand. The Augsburg police department wrote that the man making the claim had been known to them since 1927 as a schizophrenic and believed he possessed supernatural powers. But this shouldn't have been a reason to ignore him—after all, this psychic was no crazier than many Germans, as well as many historians and journalists who at the time still firmly believed in the Nazi connections to Elser's attack.

In 1946, the same year that Niemöller announced his theory, the historical truth found a controversial proponent. With his statement that Elser had acted alone, Gisevius was honoring the legacy of his friend Arthur Nebe, who had been executed. As early as December 1939, Nebe had stated that Elser had carried out the assassination

attempt on his own. Twenty years later, Gisevius expanded significantly on this thesis in a fascinating study on Nebe.

The first step toward a fundamental change in public opinion was
made with a film broadcast in 1965 by NDR. In the discussion following the broadcast, which included Heinz Boberach of the German
Federal Archives, Elser was considered by the participants to be the
sole perpetrator of the assassination attempt. In East Germany, the
producers managed to track down former prisoners who had built up
an archive on Sachsenhausen, but they were so mistrustful of the West
that they were unable to deal with the Elser question. The assassin
remained taboo in the East until the end. He appeared in none of the
works on antifascism—for East German history the attack simply did
not exist.

During the television discussion, it turned out that several of the
experts had already read the unpublished transcript of the interrogations. The Ministry of Justice in Bonn had turned over the recently
rediscovered transcript to the Federal Archive in Koblenz in 1958. It
was nevertheless another twelve years before it was finally published.

The appearance of the essay by Anton Hoch in 1969 and the
edition of the Berlin interrogations by Lothar Gruchmann in 1970
sparked a discussion in Heidenheim that resulted, in 1971, in naming
a small park in Schnaitheim the "Georg Elser Gardens." The next
year, the Heidenheim chapter of the Association of the Victims of
Nazi Persecution erected a simple stone memorial with a bronze
plaque on the site. In 1979, Hermann Pretsch, a Catholic priest in
Schnaitheim, seized upon the occasion of the demolition of the
Bürgerbräukeller in Munich to write a wide-ranging newspaper article on Elser. As Pretsch had observed, doubts had arisen with regard
to Elser's actions, even in Schnaitheim where the craftsman had conducted his first test with explosives: "Even contemporaries of Elser's, workers in Schnaitheim, who before the war had belonged to
the German Communist Party—even they admit that the suspicion
among their ranks has not completely disappeared, even though it
cannot be supported by a single fact."

The English Germanist Joseph Peter Stern dealt with Elser in a
somewhat unconventional way in his book *Hitler: The Führer and*

the People, which appeared in 1978. Suddenly even the *Frankfurter Allgemeine* conceived an affinity for the much maligned assassin. For Stern, Elser was "the man without ideology—Hitler's true antagonist." Stern was opposed to overemphasizing the July 20 attack, but then glorified Elser as a classic exemplar of the "little man." He found in him "simple moral and political ideas" and felt that Elser was not capable of abstract thought. He found him old-fashioned like the world of craftsmen that was disappearing along with him. Even if Stern ultimately elevated him a bit too much by juxtaposing him with Kafka's sense of the world, his interpretation nonetheless enriched the discussion over the next twenty years. Of course, ascribing to Elser a lack of ideology meant ignoring many of his social motives. His commitment to workers' causes became obscured; his individuality was lost.

In the late 1970s, Elser's standing continued to improve. There were many new publications about him including a play by Peter Paul Zahl, a biography by Helmut Ortner, as well as a flood of newspaper articles, which familiarized the public with the information available at that time. But no one went looking for new materials.

Since 1988, the Georg Elser Study Group in Heidenheim has succeeded in opening new avenues of investigation. The founder of the group was Gerhard Majer, who wrote the play *Schorsch: The People's Assassin.* The book by the study group is still essential reading for anyone interested in the case. Many members were annoyed by the local glorification of Rommel while hardly a word was said about the resistance fighter Georg Elser, and they were dissatisfied by the lack of public recognition in Elser's hometown of Königsbronn. The mayor there would send inquiring journalists to Heidenheim. After a lecture in Heidenheim in 1979, Georg Elser's cousin Hans Elser received a personal challenge from Stern to undertake something on Georg's behalf.

With the release of the Elser film by Klaus Maria Brandauer in 1989, Georg Elser became known throughout Germany. At the premiere, Georg's brother Leonhard Elser, his friend Eugen Rau, and his son Manfred Bühl sat next to Brandauer.

If recognition is to be lasting, it requires public memorials in addition to published materials. After the one in Schnaitheim was established, Koblenz followed suit in 1983 with a plaque at the spot where Elser was arrested in the garden near the border. It was placed there on the fiftieth anniversary of Hitler's assumption of power and was accompanied by the usual debates. In these, Elser was at least not accused of being in the SS, but the assassination attempt was viewed with some defensiveness. The conservative elements in Konstanz wanted nothing to do with the whole subject, but the progressive side adopted the cause of seeking recognition for the resistance fighter. The local paper, the *Konstanzer Anzeiger*, expressed understanding for the reluctance of some, claiming the lack of much local connection to Elser, but thereby demonstrating its own lack of familiarity with the subject: "It is not even known how long the woodworker from Königsbronn lived in Konstanz." A glance at the transcript of the interrogation would have answered this question within a few minutes.

In 1989, ten years after the Bürgerbräukeller was demolished, the city administration of Munich installed a memorial plaque on the very spot where the pillar with Elser's bomb had been located, now within the new Gasteig cultural center that was built on the site. The location of the plaque—it is mounted flush with the floor—and the cramped text make this tribute to Elser's memory almost invisible. Anyone who does not know about the plaque will probably walk past without noticing it.

The same year, a Georg Elser Square was established in the Peterhausen section of Konstanz. It is actually little more than a grassy area next to the police station. There is no traffic through the square, no one lives there, and the name does not appear in the postal listings. Finally, in 1995, a plaque appeared in Königsbronn, mounted on the building that was to house the Georg Elser Memorial. In the Elser Memorial there are photographs (which are also on permanent display in Berlin) and possessions of Georg Elser's, such as his musical instruments, clocks for which he fashioned ornamental cases, and a workbench that he built for his little brother Leonhard.

In 1997, after much resistance and a great lack of interest on the part of Munich officials, a local initiative succeeded in getting a Georg Elser Square established. It is located on Türkenstrasse, close to the room Elser lived in and the workshops of the craftsmen who unwittingly assisted him in preparing for the attack. The most recent activity of this kind to date was the decision by the City of Stuttgart to name a stone stairway connecting Diemershaldenstrasse and Gerokstrasse the Georg Elser Stairs. It should be noted, however, that when Georg's sister Maria Hirth was living there in 1939, it was on the other side of the valley, at Lerchenstrasse 52, next to the Hoppenlau Cemetery.

In 1997, the Memorial to the German Resistance in Berlin was at last able to achieve general recognition for Elser with its excellent exhibit. Since then, two duplicates of the exhibit have been on tour throughout Germany. In the meantime, lexicographers have recognized Elser's status as a resistance fighter—his name appears in all the latest reference works.

Acknowledgments

I WOULD LIKE TO express my gratitude to Professor Peter Ecke of the University of Arizona for meticulously comparing my translation with the original text. His thoughtful suggestions and criticisms have led to much discussion and many improvements.

William Odom
Vienna, 2012

Bibliography

As this book was originally published in German, the sources used by the author are not all available in English. Rather than translate the material, the author and translator chose to include the sources in their original form.

ARCHIVE

Basel (Öffentliche Universitätsbibliothek), Berlin (Bundesarchiv), Bern (Schweizerisches Bundesarchiv), Bonn (Archiv der sozialen Demokratie in der Friedrich-Ebert-Stiftung), Frankfurt/Main (Deutsches Rundfunkarchiv), Frauenfeld (Kantonsbibliothek), Friedrichshafen (Archiv des Zeppelin Museums), Freiburg / Breisgau (Erzbischöfliches Archiv), Heidenheim (Stadtarchiv), Heilbronn (Stadtarchiv), Koblenz (Bundesarchiv), Königsbronn (Georg-Elser-Gedenkstätte), Constance (Stadtarchiv), Limburg (Diözesanarchiv), Ludwigsburg (Staatsarchiv), Mainz (Dom- und Diözesanarchiv), Munich (Institut für Zeitgeschichte, Staatsarchiv), Nuremberg (Staatsarchiv), Potsdam (Brandenburgisches Landeshauptarchiv), Sachsenhausen (Archiv der Gedenkstätte des KZ Sachsenhausen), St. Gallen (Staatsarchiv), Stuttgart (Landeskirchliches Archiv), Trogen (Kantonsbibliothek)

LITERATURE

Ackermann, Volker: Nationale Totenfeiern in Deutschland. Stuttgart 1990

Albrecht, Ulrike: Das Attentat. München 1987

Bakels, Floris B.: Nacht und Nebel. Der Bericht eines holländischen Christen aus deutschen Gefängnissen und Konzentrationslagern. Frankfurt a.m. 1979

Baur, Hans: Mit den Mächtigen zwischen Himmel und Erde. Coburg 91993

Behrenbeck, Sabine: Der Kult um den toten Helden. Vierow 1996

Berthold, Willi: Die 42 Attentate auf Adolf Hitler. München 1981

Best, S (igismund) Payne: The Venlo Incident, London o.J. [1950]

Bleiber, Beatrice, und Helmut (Hg.): Die Rückseite des Hakenkreuzes. München 21994

Boberach, Heinz (Hg.): Meldungen aus dem Reich. Die geheimen Lageberichte des Sicherheitsdienstes der SS. 17 Bände. Herrsching 1984

Boelcke, Willi A. (Hg.): Kriegspropaganda 1939–1941. Stuttgart 1966

Bramsted, Ernst K (ohn): Goebbels und die nationalsozialistische Propaganda 1925–1945. Frankfurt a.M. 1971

Brissaud, André: Die SD-Story (The SD story). Zürich 1975

Broszat, Martin/Froehlich, Elke: Alltag und Widerstand. Bayern im Nationalsozialismus. München 1987

Burchardt, Lothar/Schott, Dieter/Trapp, Werner: Konstanz im 20. Jahrhundert. Konstanz 1990

Bumke, Oswald: Erinnerungen und Betrachtungen. Der Weg eines deutschen Psychiaters. München 1952

Buzengeiger W.: Tausend Tage Dachau # 309. O. O. u. J. (Ulm 1998)

Carls, Hans: Erinnerungen eines katholischen Geistlichen aus der Zeit der Gefangenschaft. Köln 1946

Christel, Albert: Apokalypse unserer Tage. Erinnerungen an das KZ Sachsenhausen. Frankfurt a.M. 1987

Deutsch, Harold C(harles): Verschwörung gegen den Krieg. Der Widerstand in den Jahren 1939–1940. München 1969

Deutschland-Berichte der Sozialdemokratischen Partei Deutschlands (Sopade). 6. Jg., 1939, Heft 9, Nachdruck Salzhausen 1980

Domarus, Max (Hg.): Hitler. Reden und Proklamationen 1932–1945. Würzburg 1963

Dörner, Bernward: Gestapo und ‹Heimtücke›. In: Gerhard, Paul/ Mallmann, Klaus-Michael (Hg.): Die Gestapo – Mythos und Realität. Darmstadt 1996, S. 325–342

Dornier, Claude: Aus meiner Ingenieurlaufbahn. Zug 1966

Dornier. Die Chronik des ältesten deutschen Flugzeugwerks. Friedrichshafen 1983

Duffy, James P./Ricci, Vincent L.: Target Hitler. The Plots to Kill Adolf Hitler: London 1992 (darin viel Unsinn, der nicht aussterben will)

Elser, Georg: Autobiographie eines Attentäters. Der Anschlag auf Hitler im Bürgerbräu 1939. Hg. und eingeleitet von Lothar Gruchmann. Stuttgart 1989 (1. Ausgabe 1970)

Gegen Hitler – gegen den Krieg!Georg Elser. Hg. vom Georg-Elser-Arbeitskreis. Heidenheim 1989

Gisevius, Hans Bernd: Bis zum bitteren Ende. 2 Bände. Zürich 1946

Ders.: Wo ist Nebe?Zürich 1966

Goebbels, Joseph: Die Tagebücher. Teil 1, Bd. 3. München 1987

Goldschmitt, Franz: Zeugen des Abendlandes. Saarlouis 1947

Gritschneder, Otto (Hg.): Ich predige weiter. Rupert Mayer und das Dritte Reich. Rosenheim 1987

Groscurth, Helmuth: Tagebücher eines Abwehroffiziers 1938–1940. Stuttgart 1970

Gross, K. A.: Zweitausend Tage Dachau. O. O. u. J. [um 1947]

Gruchmann, Lothar: Georg Elser, Tischlergeselle und Attentäter. In: Manfred Bosch, Wolfgang Niess (Hg.): Der Widerstand im deutschen Südwesten 1933–1945. Stuttgart 1984, S. 291–298

Harder, Alexander: Kriminalzentrale Werderscher Markt. Bayreuth 1963

Hassell, Ulrich von: Vom andern Deutschland. Zürich, Freiburg 1946

Heiber, Helmut: Der Fall Grünspan. In: Vierteljahreshefte für Zeitgeschichte, 5, 1957, S. 134–172.

Herbst, Ludolf: Die Krise des nationalsozialistischen Regimes am Vorabend des Zweiten Weltkrieges und die forcierte Aufrüstung. In: Vierteljahreshefte für Zeitgeschichte, 26, 1978, S. 347–392

Hess, Sales: Dachau. Eine Welt ohne Gott. Nürnberg 1946

Hitler, Adolf: Aufrufe, Tagesbefehle und Reden des Führers im Kriege 1939/41. Karlsruhe 1941

Ders: Es spricht der Führer. Gütersloh 1966

Hitlers politisches Testament. Hamburg 1981

Hoch, Anton: Der Attentäter aus dem Volke. In: Ders./Lothar Gruchmann: Georg Elser: Der Attentäter aus dem Volke. Der Anschlag auf Hitler im Münchner Bürgerbräu 1939. Frankfurt a.M. 1980 (1. Fassung 1969)

Hochhuth, Rolf: Panik im Mai. Reinbek bei Hamburg 1989

Ders.: Teil 38. Dankrede für den Basler Kunstpreis 1976. Reinbek 1979

Hoffmann, Peter: Die Sicherheit des Diktators. München, Zürich 1975

Ders.: Widerstand – Staatsstreich – Attentat. München 1979

Hrdlicka, Manuela R.: Alltag im KZ. Das Lager Sachsenhausen bei Berlin. Opladen 1992

Joos, Joseph: Leben auf Widerruf. Begegnungen und Beobachtungen im KZ Dachau 1941–1945. Olten 1946

Kershaw, Jan: Der Hitler-Mythos. Stuttgart 1980

Kimmel, Günther: Das Konzentrationslager Dachau. Eine Studie zu den nationalsozialistischen Gewaltverbrechen. In: Bayern in der NS-Zeit. Bd. II, Teil A. München, Wien 1979, S. 349–413

Kleinschmidt, Heiner/Bohnert, Jürgen (Hg.): Heidenheim zwischen Hakenkreuz und Heidenkopf. Heidenheim 1983

Klemperer, Klemens von: Die verlassenen Verschwörer. Berlin 1994

Kornbichler, Thomas: Adolf-Hitler-Psychogramme. Band II. Frankfurt a.M. 1994

Kupfer-Koberwitz, Edgar: Die Mächtigen und die Hilflosen. Als Häftling in Dachau, 2 Bände. Stuttgart 1957

Lang, Jochen von: Die Gestapo. München 1990

Langbein, Hermann: Die Stärkeren. Ein Bericht aus Auschwitz und anderen Konzentrationslagern. Köln 21982 [S. 58–88 Dachau]

Langemann, Hans: Das Attentat, Hamburg o. J. [1956]

Luik, Arno/Thomma, Norbert: «Ich sprenge die Regierung in die Luft». In: die tageszeitung, Berlin, 31. 3. 1995, S. 12f.

Mallmann, Klaus-Michael/Paul, Gerhard: Das zersplitterte Nein. Saarländer gegen Hitler. Bonn 1989

Mang, Thomas: Retter um sich selbst zu retten. Die Strategie Rückversicherung, Dr. Karl Ebner, Leiter-Stellvertreter der Staatspolizeistelle Wien 1942–45. Magisterarbeit Wien 1998 [darin über den Gestapochef F. J. Huber]

Meienberg, Niklaus: Es ist kalt in Brandenburg. Ein Hitler-Attentat. Zürich 1980

Michelet, Edmond: Die Freiheitsstraße. Dachau 1943–1945. Stuttgart 1960

Müller, Josef: Bis zur letzten Konsequenz. München 1975

Naujoks, Harry: Mein Leben im KZ Sachsenhausen 1936–1942. Berlin 1989

Neher, Franz Ludwig (unter Pseudonym Peter Hilten): Einer gegen Hitler. In: Echo der Woche vom 10. 12. 1948 – 25. 2. 1949

Neuhäusler, Johannes: Kreuz und Hakenkreuz. Der Kampf des Nationalsozialismus gegen die katholische Kirche. 2 Bände S. München 1946

Ders.: Wie war das in Dachau? Ein Versuch, der Wahrheit näherzukommen. München 31961

Odenwald, Gottfried: Georg Elser und Karl Kuch. In: Heimat-und Altertumsverein Heidenheim an der Brenz, Jg. 1995/96, S. 288–306 [Weiterentwicklung der von Vollmer ausgehenden Märchen]

Ortner, Helmut: Der Einzelgänger, Rastatt 1989, 2. Aufl.: Der einsame Attentäter. Göttingen 1993

Peis, Günter: Zieh' dich aus, Georg Elser! Bild am Sonntag, ab 8. 11. 1959 (mehrteilige Serie)

Petry, Ernst / Peis, Günter: Der Attentäter. In: Der Stern, Jg. 1964, Nr. 18–20

Picker, Henry: Hitlers Tischgespräche im Führerhauptquartier 1941–42. Stuttgart 31976

Pretsch, Hermann: Wohin mit dem Schnaitheimer Schreiner? In: Stuttgarter Zeitung, 10. 11. 1979

Renz, Ulrich: Lauter pflichtbewußte Leute. Köln 1989

Rosenberg, Alfred: Das politische Tagebuch. München 1964

Rost, Nico: Goethe in Dachau. Hamburg 1981

Rothfels, Hans: Die deutsche Opposition gegen Hitler. Krefeld 1949

Rovan, Joseph: Geschichten aus Dachau. München, Zürich 1992

Rürup, Reinhard (Hg.): Topographie des Terrors 7. Aufl. Berlin 1987

Sauer, Paul: Württemberg in der Zeit des Nationalsozialismus. Ulm 1975

Schätzle, Julius: Wir klagen an! Stuttgart o. J. [1946]

Schellenberg, Walter: Hitlers letzter Geheimdienstchef. Rastatt 1986 [Erinnerungen]

Scheytt, Stefan / Schrön, Oliver: Unerschrocken zugepackt – Von den Nazis belohnt – Ein Orden aus Bonn: Der Mann, der Georg Elser verhaftete. In: Die Zeit, Nr. 48, 24. 11. 1989 [über Waldemar Zipperer]

Schlumberger, Hella: Türkenstraße. München 1998

Schmädecke, Jürgen / Steinbach, Peter (Hg.): Der Widerstand gegen den Nationalsozialismus. München, Zürich 1985

Schnabel, Thomas (Hg.): Formen des Widerstandes im Südwesten 1933–1945. Ulm 1994

Schoebe, Gerhard: Die Hitler-Rede vom 8. November 1939. Hamburg 1960

Schwäbische Tüftler. Stuttgart 1995, S. 28–33 [Ausstellungskatalog]

Seeger, Andreas: Gestapo-Müller. Berlin 1966

Sheppard, Stephen: Georg Elser. Roman. München 1989

Sigel, Robert: Im Interesse der Gerechtigkeit. Die Dachauer Kriegsverbrecherprozesse 1945–1948. Frankfurt a.M. 1992

Sigl, Fritz: Todeslager Sachsenhausen. Berlin 1948, Nachdruck 1986

Steinbach, Peter/Tuchel, Johannes: «Ich habe den Krieg verhindern wollen». Georg Elser und das Attentat vom 8. November 1939. Berlin 1987

Steinbach, Peter: Johann Georg Elser: «... seinem Ziele denkbar nahe gekommen». In: Zeitgeschichte, Wien, Jg. 1990, S. 349–363

Stern, Joseph Peter: Hitler. Der Führer und sein Volk. München 1978

Strasser, Otto: Hitler und ich. Konstanz 1948

Tuchel, Johannes / Schattenfroh, Reinhold: Zentrale des Terrors. Prinz-Albrecht-Straße 8. Das Hauptquartier der Gestapo. Berlin 1987

Vermehren, Isa: Reise durch den letzten Akt. (10. 2. 44 bis 29. 5. 45). Hamburg 1946 [S. 171–179 über Dachau und Elser]

Wachtel, Joachim: Claude Dornier. Planegg 1989

Weisz, Franz: Die geheime Staatspolizei. Staatspolizeistelle Wien 1938–45. Diss. Wien 1991 [darin über F. J. Huber]

Wunderlich, Rudolf: Konzentrationslager Sachsenhausen bei Oranienburg 1939–1944. Frankfurt a.M. 1997

Zahl, Peter-Paul: Johann Georg Elser. Ein deutsches Drama, Berlin 1982. [die Heidenheimer Fassung Grafenau 1996]

Zittel, Bernhard: Die Volksstimmung im Dritten Reich im Spiegel der Geheimberichte des Regierungspräsidenten von Schwaben. In: Zeitschrift des Historischen Vereins für Schwaben, 66, 1972, S. 1–58

Zoller, Albert: Hitler privat. Erlebnisbericht seiner Geheimsekretärin. Düsseldorf 1949